Praise for Flight to Financial Freedom: Navigating Secure Futures

"Thor McIlrath artfully weaves together his experiences as a pilot and a financial planner - two domains where it's equally crucial to both set a plan upfront, and be prepared for mid-course corrections along the way - to guide readers through setting their own retirement plan."

Michael Kitces: MSFS, MTAX, CFP®, CLU, ChFC, RHU, REBC, CASL, Head of Planning Strategy for Buckingham Wealth Partners & Host of the Financial Advisor Success Podcast

---

"In 'Flight to Financial Freedom,' Thor McIlrath leads readers on a journey towards financial success and fulfillment. As a man who truly cares for his clients and readers, Thor's humility, passion, and commitment are evident throughout this invaluable book."

Brett Machtig: AIF®, CWS®, RMA®, Financial Advisor, Managing Partner of The Capital Advisory Group & Author of "Your Guide to Financial Freedom" and "Retirement Unlocked: Unraveling Retirement Planning and Investment Risk Strategies"

"Thor willingly took my call when I wanted to learn more about how he built his firm. He quickly turned into a mentor and helped me get out of the world of large broker dealers to become a fiduciary for my clients. Thor has a heart to educate and empower people in their personal finances. There is no doubt that thousands of families are better off financially because of his commitment to education in personal finance. I am forever grateful for Thor's friendship and willingness to share his knowledge freely to help me."

Alex Goldberg: CFP® & Co-Founder of Periscope Wealth Advisors

"Thor exemplifies everything one should look for when entrusting someone to manage money on their behalf. Most financial advisors today are more concerned about their personal business and acquiring more assets to manage than upholding their fiduciary duty to their clients. This fiduciary duty requires an advisor to put the client first and focus on helping the client meet their financial objectives. Thor is committed to that in every way: he's committed to helping clients maximize their risk adjusted returns, he's committed to Shareholder Primacy, and he's committed to doing so openly and transparently which is a breath of fresh air."

Matt Cole: PhD, CFA, Chief Executive Officer & Chief Investment Officer Strive Asset Management

---

"Thor has provided great insight by putting together a strong mixture of the pressing conversations needed in financial planning to help clients benefit in these changing times! Well done, Thor!"

Jeff Rattiner: CPA, CFP®, MBA & President JR Financial Group,Inc./Rattiner's Financial Planning Fast Track, Inc.

Flight to Financial Freedom

Navigating Secure Futures

Thor McIlrath

Flight to Financial Freedom
Navigating Secure Futures

ISBN 978-1506-911-53-3 HCJ
ISBN 978-1506-911-54-0 PBK
ISBN 978-1506-911-55-7 EBK

January 2024

Published and Distributed by
First Edition Design Publishing, Inc.
P.O. Box 17646, Sarasota, FL 34276-3217
www.firsteditiondesignpublishing.com

This book is dedicated to the Creator of all who designed each of us for a purpose and endowed us with unique and purposeful talents.

I also dedicate this book to each of my talented co-workers at McIlrath and Eck who strive for excellence, and my wife and life partner Heather who has encouraged me through the decades of long hours away from home and empowered my own unique talent in personal finance.

FOREWORD

WRITTEN BY JEFF RATTINER

Financial planning is a very rewarding profession because it provides an opportunity for financial advisors to help their clients be prepared for their financial future. It allows practitioners to assist and ultimately become a significant part in helping with client concerns while developing an appropriate strategy in helping them stay focused. It is important for clients to plan early and monitor their situations closely because things change quickly. Clients need to be on top of their situations early to help ensure they are still on track to reach their goals. From an advisor's standpoint, it is personally rewarding to assist our clients with their objectives from the very beginning of their relationship with us and throughout the years, in helping them understand and realize what it takes to be financially successful.

Thor McIlrath understands that. Serving in the U.S. Coast Guard, and as an established practitioner for many years, Thor understands the importance of being there in assisting others to reach their potential. His approach to tying client information together in helping them reach their objectives through the financial planning process is practical and well-thought out.

Throughout his book, Thor helps define specific strategies in a very direct and understandable format. Each chapter starts with an important quote and includes many other quotes throughout. His book breaks down necessary information to understandable dialogue that readers can incorporate in addressing and fulfilling their financial and personal situations. His discussion on how advisors can assess and deal with conflicts of interest is appropriate. He provides sufficient detail for readers to truly grasp the many situations he brings to the table.

Thor shows the reader what it takes to be successful. For example, Thor discusses why many small businesses die a premature and often an unnecessary death because the owner failed to be successful. His discussion on inflation and ways to deal with it is appropriate in the current environment we live in. All the chapters provide the reader with a necessary understanding of the issues that can develop. His advice on aspects involving insurance, tax management, retirement and real estate is practical. His discussions on technical topics, such as asset allocation, investment topics, and estate planning are detailed and informative.

Thor uses his experience and discusses what he's done throughout his career, such as using a team approach, to provide readers with opportunities to help size up the situations before acting. He provides examples of existing clients and prospects looking for his expertise in helping them in their current and future situations. He provides an understanding of the marketplace and the importance of incorporating financial planning into the overall macro picture.

As a professional educator, author and speaker on financial planning subject matter, one of the biggest challenges is in providing a workable model where key concerns can be raised, significant exposures defined, and recommendations and strategies can be thought through. The result would evolve into the development of a game plan to be implemented which would help address these key and critical issues. This financial planning model would help those individuals who aspire to see a more complete picture and understanding of their immediate situation and a concise strategy to follow.

Thor captures that essence in his book. His direct and hands-on approach will satisfy readers in developing a workable blueprint to bring together the importance of financial planning. If you want to read a book that delivers a bottom-line approach towards understanding and developing a solid game plan for approaching financial planning matters, you will not be disappointed.

Jeff Rattiner, CPA, CFP®

President and CEO, JR Financial Group, Inc. and Rattiner's Financial Planning Fast Track, Inc.

Educator, Author, and Speaker

Flight to Financial Freedom

Navigating Secure Futures

Contents

INTRODUCTION

As I write this, our state of Washington and much of the rest of the country is in lockdown due to the COVID-19 pandemic. Tens of millions of people have lost their jobs. Untold numbers of small businesses will likely never recover. Investment portfolios have been eviscerated. People are sequestered, anxious and angry.

By the time you read this, the nation will have recovered and the pessimism and alarm that permeates the mass media will have been replaced with other news, hopefully of a less dire nature. We will have had a presidential election and half the country will celebrate while the other half will predict calamity.

There have been many times in our nation's history when uncertainty and fear ran rampant as the economy suffered yet another unexpected blow. My parents related the frightening experience of the country being plunged unpreparedly into World War II, just as the world was recovering from the decade of the Great Depression. Subsequent economic adversities included stock market plunges in 1962, 1973, 1987's Black Monday, the technology bubble collapse of 2000-01, 9/11 and the financial crisis of 2008-09 and resulting great recession.

Each economic setback was accompanied by "expert" analysis identifying the event as being "different this time." Each time, the financial markets recovered, demonstrating a remarkable ability to anticipate a better tomorrow, despite the bad news of the day. I have no doubts that the current crisis, despite the tragic loss of life, businesses, and the attendant financial and emotional suffering, will eventually subside and our nation will, once again, display amazing economic resiliency.

During times like these, people whose financial focus has been on the pursuit of ever-higher investment returns are rudely reminded that having a sound financial strategy on which to base investment decisions is the more valuable asset. If there are any positive developments from this pandemic, perhaps one will be that more people will become aware of the importance of establishing a personalized financial strategy.

Our firm is fortunate to have an intelligent client base with varied and plentiful life and work experience. Many are engineers and managers in nearby companies including Boeing, Microsoft and Paccar. Others are educators and technicians working in the public sector. We also have many clients who are tradespeople or people who work in non-supervisory positions at these firms. Interestingly, we've found that neither a person's job designation nor their amount of formal education has much to do with their perspective on planning for retirement. The common thread among all of our clients is the recognition of the importance of having a thoughtful financial strategy that will help them weather the inescapable perils of free markets. These are not people whose first question upon meeting me was, "What kind of investment performance can I expect?" These are people who have done their homework, accumulated significant 401k and pension assets, and want an advisor or coach who can deliver more than just peace of mind.

Occasionally, a prospective client will give me a list of fairly extensive questions and I embrace it. I understand that as their financial advisor, I'm expected to bring something tangible to the table in terms of retirement planning, tax management, risk mitigation, income distribution, real estate strategies and other services designed to enhance their financial futures. An aspect often ignored is the counsel to help avoid the common destructive behaviors that jeopardize the retirement portfolios and financial stability of people who fall prey to these biases when making financial decisions.

My hope is that this book will help you learn some financial basics to improve your financial life and provide information to help guide you through the myriad of decisions you will make throughout your working years and into and through retirement. So many inadvertent (and avoidable) errors are made regarding pension distribution choices and Social Security benefit start dates. These and numerous other choices are part of a financial strategy that can then move on to decisions regarding what kind of blended investments are optimal for your individual circumstances. A major component of your strategy should be planning for survival of worst-case market scenarios. Today's access to technology makes it inexcusable not to have that information.

These fundamental concepts can be shared with succeeding generations to help them improve their financial lives in a world increasingly enthralled with DIY. It's incumbent on every American to understand the changes occurring as a result of pensions being phased out and greater personal responsibility for retirement savings. Unfortunately, our educational system overlooks the need for basic financial knowledge, as if it has no importance in student's adult lives. It is crucial information that should be required before students are allowed to graduate with a high school diploma.

I was taught that an education is the biggest equalizer but I now believe that 401ks, IRAs and other deferred compensation schemes are the biggest financial equalizers in modern history. I know many people that went to work at Boeing or other companies in the area right out of high school and were fortunate to meet someone at work who cared enough to mentor them regarding saving for the future. Those who diligently saved 15-20% from the start are likely destined to become multi-millionaires by the time they retire, but more on this in the pages ahead. Remember though, we are not trying to build personal wealth for the sake of it, we are simply trying to morally and ethically create financial freedom!

Who listens to their parents at age 22? Almost no one. But some will listen to an older worker or supervisor who takes an interest in them and advises them to save, and so they do.

Today, at age 54, being an average worker at Boeing, they may have $800k to $1MM in their account. That's a fabulous equalizer, not only for people whose education stops after high school, but also for those who may have had a comfortable upbringing and whose parents paid for their college education. They might even have received a car while attending school. Despite those financial advantages, they will likely graduate with no better understanding of money concepts than their less educated counterparts.

A good financial strategy allows us to do the things we love best in life. For me, one of those things is owning and flying my own airplane. My interest in planes began with building model airplanes in my youth. The interest carried over into adulthood when I became a pilot and eventually built my own plane. After a stint in the US Coast Guard followed by college, I imagined I would become either a professional pilot with the airlines or have a successful business career where I could afford to do my own private flying. I chose the latter.

Being a licensed pilot opens up a great many adventures, as well as an occasional opportunity to simply do something nice for someone deserving. Recently, I took a terminally ill friend—who is also a pilot—on what was to be his last flight. We had no specific flight plan; we just lazily flew around and over some of the places that were meaningful in his life. We flew over the house where he and his recently deceased wife had lived together for 60 years. It was a beautiful, if bittersweet, flight, seeing him reminisce as we meandered about with no plan and no timeline. I remember thinking how much easier life would be if it could be idly enjoyed, without having to plan, and with no timeline for accumulating funds for retirement.

Certain types of flying don't really need a detailed plan. However, if you're going to fly outside of, say, 50 miles from your home airport, and especially if you're carrying passengers, you should probably have a flight plan. It can be something as simple as a plan drawn up on a knee board, with alternate airports listed should something go wrong; or it could be a detailed strategy entered into modern navigation equipment. As a pilot, you're always looking for a safe way out in case of an unexpected weather change, or something goes wrong with an engine, or if a strong crosswind at your airport is beyond your airplane's ability to land, or any other unplanned contingency. Really good, old-time pilots become weather experts. Those that don't often never get old. A commitment to lifelong learning and respect for safety and rules have distinct parallels to planning your financial strategies.

Being proactive and using the small incremental change in flight are one of the many hallmarks of a good pilot. Even major airline pilots have to make deviations in flight and travelers wouldn't get on planes if they thought the pilot didn't have a flight plan.

An important financial lesson can be learned from flying: even if you have a well-crafted plan, you'll likely make revisions. Similarly, changes occur in our lives that require reassessing our financial strategy. More about this later.

Many advisors continue to believe their value lies in providing asset allocation and picking the right investments. For decades, I've been railing against that mistaken belief. As a firm, we provide those services for clients who request it, but we can do so much more for them in the area of planning and strategy. For example, proper tax planning alone can be worth 100-200 basis points annually (100 basis points = 1%, 200 basis points = 2%) and that's a big deal for someone with a million-dollar portfolio. Errors related to defined benefits, pensions and Social Security distributions can have significant financial consequences

Yet, financial planning has always taken a back seat to asset allocation strategies and finding hot stocks. If you were to ask a large room of investors if they have read any books on investing, many would raise their hands. If you asked the same question about books on financial planning, I suspect few would respond affirmatively. There is a great need for better understanding of the critical role of financial planning, or as I prefer to call it, financial strategy, because comprehensive planning—like a good flight plan—requires more than drawing up a financial route. It calls for following up with a consistent methodology that includes flexible strategy, continuous monitoring and occasional revisions. Done properly, it is a more sophisticated methodology than most people imagine and can also provide a greater long-term effect on investment portfolios than active investment strategies.

I believe a systematic financial strategy grounded in a proven well-grounded investment philosophy is what the majority of knowledgeable investors will demand from advisors in the future. Robo advisors already do a better job of asset allocation than what most advisors can create. There is ample research to indicate passive investing using ETFs and similar products will outperform the vast majority of active investment platforms over time. People need to understand tax ramifications, distribution decisions, and income streams, and how to maximize that income at various points in their life. And that represents just the start of thorough planning strategy. Subsequent issues include living trusts, late life insurance decisions, helping the kids buy their first home, setting up an LLC, gifting considerations and more.

We modestly consider ourselves experts in the area of financial strategy because we have done so much of it for so long. It's the core of our business and we believe these decisions have far-reaching consequences that are too important to give short shrift or tackle with best guesses. If all you need is a flu shot, you can get it at the local clinic or drug store. If you need major surgery, do your research, seek referrals for specialists, and chose your surgeon carefully.

Earlier this year, a member of my team needed fusion surgery on his vertebrae. After doing his homework, he was referred to a surgeon who regularly performed a half dozen surgeries back-to-back, three days a week, but there was a four-month wait! I told our esteemed associate, "That's the guy you want."

Whether financial strategy, piloting a plane or spinal surgery, if you specialize in one thing and do it all the time, the odds of success will likely be in your favor. That surgeon has treated thousands of spinal cord injuries and it is highly unlikely he will encounter anything he hasn't dealt with before. Likewise, I do all sorts of financial plans for one type of clientele: those seeking retirement income planning. It typically involves tax planning, benefits review, real estate, risk management, portfolio management, and additional aspects of planning. The ability to do it well lies in focusing on the specialty for a long time. In doing this, the likelihood of encountering issues that haven't been seen before is minimalized.

Fear and Greed Sell

One of the unwritten but widely understood tenets of selling is that people's prime motivators are fear and greed. It's the low hanging fruit for salespeople. This is particularly true when the product being pitched is a stock, real estate or insurance, and it's the reason investors were blindly scooping up tech stocks in the 90's. It's the underpinning for the financial crisis of 2008 and the ensuing recession. It's why people like Bernie Madoff are able to utilize Ponzi schemes to rob trusting investors of their life savings. This is the methodology I was taught to sell investments when I first entered the industry.

Fear is commonly used to sell insurance, not just by the fast-talking stereotypes perpetuated in the movies but collectively by some of America's largest and most recognized brokerage firms, one of the biggest perpetrators being Fidelity Investments. A 2019 press release from the firm states, "According to Fidelity, a 65-year-old couple retiring in 2019 can expect to spend $285,000 in healthcare and medical expenses throughout retirement."

That statement is misleading, however. Medicare Advantage plans limit annual out-of-pocket expenses to $6,700 for in-network services and $10,000 for out-of-network services, as of 2019.

Fidelity, like some other brokerage, mutual fund and insurance firms, is selling fear as much as it is selling annuities, long term care insurance and expensive mutual funds. In my experience helping people cope with decisions around these products, I've found that a lot of middle-class families who have done a good job of saving are not doing the things they would like to be doing because they fear potential healthcare costs as they age. An independent analysis of their situations frequently reveals they worry needlessly, often because of the amount of money they have been convinced they will need for medical costs. Many of these people are emotionally paralyzed and unable to enjoy what should be a fulfilling retirement because they have been fed so much fear. We find that most people who have saved diligently for retirement throughout their working years have sufficient resources to do the things they yearn for, often more than what they would believe.

Early in my career, I realized I didn't want to be a "fear and greed" salesman. Matter of fact, I didn't want to be a salesman at all. I concluded that if there was a way to show people why a financial strategy was so important, then most everyone would want to do it. I read where 85% of all businesses fail in the first 5 years, according to the bureau of labor statistics. If people did a preemptive business plan, many would discover that their business model is unworkable. It could save them a lot of money, work and frustration. Similarly, if everyone within 10 years of retirement consulted a professional coach, they would learn whether they are on track for a happy retirement. For many, they could stop worrying and start planning those trips.

Happy People

I mentioned earlier that I enjoy working with bright people, even though it means regularly being challenged and occasionally being grilled. The engineers that comprise the bulk of our client base tend to be bright, positive people, and as an advisor, it's more gratifying to be around positive people every day. As a firm, we can do more to help these people achieve their dreams because they are aspirational and, frankly, they tend to have good saving habits, which gives us more to work with in planning for retirement and making decisions. For clients without adequate resources, we often find one of 3 variables works; work longer, save more, or take more investment risk.

Every month, one or two people who come in to discuss their financial affairs with me make me realize I'm sitting across the desk from someone great. It typically happens with regularity among people of managerial level experience. I can't help but silently ask myself, "What makes this person so special? What makes them so optimistic?" Invariably, these people are earning a high income, but it's not the money they earn that makes them special. The reason they earn a high income is not primarily because of their brains or experience, it's their attitude! It's a confident, upbeat, empathetic bearing that separates them from others, and it's self-evident after sitting and talking to thousands of people over almost 30 years the way that I have. These people communicate easily and get along with others effortlessly. Their lack of self-aggrandizement, despite their career achievements, is truly refreshing. They have no need to impress and yet are inordinately impressive, while they make you feel special.

I'm grateful to be of service to people who have taken varied career paths, who along the way have put faith in tried-and-true tomes such as put 10% of your income away, spend less than you earn, plan for a rainy day and prepare with diligence.

Chapter One

The Flight Plan

Statistics indicate that roughly half of the pilots involved in accidents failed to file a flight plan before taking off. Weather briefings, weight and balance calculations, elevations and diagrams are all part of the information related to a flight. It takes effort, but seasoned pilots would never fly without one. Going through life without a sound financial plan is like getting into a plane and taking off without a flight plan. Despite the endless advertising campaigns from the financial industry regarding the importance of financial planning, a lot of people meander through their lives without one.

Perhaps no financial topic garners more discussion than retirement planning. It is—and has been—the focus of countless marketing campaigns by insurance companies, brokerage firms, banks and other members of the financial community for as long as I have been a financial advisor.

When our viewing preferences are not being interrupted by discount brokerage firms touting DIY stock picking for fun and profit, we are subjected to commercial assaults from banks and insurance firms, warning us of the dire consequences of failing to correctly plot our financial futures. Financial magazines, journalists and 24/7 financial news shows join the chorus, often parroting the "Here's how much you will need to retire comfortably" scare tactics of the major advertisers and self-anointed industry "experts."

Yet, despite the nonstop barrage of advice, much of the populace remains thoroughly confused and, sad to say, poorly advised when it comes to plotting what should be the best years of their lives.

Countless articles have been written on the alleged perils awaiting retirees. Writing for AARP, Jane Bryant Quinn warns of "4 Unexpected Expenses to Prepare for in Retirement." These include nursing homes, bear markets, overspending and medical problems.[1]

Another AARP piece, "Help! I'm 70 and Worried I'll Run Out of Money," reports on a Fidelity Investments survey that found 39 percent of baby boomers entered their partnership in debt. Of those, 30 percent said it had a negative impact on how the couple got along and 44 percent worried about having enough income in retirement, a stress exacerbated by a lack of communication and joint planning. The poll went on to say that "more than half of the couples disagreed about how much they need to save by the time they reach retirement to maintain their lifestyle, and even more concerning, 46 percent admitted they have no idea how much they need."[2]

Articles in the professional media frequently express similar sentiments. A 2016 piece in the *Journal of Accountancy* claims, "As the 4 million people retiring this year think about the future, they fear outliving their money more than anything else." Forty-one percent of CFP financial planners say running out of money is their clients' top concern about retirement—including those clients who have a high net worth, according to a survey conducted recently by the AICPA. The elderly are living longer than their projected longevity and, as a result, are running out of money, said Susan Tillery, CPA/PFS, chair of the AICPA's PFS Credential Committee. The fear of running out of money in retirement has always been present. However, we are at a demographic crossroads where the Baby Boomers, who hold the largest amount of retirement assets, are supporting both their parents and their children. This has *amplified the fear*."[3]

When I see phrases like "amplified the fear," I am reminded of the adage I learned as a neophyte financial salesman, that is, what sells is "fear and greed." I didn't want to be a peddler of that message as a new member of the financial industry and that resolve has remained my pledge through three decades of advisory work. The industry has an obligation to shoot straight with their clients when it comes to money and retirement, but there's no reason to frighten them in order to sell financial products or services, in my opinion.

Without question, the decade prior to when you intend to retire is, in particular, an important time for thoughtful planning. I prefer to call it "life planning" because your retirement could well be a longer period of time than your working years. But contrary to what most in our industry promote, that is, "you're probably not financially prepared for retirement," I find just the opposite is true, at least among the 1,200 clients our firm serves. Most have saved more than an adequate amount for a fulfilling retirement, and most have—or will have—eliminated any significant debt prior to retiring.

People are much more knowledgeable and far less gullible about financial matters than in the past when they were sold life insurance products as an investment strategy. I recall one egregious example some years back when a Boeing employee was induced to pull out roughly half a million dollars from his retirement account while he was still working there and put it into whole life insurance. Happily, that sort of exploitation is less prevalent today with so much information available for those who choose to educate themselves.

By and large, people have come to the realization that pensions are going away and that they need to find other means to align what they can save with what they plan to do in retirement. Happily, they have numerous options to help them get that done. For example, workers changing companies can leave their current 401k savings where they are, roll them over into the new employer's plan or opt for an IRA rollover—strategies not possible when I first began advising clients 30 years ago.

What many are surprised to learn is they may also do a reverse rollover: roll their IRA money into their 401k account. There are several reasons why someone might want to do a reverse rollover. One is in preparation for a backdoor or mega backdoor Roth IRA conversion.

Thirty years ago, the maximum 401k annual contribution for an individual was $7,000. For 2023, the maximum is $22,500 with a $7,500 catchup contribution for those age 50 and older. There is also an after-tax 401k that does not get much press but can be a highly beneficial option for those who have maxed out their traditional or Roth 401k contributions at $20,500. The after-tax feature allows them to contribute up to an additional $40,500 to their after-tax account. More about this in a later chapter.

For years, corporations have been shedding their traditional pensions where employees are guaranteed a specific level of benefits in favor of 401k and other retirement savings accounts that compel employees to shoulder more of the risk. The younger you are, the less retirement security you can expect from your employer.

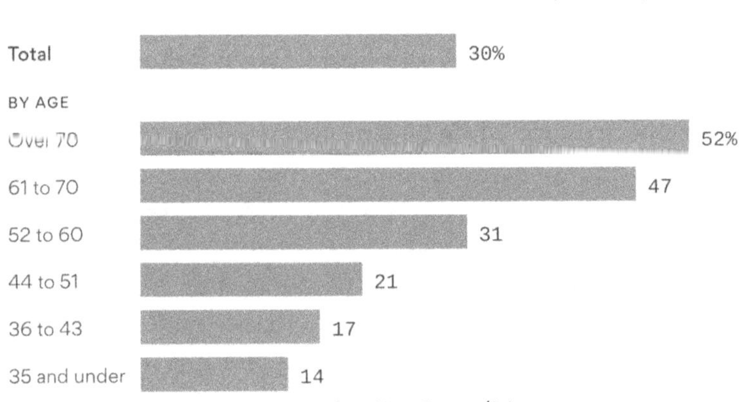

(Graphic 1.1 Households with a Defined Benefit Pension)

Recently, lower interest rates and higher longevity rates have prompted companies to offload their pension plans and offer lump-sum payments to workers. Among Fortune 500 companies, only 81 sponsored a pension plan in 2017, down from 288 in 1998, according to Prudential. At the same time, the number of pension risk transfer deals rose to 493 in 2018 from 203 in 2012, according to the LIMRA Secure Retirement Institute, a nonpartisan research center.[4]

A pension risk transfer occurs when a defined benefit pension provider offloads some or all of the plan's risk (e.g., retirement income liabilities to former employee beneficiaries). The plan sponsor can do this by offering vested plan participants a lump-sum payment to voluntarily leave the plan early (buying out employees' pensions) or by negotiating with an insurance company to take on the responsibility for paying those guaranteed benefits.[5]

Underfunded Pensions

Your Benefits Are Guaranteed...Sort Of

In 1974, then-president Gerald Ford signed into law the Employee Retirement Income Security Act (ERISA) which established the Pension Benefit Guaranty Corporation (PBGC), which ensures the benefits in private-sector defined benefit plans. It guaranteed "basic" benefits for participants in the event that their employer-sponsored defined-benefit plans became insolvent. For 2023, eligible participants can receive a maximum pension of $6,750 per month or $81,000 per year if they are 65 years old, assuming they choose a straight-life annuity. Like Social Security, early retirement reduces the benefit while retirement after age 65 increases the benefit. For example, the 2023 maximum benefit for someone who retires at age 45 is $1,687.50 per month, while someone who retires at 75 is entitled to the maximum benefit of $20,520 per month. The PBGC does not cover defined-contribution plans, such as a 401(k) or 403(b).[6]

By the end of fiscal year 2021, PBGC's positive net position was $481million—in sharp contrast to the negative net position of $63.7 billion at year's end 2020. The single-employer program, composed of about 23,400 plans, accounted for a surplus of $30.9 billion compared to the $15.5 billion at the end of 2020.[7] A multiemployer plan is a pension plan created through an agreement between two or more employers and a union. The employers are usually in the same or related industries, like construction or transportation.

Multiemployer plans are run by a board of trustees, with an equal number of employer and union trustees.

PBGC faces an immediate and critical challenge with its multiemployer program.

In 2014, Congress passed the Multiemployer Pension Reform Act (MPRA) that enacted several reforms, among them providing the option under certain conditions to reduce the retirement benefits of current retirees to avoid plan insolvency in severely underfunded plans. While the reforms were ostensibly intended to improve the program's financial condition, PBGC's projections suggest that the insolvency of the multiemployer program remains highly likely within the next few years and officials predicted the act's changes would only forestall insolvency by about an additional three years.[8]

Of course, this was not the plan when the PBGC was created. ERISA required that the PBGC be self-financing, a mandate that continues to the present day. But something went wrong along the way, leading to the current multiemployer program's near-$54 billion deficit. The PBGC was not intended to need funds from the U.S. Treasury. But proposed legislation provides tens of billions of dollars from the Treasury, and a limitless amount after that. If this were a private company, any insurance commissioner would have closed it down long ago. No rational customer would pay premiums to an insurer unable to pay its committed benefits in return.[9]

Public sector pensions may not be in much better shape. The American Legislative Exchange Council (ALEC) published a report in 2018—Unaccountable and Unaffordable—on unfunded public pension liabilities. According to the authors' research, all states combined have about $6 trillion in unfunded pension liabilities. The report investigated 280 state-administered pension plans, including the ones in our state of Washington, and examined their current assets and liabilities.

The pastor of an Evangelical Lutheran Church in America (ELCA) came in to see us when he received a 60-day notice that his pension with ELCA was about to be reduced by 50%. It represented virtually all of his savings, and ELCA being a nonprofit, his savings were not covered by the PBGC. He and his wife also had no money due from Social Security since they opted not to pay into it, believing their ELCA pension would meet their retirement needs. They now faced their upcoming retirement almost destitute as a result of ELCA's mismanagement.

This can happen to almost anyone in a nonprofit or public sector, and does with increasing regularity as the pension promises of state and local governments and other organizations responsible for people not employed in the private sector unravel.

As of the end of 2018, 48 of the 50 states in the U.S. have underfunded public pension plans. That means every state except South Dakota and Wisconsin lacks sufficient money to pay the promised retirement benefits of teachers, police officers, firefighters and other employees of those state governments.

The shortages are especially alarming in five states that currently have less than 50% of the funds needed to pay their public employees' pension benefits. The worst, Kentucky, has just 33.9% of the needed funds, followed by New Jersey (35.8%), Illinois (38.4%), Connecticut (43.8%) and Colorado (47.1%).[10]

Put another way, here's what every man, woman and child in each state would have to contribute to fully fund that state's public employee's promised benefits:

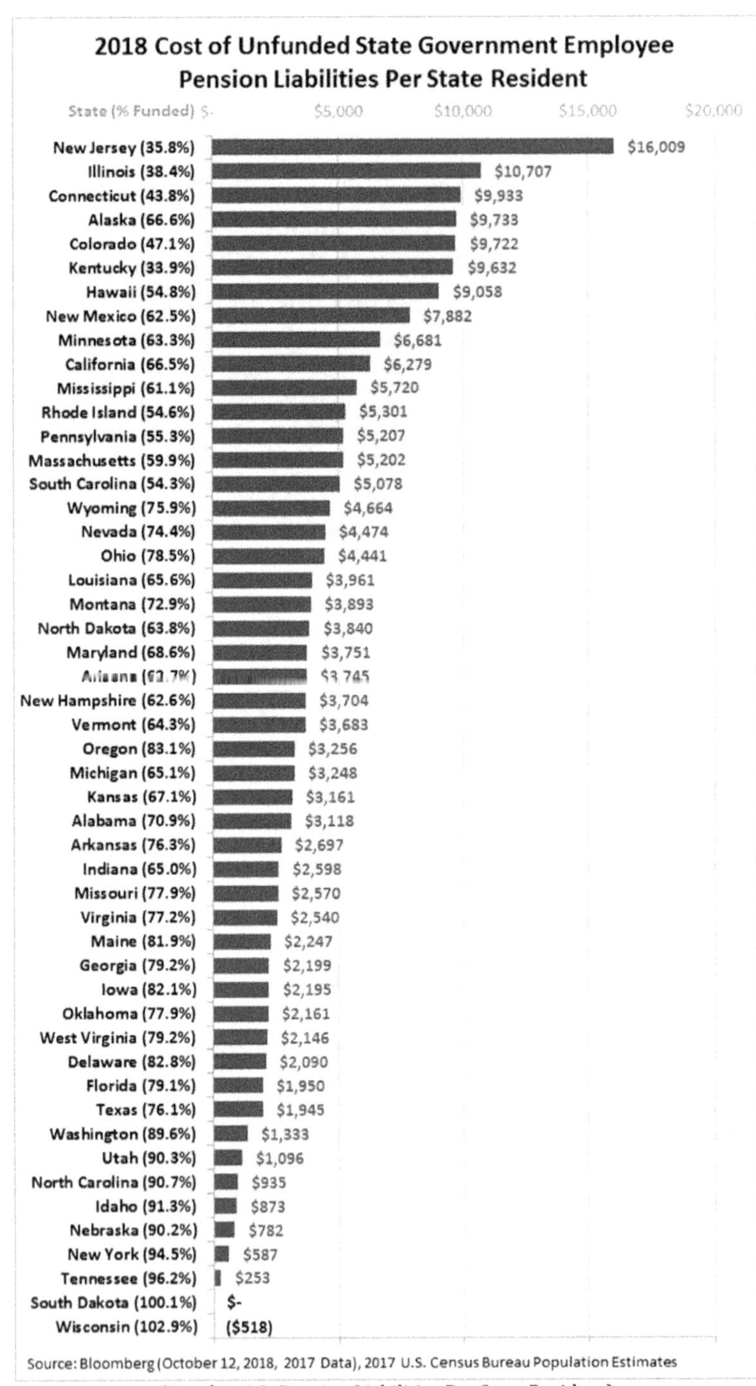

(Graphic 1.2: Pension Liabilities Per State Resident)

The authors conclude that one of the main contributors to such underfunding of public pension plans is unrealistic discount rates, "an investment return, expressed in percentages that the retirement plan's managers hope to achieve." Instead of using risk-free rates, plan managers calculate pension funds using assumed, and overly optimistic, rates of return.[11]

Over time, the purchasing power of retirement income decreases due to inflation. Cost of living adjustments (COLAs) help insulate retirees from the effects of inflation and are a vital facet of most state employee pension plans. But at least 29 states have attempted to shrink pension costs by reducing, suspending or eliminating post-employment COLAs since 2009.

These cuts to pension COLAs have faced legal challenges and courts have issued a conflicting range of opinions on the constitutional issues involved. COLA reductions in Colorado, Minnesota, New Jersey, New Mexico, South Dakota and Washington state courts have withstood constitutional challenges, as well as in the First and Fourth Circuits of the U.S. Courts of Appeals. Similar reductions have been struck down in Arizona and Illinois and, in part, in Oregon.[12]

What happens if the COLA adjustment is slashed or discontinued for a state's teachers, firefighters and members of the police force? What happens if the plan becomes insolvent and can only pay out 75% of its promised benefits, or less? What happens if there is another massive economic downturn and some of these pensions go under? The taxpayers are on the hook but there may not be enough revenues to resolve or rectify the problem.

As an advisor, I feel it's my responsibility to caution my government employee clients about the possibility of these contingencies and whether they're relying too heavily on promises that may not be fulfilled. We need to ensure that there are other resources in place to offset such an eventuality. For those working in the private sector, some companies, like Boeing and Microsoft, are so solid and well-funded that their employees need not worry too much about their pensions.

Bloomberg Business ranked Boeing's Voluntary Investment Plan (VIP) second among large companies' 401(k) plans in its 2015 rankings. ConocoPhillips, Amgen and Citigroup were other top finishers.

These pension shortfalls occur not because Americans are ignorant or careless. Most working people, whether in the public or private sector, are conscientious people who accept responsibility for their financial futures. Most are reasonably savvy when it comes to saving and investing. But even the brightest people can overlook the nuances of finance. People can be smart and educated, but they still make mistakes with their money. Sometimes, as in the case of the pastor, it's misplaced trust in an employer to exercise proper fiduciary responsibility. In many instances, arcane tax laws or enigmatic savings account provisions trip people up. Ask the average worker to explain savings account distribution options, reverse rollovers or the effect of inflation on future purchasing power and watch their eyes glaze over. It's not a matter of being uninformed; it's a function of the complexity of our tax laws and financial universe.

The effect of inflation on future purchasing power is an important but often overlooked aspect of planning, as Graphic 1.3 illustrates. The modest inflation rate for the past decade ended with a thump in 2021, quadrupling to 4.7% from the previous year's1.2%. And as people barely began to take notice of the effect, inflation soared again in calendar year 2022 to an alarming 8.0%. The year 2023 doesn't promise to be much better, with inflation greeting the new year at 6.4% in January.

In 2022, inflation hit its highest level in four decades, according to consumer price index data. Not all goods and services were similarly affected. For example, butter was up 31.4% from the previous year; fuel oil jumped 41.5%; eggs soared 59.9% and food at elementary schools rose an astounding 305.2%. The deleterious effect on purchasing power is obvious.[13]

Apply that math to the family sedan you might be shopping for in 2028 and the alarming impact of inflation becomes clearer.

Average Inflation	2%	3%	4%	5%	6%
Today	$ 1.00	$ 1.00	$ 1.00	$ 1.00	$ 1.00
5 Years	$ 1.10	$ 1.16	$ 1.22	$ 1.28	$ 1.34
10 Years	$ 1.22	$ 1.34	$ 1.48	$ 1.63	$ 1.79
15 Years	$ 1.35	$ 1.56	$ 1.80	$ 2.08	$ 2.40

(Graphic 1.3: Average Inflation)

My wife works for a Canadian airline. She is scheduled to receive a $2,600 monthly pension when she reaches age 65. Currently, the airlines' pension plan is 102% funded. It had been insolvent at one point but the company successfully turned things around and the plan is now solvent. Canadians do not have 401k plans but there are employer pension plans, which may be employer-sponsored, self-directed or a mixture of both.

All employed Canadians pay into the Canada Pension Plan (CPP) or Quebec Pension Plan (QPP). Canadians are eligible to stop working and start collecting CPP/QPP at 65 years old, or at age 60 at a reduced rate. The purpose of CPP is to supplement other retirement savings. It is not near enough money to live off of entirely upon retirement and is considered taxable income in Canada. There is also an Old Age Security Pension (OAS) that everyone in Canada qualifies for once they hit the age of 65, even if they've never been employed. Canadians do not pay into the plan as they do with CPP. Payments reflect a person's earned income due to ongoing contributions made during their working years.

Another option for Canadians is a Registered Retirement Savings Plan (RRSP), a retirement savings account where employee contributions and earnings are not taxed until withdrawn, ostensibly for retirement. RRSPs can be funded with a variety of investment vehicles. Finally, there is the Tax-Free Savings Account (TFSA), which works like a savings account. Individuals set aside whatever amount they wish—

up to a government-set maximum—and can remove it whenever they wish without penalty. The money in a TFSA typically accrues a higher rate of interest than a traditional savings account and the interest is tax-free.[14]

When compared to Europeans and most other countries, Americans, perhaps by necessity, are savvier about financial matters. In America, your financial future is largely a DIY proposition. In most European countries, working with a fiduciary financial advisor such as a CFP is typically reserved for the wealthy. This is not as true in America where are great deal of investment accumulation happens in employer-based retirement plans such as 401Ks

For example, brokerage firms like Fidelity Investments and Genworth Financial pump out a ceaseless stream of statistics on retirement and the associated costs. In its annual Retiree Health Care Cost Estimate, Fidelity estimates that a 65-year-old couple retiring in 2019 can expect to spend $285,000 in healthcare and medical expenses throughout retirement, net of taxes.

Does that seem excessive? According to HealthView Services—a firm that produces healthcare cost-projection software—a healthy 65-year-old couple retiring in 2019 will need more than $387,000 to cover healthcare expenses, including Medicare Parts B and D.

According to consulting firm Milliman, the average healthy 65-year-old couple retiring in 2019 will spend $369,000 on healthcare in retirement, based on Medicare costs coupled with projected healthcare inflation rates.[15]

As you can see, the estimates regarding retirement healthcare costs vary wildly. One thing they have in common is to scare the pants off people. Remember, fear sells. These so-called "studies" typically fail to provide detailed information on how the study was conducted or why the assumptions used were chosen. When I discuss these statistics with independent experts on Medicare supplement policy, they say that – mathematically – these projected out-of-pocket estimates are a virtual impossibility. Again, much more about this topic in a later chapter.

Income Protection

Over the years, I've encountered numerous instances where people's financial futures were either rescued or decimated, based on whether they had adequate income protection. This is another topic I will cover in greater detail in a later chapter, but a specific case comes to mind that is worth telling here.

A single woman, age 57, was diagnosed with a debilitating brain disease. She had crafted a successful career and was earning $150k annually from her telecommunications employer when diagnosed. Because she had previously purchased a long-term disability policy, she was entitled to receive $5k monthly from her insurance carrier, money that was tax-free. She also receives $3k monthly from her employer's disability coverage but must pay taxes on that benefit. She had accumulated roughly $500k in her free Roth and tax-deferred 401k accounts combined but owed about $100k on her mortgage. She told me that without that $5k tax-free disability payment, she would not have been able to maintain her modest lifestyle and would have been forced to sell her home.

This example illustrates the importance of proper life planning strategy, including an assessment of whether a person or couple's income needs to be protected. The majority of people I serve who are within ten years of retirement could survive a situation like this without income protection because they have little or no debt, they accumulated sufficient savings, or their spouse would just have to work longer. Things can usually be adjusted. The other 25-30% of my clients who lack income protection could be in big trouble without it. For someone who is on their own and lacking a funded defined-benefit pension, the result could be a bleak future, if not financially catastrophic.

If the worst case for these people would mean losing assets and going backwards financially, they should put a price tag on that and decide if it's a risk worth taking. The biggest financial risk people within 10 years of retirement face is usually the risk of loss of income.

What Does it Cost to Retire Comfortably?

As mentioned, most of our clients live here in the state of Washington. Most who are retired are able to live comfortably on $90-100k a year. A good number live on $60k a year or less. They can do this, even in an area like Puget Sound, where living expenses are above the national average, because they have no mortgage or other debt. They travel abroad regularly, enjoy various hobbies and activities and are able to visit their children and grandchildren living in other parts of the country without straining their budget. We have retired clients living in expensive areas like Snohomish on $60k a year who budget upwards of $10k annually on travel for the first 10-15 years of their retirement. Again, they can do it because they are shrewd shoppers and have zero debt. Out of that $60k they might budget $600 a month for food and another $400 a month for property taxes, and they're not living in hovels. Their net worth might be a million or more and they live on $60k a year of retirement income off their investment portfolio. Individuals today typically receive $2000-2500 monthly from Social Security (SS) and if married, their spouse automatically qualifies for another $1000-1250. The SS usually takes care of most of their basic needs by itself. If someone is living on a total of $70-80K annually in a safe, scenic environment and doing what they wish, I believe that's the definition of a satisfying financial retirement.

These people are typical clients, not exceptions. We create planning strategy for people like this every day. It's extremely rewarding to see them enjoying a fulfilling retirement because of the planning we did together years before.

If you haven't already done so, I urge you to spend some time thinking about what you want your retirement to be like, what you want to do during a span of years that could well be longer than your working years. Remember that the retirement years for most people are not linear. You will likely experience different "seasons" of your retirement, with the earlier years more active, the middle years divided between doing the things you enjoy and waiting for the results of medical tests, and the final years, whatever they hold.

What many people fail to understand is that retirement has these different stages and there is a pronounced financial dichotomy between them. The mantra of most financial advisors is that you should limit your income distributions to a consistent 4% so as to preserve your investment principal. But if you plan to travel extensively during your early retirement years while you are still young enough to fully enjoy the experience, you can actually pull down more of your resources during this period if that's the lifestyle you choose. It may violate the traditional distribution code but this may be fine if you expect the later years of retirement will be less active, hence you will be spending less money. You simply throttle back when those "not as active" years arrive.

A fiduciary is obliged to offer advice that is in his/her clients' best interests. Part of meeting that obligation is to understand the motives and desires of each client. Not everyone has the same vision of what retirement should be. For some, travel means international travel and first-class accommodations. For others, it means hooking a popup trailer to their car and travelling around the U.S. to see their grandchildren. Keep in mind you will experience different stages of your retirement and your priorities will change. Chances are, you have more flexibility than you think with the resources available to you if you choose. Maybe you can pull out 5-8% distribution for a few years, deplete some of your safe assets and survive any market drops that may happen because you're going to throttle back in the later years when you're not going to be so active. Don't think in terms of actuarial tables. Reject the notion that you can only take 4% withdrawals for the rest of your life when what you want to do is enjoy the earlier years to their fullest and you have enough cash reserves on hand, thanks to the planning you did and the elimination of debt.

Chapter Two

Tax Management

In my experience, many people overestimate the amount of taxes they will pay in retirement. A married couple with $100k annual income filing jointly, for example, shouldn't have to pay very much in income taxes at all. Their 2023 standard deduction is $27,700 and the over age 65 deduction is an additional $2,800 for a total of $30,500, reducing their AGI to about $69,500. The 2023 tax rate is 10% on the first $22,000 and 12% on AGI from 22,000 to $89,450, which means they will pay $2,200 + $5,700 or a total of about $7,900 in taxes. (Income tax only, WA state.)

Retirees see advertisements or are told by someone selling investment products that they face a significant tax liability but it's usually not true. They would have to be in a high tax bracket and have a good deal of income from non-tax deferred accounts to realize a large tax liability. I have wealthy retired clients with $200k in taxable annual income and their overall effective tax rate (couples filing jointly) for 2023 is roughly 24 %. (see graphic 2.1)

Tax Rate	Taxable Income (Single)	Taxable Income (Married Filing Jointly)
10%	Up to $11,000	Up to $22,000
12%	$11,001 to $44,725	$22,001 to $89,450
22%	$44,726 to $95,375	$89,451 to $190,750
24%	$95,376 to $182,100	$190,751 to $364,200
32%	$182,101 to $231,250	$364,201 to $462,500
35%	$231,251 to $578,125	$462,501 to $693,750
37%	$578,126 or more	$693,751 or more

(Graphic 2.1 2023 Tax Brackets)

Long-term capital gains tax for marrieds in 2023 is zero up to $89,250 in income and 15% from $89,250-$553,850. Qualified dividends are taxed the same.

Taxation of Retirement Savings

I will discuss the traditional and Roth versions of IRA and 401(k) plans in detail in chapter three. For tax consideration purposes, here are some basics.

Once retired, most people will be in a lower tax bracket than during their peak earning years. In retirement, some types of income are taxable while other types are not. Federally taxable income includes withdrawals from your 401(k) and traditional IRA. Income from pensions, annuities or investment real estate is also subject to taxes, as is income from dividends, interest or capital gains from stock sales. Depending on your other income, Social Security benefits may also be taxable up to 85%.

Income from a Roth IRA or Roth 401(k) is not taxable. Interest income from municipal bonds is exempt from federal taxes, as well as state and local taxes if you buy bonds issued by your resident state. If you are married filing jointly, you pay zero capital gains tax on investments you sell in 2023 if your taxable income is $89,250 or less.

The 2023 contribution limit for employees who participate in 401(k) and 403(b) plans is $22,500. The catch-up contribution limit for employees aged 50 and over is $6,500.

The 2023 contribution limit to an IRA is $6,500, with an additional over-age 50 catchup limit of $1,000. The deductible contributions are subject to phase-out ranges based on annual income limits.

The same contribution limits apply to a Roth 401(k) or Roth IRA, the difference being that the contributions are not deductible when made but there is no tax due when the funds are withdrawn, presumably during retirement. To qualify for a Roth IRA, individuals must earn no more than $153,000 and couples must earn no more than $228,000. There are no income limits for a Roth 401(k).

An additional option for the 401(k) is non-Roth after-tax contributions. That is, contributions made from compensation with dollars that have already been taxed. The total annual contribution limit for a 401(k) is $61,000 or $67,500 for those age 50 and older.

Roth IRAs also allow tax-free withdrawals of earnings on contributions after a five-year holding period under certain conditions, including reaching age 59½, being disabled or using the funds for first-time home-buying expenses.[16]

Standard vs Itemized Deductions

When filing taxes, you can claim the sum of your itemized deductions, provided you don't claim the standard deduction. Itemized deductions include state and local taxes, mortgage interest, medical expenses and charitable donations among others. Capital losses for the year are not included so they are not a consideration for whether or not to itemize.[17]

The federal standard deduction virtually doubled as a result of The Tax Cuts and Jobs Act of 2017 (TCJA), eliminating the need to itemize for many taxpayers. However, charitable donations to qualified charities remain an itemized deduction, subject to AGI limits, which were raised from 50% to 60% in TCJA. The AGI limit for capital assets like stock or real estate remains at 30%.[18]

Allocating Investments

The tax benefits for maximizing and properly compartmentalizing contributions during your accumulation phase can be significant. Choosing the appropriate investments for taxable and non-taxable retirement accounts cannot be understated. Proper investment management allows tax-efficient investing without necessarily sacrificing performance.

Almost any type of investment is permissible inside an IRA, including stocks, bonds, mutual funds, annuities, unit investment trusts (UITs), exchange traded funds (ETFs) and even real estate. Life insurance, derivatives, collectables, personal real estate and most coins are not allowed inside an IRA but are permitted inside a self-directed IRA.[19]

The difference between a traditional IRA and a self-directed IRA is that the latter allows investors to hold alternative investments, principally because the investor is responsible for managing his or her own account.

Mutual funds and ETFs are the most common investment options for 401(k) plans, although other investments may be available. There are infinite variations of both options. Mutual fund types include aggressive growth, balanced, value, conservative, target-date and other specialized funds. Your tolerance for risk, years to retirement and amount needed are determining factors.

An important consideration for the funds chosen is whether they will be held in a tax-deferred IRA or 401K, or in a taxable retail brokerage account. If held in a brokerage or vendor direct account that is not tax deferred in any way, you should be sensitive to the tax management of the fund. Mutual fund managers are driven and evaluated by performance. They are typically not concerned with whether they are creating short-term or long-term capital gains when they sell stocks. They don't know you, your circumstances or how your tax situation might be affected by how they manage their fund. If you hold mutual funds inside of a brokerage account that's not tax deferred, you must be aware of the potential tax ramifications.

A key consideration is the fund's turnover ratio, a measurement of the percentage of the fund's holdings that are replaced during the year. If a fund holds 50 different stocks and replaces (turns over) 25 of them during the year, its turnover ratio is 50%. A low turnover ratio—generally considered to be 20% or less—indicates a buy and hold strategy for actively-managed mutual funds. Passively managed funds, such as ETFs and index funds, are inherently low turnover. In general, a higher turnover fund will have higher trading and tax costs than a fund with lower turnover. The higher tax costs mainly arise from capital gains distributions—taxes generated by the mutual fund selling securities that have gained. Trades often have their own transaction fees as well.[20]

Funds more sensitive about capital gains tax liabilities tend to have lower turnover ratios and deliver higher net returns. This is one reason for the popularity of ETFs, especially for affluent investors with large sums in non-tax deferred accounts.

Because of the way they are structured, mutual funds tend to incur more capital gains taxes than ETFs, which incur capital gains tax only when they are sold by the investor. Mutual funds pass on capital gains taxes to investors throughout the life of the investment.[21]

Another advantage of ETFs is better transparency. Actively-managed ETFs—the most transparent iteration—must, by law, disclose their full portfolios every day. Mutual funds, on the other hand, are only required to disclose their portfolios on a quarterly basis with a 30-day lag. ETF investors can sell to another investor anytime they wish, much like a stock. One caveat is fixed-income ETFs, which have higher turnover and are less tax efficient than the more common equity-based ETFs. When mutual fund investors want to cash out, the fund manager must sell securities to raise cash to meet those redemptions.[22]

When planning for retirement, if you haven't maxed out your 401k or IRA contributions—which potentially represent a great deal of money—you should prioritize that before buying stocks in a brokerage account or pursuing other strategies, such as paying down your mortgage.

On the other hand, if all of your retirement money is in tax deferred accounts, you can ignore the tax management issue, other than in the case of some Roth conversions.

Bunching Deductions

For a married couple, the 2023 standard deduction of $27,700 (and an additional $2,800 for those over age 65) is so large that most people will not have sufficient deductions to itemize. But for those who do itemize, "bunching" deductions can be beneficial.

As the term implies, bunching refers to paying two-year's worth of deductible costs in a single year in order to itemize them on your tax return. Essentially, you bunch deductions for both years and claim them one year, then take the standard deduction the next. The strategy maximizes deductions, assuming you have enough of them over the two years to exceed the standard deduction by enough to make the effort worthwhile. Examples include medical expenses, property taxes and charitable contributions. People who are philanthropic or fund charities, in particular, tend to bunch deductions. Many of them like to make a consistent, ongoing contribution each year.

If you haven't previously done so, once you reach the age of 70½ where you have to begin taking required minimum distributions (RMD) from your traditional IRA, you might consider charitable donations to a charity, church or foundation directly from that account, which lets you avoid income tax on up to $100,000 per year. (Bear in mind that if you contribute from your IRA, you can't also claim a deductible charitable contribution for the same amount.)[23]

Most Required Minimum Distribution (RMD) amounts must be taken each year after turning 72, this amount is calculated by dividing the owner's account balance at the end of the prior year (December 31) by the owner's current year life expectancy factor found in the IRS Uniform Lifetime Table (Graphic 2.2).

Uniform Lifetime Table

Age of Account Holder	Divisor	Age of Account Holder	Divisor
72	27.4	91	11.5
73	26.5	92	10.8
74	25.5	93	10.1
75	24.6	94	9.5
76	23.7	95	8.9
77	22.9	96	8.4
78	22.0	97	7.8
79	21.1	98	7.3
80	20.2	99	6.8
81	19.4	100	6.4
82	18.5	101	6.0
83	17.7	102	5.6
84	16.8	103	5.2
85	16.0	104	4.9
86	15.2	105	4.6
87	14.4	110	3.5
88	13.7	115	2.9
89	12.9	120+	2.0
90	12.2		

(Graphic 2.2: Uniform Lifetime Table)

The SECURE 2.0 Act decreased the late withdrawal penalty for RMDs beginning in 2023 from 50% to 25%, and allow a further reduction down to 10% if amounts are removed by the stated deadline. Another major change set forth by SECURE 2.0 involves increasing the age at which RMDs first commence from 72 to 73. This applies to account owners who turn age 72 on or after January 1, 2023.

Tax Laws Change

It's unfortunate, but a lot of products sold as "tax-advantaged" investments are based on the mistaken notion that tax rates will remain constant for the duration. I'm referring to schemes involving index annuities, non-traded REITS and other illiquid financial vehicles that fall flat when tax rates or laws change...which they invariably do. This also applies to irrevocable life insurance trusts and similar products, which might be fine were it not for the problems caused by vacillating tax rates or inflation. The roller coaster that tax rates have travelled over the past century is illustrated in graphic 2.3.

4-Feb-20

Historical Highest Marginal Income Tax Rates

Year	Top Marginal Rate	Year	Top Marginal Rate	Year	Top Marginal Rate	Year	Top Marginal Rate
1913	7.00%	1948	82.13%	1983	50.00%	2018	37.00%
1914	7.00%	1949	82.13%	1984	50.00%	2019	37.00%
1915	7.00%	1950	84.36%	1985	50.00%	2020	37.00%
1916	15.00%	1951	91.00%	1986	50.00%		
1917	67.00%	1952	92.00%	1987	38.50%		
1918	77.00%	1953	92.00%	1988	28.00%		
1919	73.00%	1954	91.00%	1989	28.00%		
1920	73.00%	1955	91.00%	1990	28.00%		
1921	73.00%	1956	91.00%	1991	31.00%		
1922	58.00%	1957	91.00%	1992	31.00%		
1923	43.50%	1958	91.00%	1993	39.60%		
1924	46.00%	1959	91.00%	1994	39.60%		
1925	25.00%	1960	91.00%	1995	39.60%		
1926	25.00%	1961	91.00%	1996	39.60%		
1927	25.00%	1962	91.00%	1997	39.60%		
1928	25.00%	1963	91.00%	1998	39.60%		
1929	24.00%	1964	77.00%	1999	39.60%		
1930	25.00%	1965	70.00%	2000	39.60%		
1931	25.00%	1966	70.00%	2001	39.10%		
1932	63.00%	1967	70.00%	2002	38.60%		
1933	63.00%	1968	75.25%	2003	35.00%		
1934	63.00%	1969	77.00%	2004	35.00%		
1935	63.00%	1970	71.75%	2005	35.00%		
1936	79.00%	1971	70.00%	2006	35.00%		
1937	79.00%	1972	70.00%	2007	35.00%		
1938	79.00%	1973	70.00%	2008	35.00%		
1939	79.00%	1974	70.00%	2009	35.00%		
1940	81.10%	1975	70.00%	2010	35.00%		
1941	81.00%	1976	70.00%	2011	35.00%		
1942	88.00%	1977	70.00%	2012	35.00%		
1943	88.00%	1978	70.00%	2013	39.60%		
1944	94.00%	1979	70.00%	2014	39.60%		
1945	94.00%	1980	70.00%	2015	39.60%		
1946	86.45%	1981	69.13%	2016	39.60%		
1947	86.45%	1982	50.00%	2017	39.60%		

Notes: This table contains a number of simplifications and ignores a number of factors, such as the amount of income or types of income subject to the top rates, or the value of standard and itemized deductions.
Sources: IRS Revenue Procedures, various years. Also, Eugene Steuerle, The Urban Institute; Joseph Pechman, *Federal Tax Policy*; Joint Committee on Taxation, Summary of Conference Agreement on the Jobs and Growth Tax Relief Reconciliation Act of 2003, JCX-54-03, May 22, 2003.

(Graphic 2.3: Tax Rates 1913-2020)

When counselling clients in this area, we emphasize the importance of flexibility because inflation and taxes are fluid elements in planning. Tax rates change, tax benefits change, inflation rates change. Tax strategies must be flexible so they can be modified in response to those changes. What we don't want to do is create strategies that cannot be undone without severe penalties or losses.

People often make financial decisions as though nothing is going to change throughout their lifetime and that is almost never the case. It's vital to construct planning and strategies that are flexible and to avoid products and strategies that cannot quickly and inexpensively be unwound.

Employee Stock Plans

Companies offer a variety of plans to encourage or reward their employees. Here are some of the more common offerings.

Employee stock options (ESOs) are equity compensation. Instead of granting shares, the company provides call options on shares of company stock. ESOs are not traded on an exchange and cannot be sold. They typically have a vesting schedule—which can be immediate or over time—that determines when employees gain full control of their options. Employees have the right but not the obligation to buy the company stock at a predetermined strike price and the options must be exercised prior to their expiration date.

Non-qualified stock options (NSOs) are generally provided at a price lower than market value and taxed as ordinary income in the year the options are exercised. The tax is based on the difference between the strike price and the price of the stock when the options are exercised. Options are taxed when exercised, and at long-term capital gains rates if they are exercised after at least a year and a day.

Qualified stock options, also known as incentive stock options (ISOs), have the same general exercise rules as NSOs but might not be provided at a lower price than market value. They are taxed at capital gains rates not when purchased but when sold.[24]

Restricted Stock Grants (RSGs) give employees the right to acquire or receive shares once certain criteria are met, such as a number of years of employment or performance incentives.

An **employee stock purchase plan** (ESPP) allows employees to purchase company stock through after-tax payroll deductions at a discounted price, up to 15%, depending on the employer. At the purchase date, the accumulated funds are used to purchase company stock on behalf of the participating employees. With a qualified ESPP there are no taxes owed on the discount at the time of purchase. A non-qualified ESPP has the same structure but without the favorable tax treatment.

An **employee stock ownership plan** (ESOP) provides a company's employees with stock ownership, often at no up-front cost. ESOP shares are considered part of employees' compensation and are typically held in an ESOP trust until the employee retires or leaves the company, when the shares are sold. Employees are taxed upon distribution, but can be delayed if rolled over into an IRA or other retirement plan and taxed as ordinary income when withdrawn.[25]

If your company has a **supplemental savings plan** (SSP), you should look into it. We have a lot of clients employed at Boeing, which has one of the largest retirement plans in the U.S. with over $60 billion in plan assets.

A Declutter Deduction

It's great to get a deduction for giving away a collectible or something you're no longer using. Sometimes, we have something that's not easily sold on eBay or Craigslist, but would make a nice contribution to a private school auction. I've done that several times for a local school. On another occasion, I had a 50-year-old John Deere riding lawn mower. I had over $5,000 invested in it but was receiving only low ball offers of less than half the value on Craigslist. So, I loaded it up on a truck and took it down to the Bargains Galore store as a charitable contribution. I told them what I had invested in it and received a $5,000 receipt. It felt better to take a small loss and get the deduction than selling it to someone trying to negotiate a bargain.

People often make inaccurate assumptions about the amount of taxes they will have to pay in retirement. The misperception is understandable, given the hype supporting the sale of "tax advantaged" investment products. In my experience, however, most people will be in a lower tax bracket once they reach retirement.

Chapter Three

Pension Plans and Deferred Compensation

When you retire, the federal government—and all but the nine states that do not charge income tax—will expect you to pay taxes on your income, both earned and unearned. That includes Social Security (special tax provisions apply if your income is above a certain level) and withdrawals from your pension, 401k and traditional IRA. You will not have to pay taxes on withdrawals from your Roth 401k and Roth IRA plans.

Financial advisors and their investor clients often based their retirement savings decisions on tax considerations. However, I regularly meet with people earning $150k, $250k or more annually and they don't always have a clear understanding of the ramifications of their choices. Given the dramatic shift in employer-sponsored retirement plans over the past 20 years or so, from defined benefits to defined contributions, it may be helpful to first explain the differences between the two.

Defined Benefit (DB) vs. Defined Contribution (DC)

In a defined benefit (DB) plan, employers are responsible for the performance and funding of their plan. If the plan's investments underperform, such as they did during the 2008 financial crisis, the cost to maintain adequate funding to offset pension obligations in defined benefit plans can become prohibitive for the employer. People are also living longer. Many will collect pension income for a longer period than they were employed. Companies are required to keep their DB plans funded and face potentially significant liability should their plans fail. In most instances, the pension benefits of a failed plan are guaranteed by the Pension Benefit Guaranty Corporation (PBGC), a federal agency created in 1974 by the Employment Retirement Income Security Act (ERISA).

The PBGC currently covers 35 million participants under defined benefit pension plans in the US, an exception being that they do not cover pension plans with 25 or fewer participants. The PBGC will pay benefits to participants of a terminated plan even if the employer has failed to pay the required insurance premiums as well.

All these factors have contributed to the massive shift from DB plans to defined contribution (DC) plans, where employees now must assume responsibility for investment allocation and, ultimately, investment performance that ensures their income goals are met— another reason to have a plan and strategy for providing ongoing financial income. Obviously, everyone would like strong investment returns, but I believe the term "investment performance" is overused and has lost meaning. If you are a super saver and retire later in life, you can likely get by just fine with poor investment performance. Even taking inflation into account, if you started saving 15% of your income from your first day of employment and are currently earning a Pacific Northwest middle-class household income of $150k a year, at an average annual investment return of 7% your retirement account would have accumulated over two million dollars after 40 years. And that number assumes an average inflation rate of 4.28%. Graphic 3.1 contains an example illustrating this accumulation.

Annual Salary
$ 150,000.00
Employee Contribution
15%
Employer Contribution
3%
Average Return (Balanced Portfolio)
7.06%
Average Standard Deviation
9.34%
40-year Inflation
4.28%
Average Real Return (for example)
2.7%

		Real Return
Year 1	$ 27,000.00	2.3%
	$ 54,626.48	-6.6%
	$ 78,044.13	7.2%
	$ 110,687.78	-3.6%
	$ 133,649.20	-15.8%
	$ 139,465.89	14.9%
	$ 187,229.61	18.3%
	$ 248,543.04	-1.3%
	$ 272,340.34	10.3%
Year 10	$ 327,386.52	-8.1%
	$ 327,953.89	-1.4%
	$ 350,207.41	19.8%
	$ 446,635.06	6.1%
	$ 501,093.99	8.8%
	$ 572,179.67	-1.2%
	$ 592,070.55	16.4%
	$ 716,448.33	-10.8%
	$ 666,404.67	8.8%
	$ 752,195.44	-5.1%
Year 20	$ 741,156.55	-9.6%
	$ 696,851.70	16.1%
	$ 836,225.01	2.6%
	$ 885,241.04	13.0%
	$ 1,027,590.61	11.4%
	$ 1,171,780.21	26.8%
	$ 1,512,527.61	-1.6%
	$ 1,515,062.04	-11.8%
	$ 1,363,645.91	17.5%
	$ 1,629,598.53	-10.8%
Year 30	$ 1,481,372.93	-12.7%
	$ 1,319,740.84	-15.4%
	$ 1,143,477.37	-1.0%
	$ 1,158,798.15	11.8%
	$ 1,322,125.33	1.5%
	$ 1,368,447.90	19.4%
	$ 1,661,285.78	-3.7%
	$ 1,626,727.35	1.3%
	$ 1,674,570.06	15.5%
	$ 1,961,357.18	1.7%
Year 40	$ 2,021,201.71	5.5%

(Graphic 3.1: Savings Plan Accumulation)

Retiring employees of companies, who either maintaining or discontinuing their DB plans, must choose whether to take an immediate lump sum distribution—which can be rolled into an IRA—or take a defined benefit income stream (such as an annuity) that pays a fixed amount each month. In that regard, one of the significant risks often overlooked in retirement planning is the impact of the afore-mentioned inflation.

Financial professionals commonly use the "Rule of 72" to calculate how long it would take to double your money, based on your rate of return.

The formula is 72 / Interest Rate.

So, for example, it takes 12 years to double your money at 6% annual interest. You would double your money in 10 years if your interest rate jumped to 7.2%.

What is less commonly cited is the use of the rule of 72 for calculating the effect of inflation. At an annual rate of 2%, inflation would reduce your money by half in 36 years. A slight increase in the inflation rate to 3% would result in your money being halved in just 24 years instead of 36, illustrating why seemingly small changes in the inflation rate can have a dramatic impact on long-term planning. An interesting side note: if your credit card charges 15% annual interest, your balance will double in just 4.8 years![26]

For a historical perspective, consider a study of investment returns over the period 1988-2004, during which defined benefit plans outperformed 401(k) plans by one percentage point. A subsequent study of the years 1990-2012—based on data from the Department of Labor's form 5500—revealed almost identical results: defined benefit plans outperformed defined contribution plans by 0.7 percent. Part of the explanation may rest with higher fees, which are deducted before returns are reported to participants. But the one percentage point shortfall understates the investment problem in 401(k) plans, since an aggregate number does not reflect the fact that more than half of participants in 401(k) plans do not follow the prudent investment strategy of diversifying their holdings.[27]

One reason for the investment success of defined benefit pensions over the years is that pension managers have access to private equity and other investment alternatives not available to individuals unless they are qualified investors—also referred to as accredited investors—individuals or entities that can purchase unregistered securities primarily due to the investor's income and net worth. Another, and I believe more important reason, why defined benefit pension plans tend to outperform individuals managing their own defined-contribution plans is that the former began with an investment policy statement, a formal financial plan that dictates how the money in the plan will be invested. The plan takes into consideration its pension obligations, the outlays the plan must cover in a given year and the expected rate of return of the assets within the plan. That cost should logically be accounted for by fixed income investments, such as corporate or investment grade bonds. The equivalent for an individual's defined contribution plan would be a defined income stream, such as from a fixed-income annuity. The balance can be described as the at-risk portion of the plan, containing investments such as equities. The thoughtful planning employed by defined benefit managers is often missing in the plans managed by individuals, who tend to move in and out of investments too often, with predictably less successful results. More about this in the chapter on "Disruptive Behaviors."

Further reinforcement of the statistics that DB plans historically performed better than DC (401k) plans comes from a 2006-2008 investment update by Towers Watson, which upheld the 1% annual performance advantage of DB plans. The possible reason may lie in the way investment results are reported, or because of a higher concentration of equities. Perhaps more logically, it might be due to the fact that DB plan trustees have a fiduciary responsibility for investment performance. They or the financial professionals hired to manage their plans typically have considerably more financial savvy than the average individual investor, as well as access to more sophisticated investment vehicles than 401(k) plan participants. As mentioned, defined benefit plans adhere to an investment policy statement which is routinely monitored, reviewed and rebalanced as necessary. While a 1% annual gain difference may not sound like a big deal, over an average worker's 40-year career, it translates into an extra $220,000 at retirement, so it is, indeed, a big deal.[28]

If you've ever visited another country and had the advantage of being accompanied by someone who lives there or has visited the country previously, you know how much more you get out of the trip than if you went on our own, not to mention the tourist traps and other pitfalls you avoid. You might draw an analogy between the investment results achieved by pension managers and DIY individual investors. A sound financial strategy and the help of a financial fiduciary can allow individuals to essentially replicate the benefits accrued to large pension plans managed by fiduciaries adhering to an investment policy. And given the availability of low-cost index funds, individual investors today have virtually the same entry cost basis for most major asset classes as large institutional investors.

The University of North Carolina did a study using faculty data (Clark, Ghent, and McDermed, 2006) to calculate and compare DB versus DC pension benefits, assuming retirement at 65 after 30 years of employment. Interestingly, they discovered that men had greater pension wealth under a DC plan—assuming an allocation of 50% stocks with 6% returns and 50% bonds with 3% returns—likely due also to higher lifetime earnings, whereas women would gain greater wealth with a DB plan because of longer life expectancies. The conclusion was that plan preferences are based on age, gender, mobility and risk aversion, among other factors.[29]

Pension Distributions from DB Plans

If you participate in an employer-sponsored retirement plan—whether defined benefit or defined contribution—you need to fully understand your distribution options. A hasty or uninformed choice can have momentous consequences, such as how much of your money will be lost to taxation, how long your money will last and whether there will be anything left for the next generations, should you wish to leave it for them. In the case of a defined contribution plan, your investment choices, as well as how you choose to take your money, and the amount and timing of your distributions are critical factors. In the case of a defined benefit plan, your employer chooses the investments. However, if you take the lump sum distribution option and roll your money from the plan into an IRA, you are now responsible for making the investing choices.

Depending on the type of plan and contributions (yours, your employers, pre-tax, after-tax), your distribution options may be limited. Not every plan offers the same payment alternatives, although that would certainly simplify things. Everyone has unique circumstances and challenges. Knowing what your options are and understanding their ramifications is important. People tend to instinctively base their distribution decisions on receiving the highest income stream or most advantageous payout. That's often not the best approach. A defined benefit pension plan offers a variety of payment options designed to benefit the participant, not the employer, who is ambivalent about which option is chosen. It's an advantage for the employee to be able to choose the alternative that best meets his or her unique situation and goals, such as max survivor benefits.

Different distribution options carry different payouts and tax consequences. You can't leave your money in an employer-sponsored plan indefinitely. You must begin taking required minimum distributions (RMDs) in the year you reach age 72 (73 if you reach age 72 after Dec 31, 2022). You may, however, qualify for an exception from taking RMDs from your current employer-sponsored retirement account if you are still working and do not own more than 5% of the business you work for. In most cases, defined benefit plans do not permit you to take distributions until you leave your employer or reach the plan's retirement age.

One of the most important benefits of working with a financial fiduciary can be pension maximization. Let's say a worker decides to retire at age 60. He has an employer pension of $2,500 a month and is eligible to receive Social Security payments of another $2,500 a month. That $60k annual income is sufficient to cover expenses for he and his wife. But if he chooses the survivor benefit option from his pension, his monthly payment is reduced to $1,750, not enough to retire. He's seemingly caught in a Catch-22.

Now let's assume that he is in good health. What we could do to maximize his pension options is to have him take out a 20-year term life insurance policy to indemnify his wife in case of his death. The premium is a fixed rate of $200 monthly for the term of the policy. He now can take the $2,500 monthly pension option and after deducting the $200 insurance premium, he is $550 a month better off than if he took the pension's survivor benefit. If he dies, his wife is protected either way and he has bought time until he reaches age 80. If his wife passes away before the policy expires, he can cancel and save the $200 monthly.

Your first decision is whether to take a lump sum payout, monthly pension payments in installments over your life expectancy or as an annuity, or a direct rollover into an IRA.[30] Like most choices in life, each has advantages and disadvantages. Monthly payments for life—typically in the form of an annuity—serve as insurance that you will receive a check every month until your death, or until the subsequent death of your spouse. The disadvantage is the loss of purchasing power over the years as a result of inflation, unless your plan is adjusted for inflation, which most private employer-sponsored plans are not.

Inflation has a way of lulling people into a false sense of confidence. The first 20 years of this millennium saw an average annual inflation rate of about 2%. That extended period of abnormally low inflation was unexpectedly interrupted by a leap to 4.7% in 2021 and another surge to

8% in 2022.[31] Today's prices are 1.75 times as high as average prices in 2000, according to the Bureau of Labor Statistics consumer price index. **A dollar today only buys 57% of what it bought in 2000.**

A lump-sum distribution, especially a large one, can carry significant tax consequences.

You may have to pay a 10% premature distribution tax if you are under age 59½ and your money will no longer be in a tax-deferred retirement account. If you choose the lump sum payment, unless you need the money immediately for an emergency, you can roll it over into an IRA.

A direct rollover is a tax-free transfer of assets from a retirement plan to a plan at a new employer or to an IRA. An indirect rollover is a tax-free transfer of assets from a plan trustee to you and then on to an IRA or second plan trustee. The indirect rollover is useful if you don't immediately have a new employer plan to roll your assets into. You can park them in an IRA until you secure a new position and open a plan with that employer as sponsor. With an indirect rollover, however, your old employer or plan administrator is required by law to withhold 20% of your distribution for federal income tax. You can claim the amount withheld as a credit on your federal income tax return, assuming you return the money to a plan within 60 days, but you lose that amount from your portfolio's tax-deferred earning potential.[32]

The advantages of choosing a lump sum and rolling it over into an IRA are that you won't have to pay taxes until you begin withdrawing the money, you can choose how to invest the money so it grows and maintains your purchasing power and you will have money available in case of a financial emergency. Your heirs or charity will inherit what's left after you die. The catch with the lump sum option is that you—not your employer or a plan trustee—are now responsible for managing your money and choosing investment options. There are also costs, such as management fees, to consider.

As mentioned, you will be responsible for taxes on your pre-tax 401k or the money you roll over into an IRA when you take distributions. If you are managing your own money and are not judicious in how much you spend, you could run out of money before you or your spouse run out of life.

One option would be to use some of the money to buy an annuity that provides monthly payments, and personally manage the rest of the money in an effort to keep up with inflation. If you chose this option, it's important to select the appropriate annuity. In my experience, investors tend to be better off with sufficient allocations to fixed income assets, such as bonds, in their IRA.

Doing that substitutes the need for a fixed income annuity, which typically invests in the same investment vehicles they have access to in the fixed income allocation of their IRA, and almost always at a significantly lower cost than that of an annuity, which usually has massive costs in the form of commissions, management fees, surrender penalties and other costs which are buried inside the insurance contract and almost impossible to find—not to mention your money is tied up for 5, 10 years or longer

Annuity Shopping

In my experience, there is usually a better, more cost-effective fixed income option than an annuity, particularly when interest rates are low. In addition, there is much documentation about the abuses associated with the sale of annuities. I've witnessed some tragic examples of individuals who were sold an annuity by a broker when other options would have been much more appropriate—and far less costly. However, if you decide you still wish to buy an annuity, it's important to understand the nuances of these vehicles and how to shop for the best option.

There are three types of annuities from which to choose: single life, joint and survivor and period certain and life. A single-life annuity offers the largest monthly payment but payments stop when you die. If your spouse will need that income after your gone, choosing the largest monthly payment may not be your best option. A joint-and-survivor annuity pays while you are alive and continues payments to your spouse or other beneficiary after your death. Typically, you can opt for either a 100, 75 or 50% joint-and-survivor annuity. The difference represents the percentage of your benefit that your spouse will receive after you're gone. A period-certain-and-life annuity pays your beneficiary for a specific number of years—typically between 5 and 20 years—after your death, then stops. The payments from this option will usually be larger than those from a joint-and-survivor annuity. A single person who wants to receive monthly payments but have some wealth pass on to heirs should he or she die young might logically choose a period-certain-and-life annuity.[33]

Your overall financial picture helps dictate which option is best for you. If you have sufficient other assets to cover your living expenses, the lump sum distribution (rolled over into an IRA to defer taxes until you decide—or are required—to take distributions) is probably the better option. If you are in poor health, the lump sum option also makes sense. On the other hand, if you or your spouse has a family history of long life and/or if there is any uncertainty about having sufficient money to last your expected lifetime, the monthly pension payment may be the right choice.[34]

The tax ramifications discussed in chapter two are another important consideration when choosing a payment option. There are ways to navigate the distribution choice minefield, but for most, the counsel of an experienced financial professional is advisable. These decisions are often irrevocable and involve substantial costs and other consequences.

Public Sector and Non-Profit Pensions

State and local government employees, as well as those working at non-profit organizations usually have access to a tax-advantaged, deferred compensation retirement plan called a 457b plan. Participants can make pre-tax contributions that compound without being taxed until withdrawn. Employees are allowed to contribute up to 100% of their salary, provided it does not exceed the applicable dollar limit for the year, which is $22,500 for 2023. Employees age 50 or older may contribute up to an additional $7,500 for a total of $30,000. Participants direct their own investments and virtually any type of investment is allowed. 457 plans are taxed similarly to a 401k or 403b plan[35], that is, when distributions are taken. Participants must begin taking distributions by age 72.[36]

Governmental 457b plans share many characteristics with qualified plans, such as 401(k) plans, whereas 457b plans maintained by non-governmental tax-exempt entities are a bit different from qualified plans or governmental 457(b) plans. The differences can be a complex issue, but for our purposes, the primary distinctions are that all employees can be included in a governmental 457 plan—with eligibility subject to sponsor discretion—whereas private tax-exempt 457 plans must limit participation to select management or highly compensated employees, with the exception of rule 414e which allows religious organizations to include all employees.

The Roth Conundrum

What we encounter most in our professional practice is individuals with significant deferred compensation who need a strategy designed to maximize their retirement income. For people like this, typically earning high annual incomes, how best to allocate their savings among the various retirement vehicles becomes a paramount consideration.

In recent years, we've noticed a tendency among these individuals to allocate increasing amounts of their retirement savings to a Roth 401k instead of fully funding their pre-tax accounts, including their 401k. The idea is to mitigate their retirement tax burden by putting more after-tax dollars into savings during their working years. While the Roth 401k (and Roth IRA) are useful planning tools, they can be counterproductive if too much money is shifted into them from pre-tax savings.

Most of our clients will be in a lower tax bracket after retirement than they are now, while still working. As an example, a retired couple withdrawing $100k annually can currently claim the standard $25,900 deduction. Those over age 65 receive an additional standard deduction of $2,800 for a married couple.

What this means is a retired couple with $100k in unearned income can still stay in the 10-12% tax bracket. Why would you pay 24% tax on today's earnings so you can save money for retirement that will be taxed at approximately half that rate? Doesn't it make more sense to put as much pre-tax money as you can into a traditional 401k and pay 12% tax when you retire instead of 24% tax today?

For those able to do so, I advise they put the maximum amount into their 401k and then make some post tax contributions—assuming their employer allows it—so they have some tax-free accumulation that they can roll to a Roth IRA when they retire or sooner. If your company allows post-tax contributions to your 401k, here's how you might go about it, depending on your income, spending and other considerations, of course.

In addition to the $22,500 pre-tax annual 401k contribution limit for 2023—$30,000 if you are 50 or older, thanks to the catch-up provision—you can contribute an additional $43,500 of after-tax contributions. The total contribution limit (pre- and after-tax) is $66,000 ($73,500 if 50 or older), minus any employer contributions. For example, if your employer contributes 3% (representing $3,000 of your income of $100,000) to your 401k, your total contribution limit would be reduced by $3,000.

The reason for making the additional contributions to your 401k instead of a savings or brokerage account is that the after-tax money you put into your 401k grows tax-free until you take distributions in retirement. Graphic 3.2 depicts the dramatic effect of making additional contributions to a 401k.

	Pre-Tax	Post-Tax	Taxable Account
Year 1	$ 30,000.00	$ 37,500.00	$ 67,500.00
	$ 66,731.62	$ 83,414.52	$ 150,146.14
	$ 100,087.69	$ 125,109.62	$ 225,197.31
	$ 126,689.05	$ 158,361.31	$ 285,050.36
Year 5	$ 156,641.59	$ 195,801.99	$ 352,443.58
	$ 161,827.55	$ 202,284.43	$ 364,111.98
	$ 200,224.53	$ 250,280.67	$ 450,505.20
	$ 243,768.74	$ 304,710.93	$ 548,479.67
	$ 277,682.72	$ 347,103.40	$ 624,786.12
Year 10	$ 328,811.31	$ 411,014.14	$ 739,825.45
	$ 334,161.31	$ 417,701.64	$ 751,862.95
	$ 365,916.57	$ 457,395.72	$ 823,312.29
	$ 424,278.70	$ 530,348.37	$ 954,627.07
	$ 521,667.21	$ 652,084.01	$ 1,173,751.22
Year 15	$ 573,143.37	$ 716,429.22	$ 1,289,572.59
	$ 764,306.10	$ 955,382.53	$ 1,719,688.73
	$ 802,386.23	$ 1,002,982.79	$ 1,805,369.02
	$ 910,205.79	$ 1,137,757.24	$ 2,047,963.04
	$ 939,153.77	$ 1,173,942.21	$ 2,113,095.98
Year 20	**$ 1,125,560.50**	**$ 1,406,950.63**	**$ 2,532,511.13**

Annual Salary (22% Marginal Tax Bracket)
$ 100,000.00
Employee Pre-tax Contribution ($27,000)
27%
Employee Post-tax Contribution ($37,500)
37.5%
Employer Contribution ($3,000)
3%
Taxable Account Contribution ($67,500)
67.5%
Average Return (Moderate Portfolio)
5.56%

Total Pre-tax Contributions
$ 600,000.00
Total Post-tax Contributions
$ 750,000.00
Total Taxable Account Contributions
$ 1,350,000.00

	Pre-Tax	Post-Tax	Taxable Account
Taxes paid pre-retirement	$ -	$ 165,000.00	$ 297,000.00
Taxes owed post-retirement	$ 135,067.26	$ 78,834.08	$ 177,376.67
Total Taxes Paid	$ 135,067.26	$ 243,834.08	$ 474,376.67
Retirement Account v. Taxable Account LifetimeTaxes	**$**	**378,901.34**	**$ 474,376.67**

(excluding dividends, distributions, sales pre-retirement)

(assume withdrawals all inside 12% marginal tax bracket, All capital gains taxed at 15%)

(Graphic 3.2 Pre- and Post-Tax Contributions)

An additional strategy to grow your retirement savings is to roll over the after-tax portion of your 401k into a Roth IRA. More about this later in the chapter.

Backdoor Roth IRA

Certain high-income earners (MAGI[37] over $138,000 for singles, $218,000 for couples filing jointly) are precluded from contributing to a Roth IRA. An alternative strategy for these people is the backdoor Roth IRA, which converts a non-deductible traditional IRA contribution into a Roth account. It's important to note that a backdoor Roth typically won't work for those with large regular IRA accounts, such as from a previous employer's rollover of a 401(k).

Any existing pre-tax IRA accounts should be evaluated as to whether they should first be rolled over into a 401k, 403 or 457b plan, a tactic known as a reverse IRA to 401k rollover, assuming the plan permits reverse IRA rollovers. Next, both a traditional IRA and Roth IRA account are opened. The 2023 non-deductible limit of $6,500 ($7,500 if over 50) is then contributed to the traditional IRA. The final step is to transfer the money in the traditional IRA to the Roth IRA. This is better done as soon as possible because any earnings in the traditional IRA become taxable when converted to Roth IRA.

The big benefit here is that while contributions to a Roth IRA are limited by income, conversions are not limited by income and are tax free.[38]

Mega Backdoor Roth IRA

To be eligible for a mega backdoor Roth IRA, you must participate in a 401k plan at work that allows after-tax contributions—not Roth 401k contributions, just after-tax contributions. Many employer 401k plans do not allow after-tax contributions, so make sure your plan does.

The first step is to maximize your after-tax 401k contributions (not straight up Roth 401k contributions). The limit on total 401k contributions for 2023 is $66,000 ($73,500 for those over 50), comprised of an employee's pre-tax limit of $22,500, plus any employer contributions. The remainder can be made up of employee after-tax contributions, assuming the employer 401k permits them. In this way, you can maximize your 401k with after-tax contributions up to the contribution limit each year.[39]

Mitigating Overall Risk

When both spouses are working and each has a 401k, one spouse will often be more comfortable with investment risk than the other. In fact, it's unusual for both spouses to be comfortable with the same level of risk. What we typically recommend is that the couple perceive their two plans as a single 401k for the purpose of allocating investments. If one spouse will be retiring sooner than the other, we would then invest that individual's 401k more heavily in low-risk investments so it becomes the primary source of income to supplement their early retirement needs. We might not have to tap into the other individual's account until several years later, so we might increase the risk level in order to secure higher returns for that account. Naturally, we can make minor adjustments as necessary via rebalancing along the way.

An example would be if one spouse is 59 and the other is 55. The older spouse, who plans to retire next year, has $750k in his account, while his younger spouse has $500k in her account. Let's say they want to pull out $40k a year as replacement of his income. We might then designate his 401k as the account with the "safer money" and shift assets so it contains a higher percentage of bonds and other fixed-income assets. We can then allocate more aggressive assets to the younger spouse's 401k to balance the overall retirement portfolio. This is how a couple can use *strategic asset allocation* to view their individual retirement accounts as a single cohesive portfolio to better meet their specific retirement needs.

Invariably, when severe volatility hits the markets, one spouse will bolt for the door. Treating the two retirement accounts as a single retirement portfolio can alleviate this fear. It's nice to be able to reassure a couple by telling them that this strategy works out better for them both. One has a higher risk profile and is more willing to sustain market ups and downs, while the other is not. But in cases where they're going to need income from one of the accounts anyway, we can decrease the risk for the spouse who is more risk adverse without compromising the overall investment results. One of the beautiful aspects of diversification is that while the broad markets may be down, there are some investments that may be up. Regardless of which direction the market is moving, there will be some non-correlated investments that typically move in the opposite direction.

The Callan Periodic Table of Investment Returns

Annual Returns for Key Indices Ranked in Order of Performance (2002–2021)

2002	2003	2004	2005	2006	2007	2008	2009	2010	2011
Glbl ex-U.S. Fixed 22.37%	Emerging Market Equity 55.82%	Real Estate 37.96%	Emerging Market Equity 34.00%	Real Estate 42.12%	Emerging Market Equity 39.38%	U.S. Fixed Income 5.24%	Emerging Market Equity 78.51%	Small Cap Equity 26.85%	U.S. Fixed Income 7.84%
U.S. Fixed Income 10.26%	Small Cap Equity 47.25%	Emerging Market Equity 25.55%	Real Estate 15.35%	Emerging Market Equity 32.17%	Dev ex-U.S. Equity 12.44%	Glbl ex-U.S. Fixed 4.39%	High Yield 58.21%	Real Estate 19.63%	High Yield 4.98%
Real Estate 2.82%	Real Estate 40.69%	Dev ex-U.S. Equity 20.38%	Dev ex-U.S. Equity 14.47%	Dev ex-U.S. Equity 25.71%	Glbl ex-U.S. Fixed 11.03%	Cash Equivalent 2.06%	Real Estate 37.13%	Emerging Market Equity 18.88%	Glbl ex-U.S. Fixed 4.36%
Cash Equivalent 1.78%	Dev ex-U.S. Equity 39.42%	Small Cap Equity 18.33%	Large Cap Equity 4.91%	Small Cap Equity 18.37%	U.S. Fixed Income 6.97%	High Yield -26.16%	Dev ex-U.S. Equity 33.67%	High Yield 15.12%	Large Cap Equity 2.11%
High Yield -1.37%	High Yield 28.97%	Glbl ex-U.S. Fixed 12.54%	Small Cap Equity 4.55%	Large Cap Equity 15.79%	Large Cap Equity 5.49%	Small Cap Equity -33.79%	Small Cap Equity 27.17%	Large Cap Equity 15.06%	Cash Equivalent 0.10%
Emerging Market Equity -6.16%	Large Cap Equity 28.68%	High Yield 11.13%	Cash Equivalent 3.07%	High Yield 11.85%	Cash Equivalent 5.00%	Large Cap Equity -37.00%	Large Cap Equity 26.47%	Dev ex-U.S. Equity 8.95%	Small Cap Equity -4.18%
Dev ex-U.S. Equity -15.80%	Glbl ex-U.S. Fixed 19.36%	Large Cap Equity 10.88%	High Yield 2.74%	Glbl ex-U.S. Fixed 8.16%	High Yield 1.87%	Dev ex-U.S. Equity -43.56%	Glbl ex-U.S. Fixed 7.53%	U.S. Fixed Income 6.54%	Real Estate -6.46%
Small Cap Equity -20.48%	U.S. Fixed Income 4.10%	U.S. Fixed Income 4.34%	U.S. Fixed Income 2.43%	Cash Equivalent 4.85%	Small Cap Equity -1.57%	Real Estate -48.21%	U.S. Fixed Income 5.93%	Glbl ex-U.S. Fixed 4.95%	Dev ex-U.S. Equity -12.21%
Large Cap Equity -22.10%	Cash Equivalent 1.15%	Cash Equivalent 1.33%	Glbl ex-U.S. Fixed -8.65%	U.S. Fixed Income 4.33%	Real Estate -7.39%	Emerging Market Equity -53.33%	Cash Equivalent 0.21%	Cash Equivalent 0.13%	Emerging Market Equity -18.42%

2012	2013	2014	2015	2016	2017	2018	2019	2020	2021
Real Estate 27.73%	Small Cap Equity 38.82%	Real Estate 15.02%	Large Cap Equity 1.38%	Small Cap Equity 21.31%	Emerging Market Equity 37.28%	Cash Equivalent 1.87%	Large Cap Equity 31.49%	Small Cap Equity 19.96%	Large Cap Equity 28.71%
Emerging Market Equity 18.23%	Large Cap Equity 32.39%	Large Cap Equity 13.69%	U.S. Fixed Income 0.55%	High Yield 17.13%	Dev ex-U.S. Equity 24.21%	U.S. Fixed Income 0.01%	Small Cap Equity 25.52%	Large Cap Equity 18.40%	Real Estate 26.09%
Dev ex-U.S. Equity 16.41%	Dev ex-U.S. Equity 21.02%	U.S. Fixed Income 5.97%	Cash Equivalent 0.05%	Large Cap Equity 11.96%	Large Cap Equity 21.83%	High Yield -2.08%	Dev ex-U.S. Equity 22.49%	Emerging Market Equity 18.31%	Small Cap Equity 14.82%
Small Cap Equity 16.35%	High Yield 7.44%	Small Cap Equity 4.89%	Real Estate -0.79%	Emerging Market Equity 11.18%	Small Cap Equity 14.65%	Glbl ex-U.S. Fixed -2.15%	Real Estate 21.91%	Glbl ex-U.S. Fixed 10.11%	Dev ex-U.S. Equity 12.62%
Large Cap Equity 16.00%	Real Estate 3.67%	High Yield 2.45%	Dev ex-U.S. Equity -3.04%	Real Estate 4.06%	Glbl ex-U.S. Fixed 10.51%	Large Cap Equity -4.38%	Emerging Market Equity 18.44%	Dev ex-U.S. Equity 7.59%	High Yield 5.28%
High Yield 15.81%	Cash Equivalent 0.07%	Cash Equivalent 0.03%	Small Cap Equity -4.41%	Dev ex-U.S. Equity 2.75%	Real Estate 10.36%	Real Estate -5.63%	High Yield 14.32%	U.S. Fixed Income 7.51%	Cash Equivalent 0.05%
U.S. Fixed Income 4.21%	U.S. Fixed Income -2.02%	Emerging Market Equity -2.19%	High Yield -4.47%	U.S. Fixed Income 2.65%	High Yield 7.50%	Small Cap Equity -11.01%	U.S. Fixed Income 8.72%	High Yield 7.11%	U.S. Fixed Income -1.54%
Glbl ex-U.S. Fixed 4.09%	Emerging Market Equity -2.60%	Glbl ex-U.S. Fixed -3.09%	Glbl ex-U.S. Fixed -6.02%	Glbl ex-U.S. Fixed 1.49%	U.S. Fixed Income 3.54%	Dev ex-U.S. Equity -14.09%	Glbl ex-U.S. Fixed 5.09%	Cash Equivalent 0.67%	Emerging Market Equity -2.54%
Cash Equivalent 0.11%	Glbl ex-U.S. Fixed -3.08%	Dev ex-U.S. Equity -4.32%	Emerging Market Equity -14.92%	Cash Equivalent 0.33%	Cash Equivalent 0.86%	Emerging Market Equity -14.57%	Cash Equivalent 2.28%	Real Estate -9.04%	Glbl ex-U.S. Fixed -7.05%

The Callan Periodic Table of Investment Returns conveys the strong ***case for diversification*** across asset classes (stocks vs. bonds), capitalizations (large vs. small), and equity markets (U.S. vs. global ex-U.S.). The Table highlights the uncertainty inherent in all capital markets. Rankings change every year. Also noteworthy is the difference between absolute and relative performance, as returns for the top-performing asset class span a wide range over the past 20 years.

A printable copy of The Callan Periodic Table of Investment Returns is available on our website at ***callan.com/periodic-table/****.*

Callan Institute

Research | Education | Dialogue

(Graphic 3.3a Callan Asset Table 2001-2021)

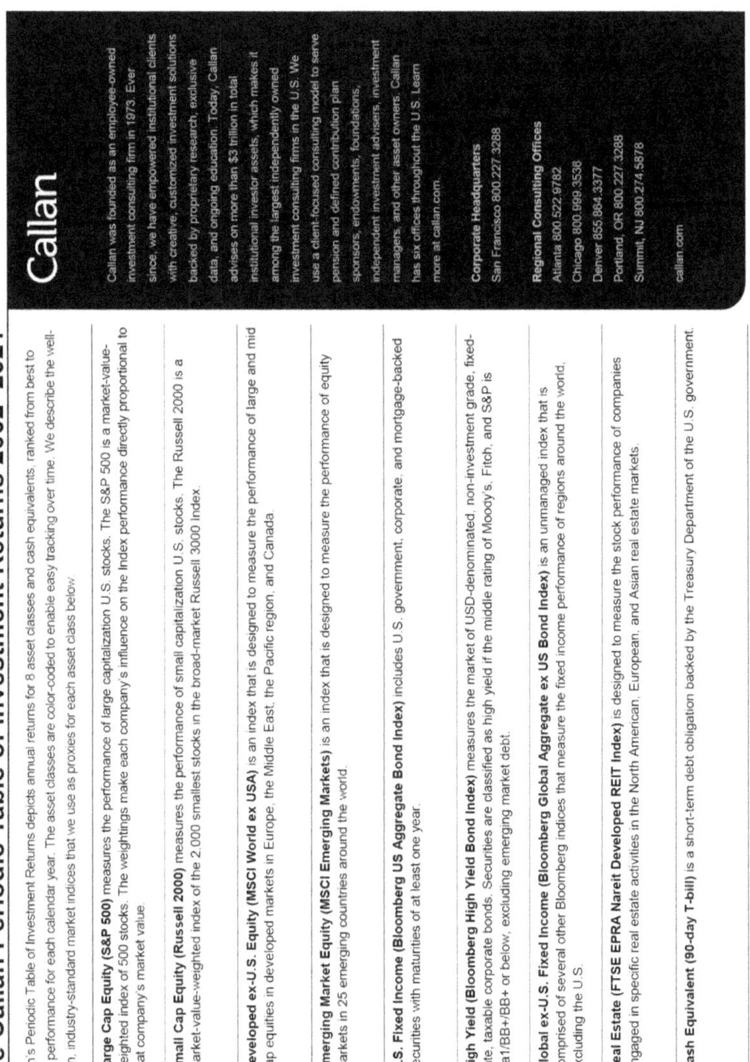

The Callan Periodic Table of Investment Returns 2002–2021

Callan's Periodic Table of Investment Returns depicts annual returns for 8 asset classes and cash equivalents, ranked from best to worst performance for each calendar year. The asset classes are color-coded to enable easy tracking over time. We describe the well-known, industry-standard market indices that we use as proxies for each asset class below.

- **Large Cap Equity (S&P 500)** measures the performance of large capitalization U.S. stocks. The S&P 500 is a market-value-weighted index of 500 stocks. The weightings make each company's influence on the Index performance directly proportional to that company's market value.
- **Small Cap Equity (Russell 2000)** measures the performance of small capitalization U.S. stocks. The Russell 2000 is a market-value-weighted index of the 2,000 smallest stocks in the broad-market Russell 3000 Index.
- **Developed ex-U.S. Equity (MSCI World ex USA)** is an index that is designed to measure the performance of large and mid cap equities in developed markets in Europe, the Middle East, the Pacific region, and Canada.
- **Emerging Market Equity (MSCI Emerging Markets)** is an index that is designed to measure the performance of equity markets in 25 emerging countries around the world.
- **U.S. Fixed Income (Bloomberg US Aggregate Bond Index)** includes U.S. government, corporate, and mortgage-backed securities with maturities of at least one year.
- **High Yield (Bloomberg High Yield Bond Index)** measures the market of USD-denominated, non-investment grade, fixed-rate, taxable corporate bonds. Securities are classified as high yield if the middle rating of Moody's, Fitch, and S&P is Ba1/BB+/BB+ or below, excluding emerging market debt.
- **Global ex-U.S. Fixed Income (Bloomberg Global Aggregate ex US Bond Index)** is an unmanaged index that is comprised of several other Bloomberg indices that measure the fixed income performance of regions around the world, excluding the U.S.
- **Real Estate (FTSE EPRA Nareit Developed REIT Index)** is designed to measure the stock performance of companies engaged in specific real estate activities in the North American, European, and Asian real estate markets.
- **Cash Equivalent (90-day T-bill)** is a short-term debt obligation backed by the Treasury Department of the U.S. government.

Callan

Callan was founded as an employee-owned investment consulting firm in 1973. Ever since, we have empowered institutional clients with creative, customized investment solutions backed by proprietary research, exclusive data, and ongoing education. Today, Callan advises on more than $3 trillion in total institutional investor assets, which makes it among the largest independently owned investment consulting firms in the U.S. We use a client-focused consulting model to serve pension and defined contribution plan sponsors, endowments, foundations, independent investment advisers, investment managers, and other asset owners. Callan has six offices throughout the U.S. Learn more at callan.com.

Corporate Headquarters
San Francisco 800.227.3288

Regional Consulting Offices
Atlanta 800.522.9782
Chicago 800.999.3536
Denver 855.864.3377
Portland, OR 800.227.3288
Summit, NJ 800.274.5878

callan.com

(Graphic 3.3b Callan Asset Table 2001-2021)

If the couple and I have established a mutual trust relationship and I know the investment profile that better suits them is outside of their tolerance for risk, I know I can take their portfolio outside of that standard deviation and they will be comfortable because we have that trust relationship. I'm able to achieve a higher risk adjusted return for them than if they were left to self-manage their accounts and had no one to show them the value of staying invested across equity classes.

Case Study

Let's assume you are age 50, earning $100k annually and making maximum pre-tax 401k contributions of $30,000 annually. Your employer makes a 3% matching contribution of $3,000. Your maximum allowable total 401k annual contribution is $73,500 (including your over 50 catch up). Deducting your and your employer's combined $33,000 contribution means you can contribute up to $40,500 post-tax into your 401k.

Your post-tax contribution also grows tax-free, not unlike a Roth, and when you retire, you can separate the post-tax portion by rolling it directly into a Roth IRA. Earnings on post-tax contributions, however, are considered "pre-tax" and are taxable when withdrawn. Roth 401k contributions and earnings accumulate tax free.

All of this can also be done in conjunction with a health savings account (HSA) which allows you to save almost $8,000 more each year, money that can be withdrawn tax-free during retirement to pay for healthcare costs, Medicare supplement premiums, long-term healthcare premiums or costs, etc. This strategy can be a tremendous boost for so-called "empty nesters" serious about building substantial retirement savings. As a couple, they could potentially contribute a combined $135,000 annually, plus their non-deductible Roth IRA contributions, plus their HSA contributions. It can represent a huge sum for retirement.

A little-known but important detail is that individuals can withdraw penalty-free from a 401k or deferred compensation plan at age 55 if they leave employment (whether laid off, fired or quit) and retire. I find many people mistakenly believe they have to draw down from some other source if they retire early.

Awhile back, an engineer working at Microsoft came in to see me. His compensation, like most senior engineers at the company, was in excess of $200k. He and his wife were saving the maximum in his 401k, another $50k in a brokerage account each year and nearly had their mortgage paid off. They were living on $70k a year and saving the rest, but they were paying a heavy tax load. He was unaware that Microsoft allowed him to make post-tax contributions to his 401k, as a number of Fortune 500 companies do.

What made the experience more interesting for me was that an advanced-degree engineer had a difficult time accepting the fact that he could grow his retirement savings so much faster by contributing the maximum to his 401k (pre- and after-tax) and allowing the money to grow tax-free versus putting his after-tax savings into a brokerage account and paying income taxes on it each year. And, as it turned out, Microsoft actually allows post-tax 401k contributions to be held in a brokerage account, so the engineer didn't have to change his choice of investments, just the structure in which they were held, to realize a significant retirement gain.

Here was a 50-year-old who hoped to retire at 55 but didn't see how he could make it happen and feel comfortable he would have enough to last through retirement. He now can put an additional $44,000 a year (including his catch up) into his 401k for the next five years and have it accumulate tax-free. At age 55, assuming a 7% compound rate of return, he will have roughly $325,000 in after-tax 401k growth, in addition to his pre-tax contribution accumulation. By the time he begins withdrawals, say at age 70, he should have approximately $1 million, just in post-tax accumulation.

This is one of the most exciting and rewarding financial strategies I have ever come across! There is no other way my client could have secured such an enormous tax-free contribution. He was evidently as excited as we were about the windfall because he shared his experience with some fellow engineers at work who have since become clients.

Options for the Self Employed

Someone who owns their own business without employees has an opportunity to secure considerable tax savings using a solo 401k plan— or what the IRS calls a one-participant 401k—which offers some unique planning flexibility. While the plan is restricted to self-employed individuals without employees, the plan can be used to cover the business owner's spouse as well. For 2023, participants can contribute up to $66,000 plus an additional $7,500 catch-up contribution if age 50 or older. Contributions are pre-tax so they reduce taxable income for the year. Distributions are taxed as income and taxes and penalties apply to distributions taken before age 59 ½. There are also solo Roth 401k plans available for post-tax investing. Self-employed individuals are both employee and employer. As employees, they can contribute up to $22,500 or 100% of their compensation, whichever is less. As employers, they can make an additional profit-sharing contribution of up to 25% of their compensation or net self-employment income—their net profit less half their self-employment tax and the plan contributions they made as employees. The limit on compensation used to calculate contributions is $330,000 in 2023. If a sponsor's spouse earns income from the business, the amount the couple could contribute could effectively double, depending on income levels. As an employee, the spouse could contribute up to the $22,500 limit (plus the 50-and-older catch-up provision, if applicable). As the employer, the sponsor could then make the plan's profit-sharing contribution for the spouse, of up to 25% of compensation.[40]

Small Businesses with Employees

As a small business owner with employees— whether a sole proprietor, partnership or corporation—you have several retirement plan options. The easiest to set up and administer is the simplified employee pension (SEP), which is based on an individual retirement account (IRA). Unlike qualified plans that must be established by the end of the business year, a SEP can be set up any time prior to the business' tax-filing deadline and does not require filing 5500 returns.

The SEP allows you as a business owner to contribute to both your employees and your own retirement savings. Contributions are made to an IRA set up for each employee participant (a SEP-IRA) and only you, the employer, can make contributions, subject to a limit of 25% of each qualified employee's total compensation or a maximum of $66,000 in 2023, whichever is less. The same 25% limit applies to contributions for yourself, based on your net earnings. Contributions grow tax-deferred until withdrawn in retirement and when made are tax deductible to the business.[41] Each year, you can decide how much to contribute on behalf of your employees. If you have a bad year, you aren't locked into making a contribution.

A similar employer-sponsored plan is the SIMPLE IRA. An important difference is that your employees can also contribute to the plan. As an employer, you have two contribution formula choices: match up to 3% each employee's annual contribution, or set up a non-elective 2% contribution of each employee's compensation—up to $330,000—without requiring employee contributions. For 2023, the employee contribution limit is $15,500 with an additional catch-up contribution of $3,500 for those 50 years and older.[42]

While a SEP IRA can be set up by any size business, a SIMPLE IRA is for businesses with 100 employees or less. Overall, the SEP plan is a better option for most small businesses because it allows for larger contributions and greater flexibility.[43]

Chapter Four

Remaining Composed When Facing Turbulence

Pilots know that given enough time in the air, they will experience severe turbulence at some point. How a pilot responds to the hazard often determines whether the plane eventually lands safely. Pilots that anticipate and prepare for turbulence and other challenges are better able to remain calm and manage their emotions during turmoil. Investors able to respond to market volatility dispassionately and stay the course avoid the financially punishing mistakes of those who react based on their emotions.

According to the 2016 Dalbar Quantitative Analysis of Investor Behavior (QAIB), in 2015 the average equity mutual fund investor underperformed the S&P 500 by a margin of 3.66%. This was not a one-year aberration but rather a long-term trend. The 20-year annualized S&P return was 8.19% compared with just 4.67% annualized return for the average equity mutual fund investor — a gap of 3.52%.

A report by the investment research company Morningstar® found that investors also experienced significantly lower returns than were earned by the very funds they were invested in. Morningstar® found that because of the timing of investors purchases and sales of fund shares, investors performed worse than if they had simply held the fund through good and bad times. Much of the discrepancy can be attributed to behavioral or cognitive biases.

History shows that mutual fund investors generally increase inflows after observing periods of strong performance. They buy at high prices when future expected returns are lower, and they sell after observing periods of poor performance when future expected returns are now higher. This results in what author Carl Richards called the "behavior gap," in which investor returns are well below the returns of the funds in which they invest. Perhaps with this observation in mind, Warren Buffett once said, "The most important quality for an investor is temperament, not intellect."

Life might be much easier for financial advisors if their clients always make rational investment decisions based on fundamentals, but that's typically not the case. Investors often act irrationally and make decisions based on emotions and innate behavioral biases. The study of these behaviors is known as behavioral finance. It first emerged in the 1980s when researchers began to explore the cracks in the efficient market hypothesis (EMH), a theory that holds the price of a stock—or virtually any investment for that matter—reflects all the information the market already knows about it, and that stocks trade on exchanges at their fair market value. The theory, widely embraced as dogma up until that point, evolved from a PhD dissertation by Eugene Fama in the 1960s, who became known as the "father of modern finance."

Advocates of EMH believe that it is impossible to outperform the overall market using market timing or stock-picking expertise, and that the only way to beat the market is to buy riskier investments. As a result, they hold that there is no advantage to be gained by searching for undervalued stocks or trying to predict market movements through either fundamental or technical analysis.[44]

Much of what is known about behavioral finance—and behavioral economics in general—is attributed to the pioneering work of Daniel Kahneman and Amos Tversky. Kahneman's bestselling 2011 book, "Thinking, Fast and Slow," summarizes much of his research. Numerous experiments exposed the irrationality of how humans make decisions and identified some 20 "cognitive biases"—subconscious reasoning errors that distort a person's perception and judgment. *New York Times* columnist David Brooks was so impressed with the work that he declared, "It will be remembered hundreds of years from now. Kahneman and Tversky are like the Lewis and Clark of the mind."[45]

Investors often rely too heavily on what is known as "System 1" thinking—instinctive judgments that arise from associations stored in our memory. These occur automatically and quickly, with virtually no effort on our part versus logically evaluating the available information before reaching a conclusion. System 1 is critical to survival. It's what makes you duck when someone on the golf course yells "fore!" or when you swerve to avoid an oncoming vehicle. But as Daniel Kahneman has demonstrated, it's also a source of bias that can result in poor decision making, because our intuitions frequently lead us astray. Other sources of bias involve System 2 thinking—reasoning that has become skewed. Cognitive limitations or unwillingness to invest the time to adequately research an investment, for example, can cause investors to focus on the wrong things.[46]

> "The illusion that we understand the past fosters overconfidence in our ability to predict the future."
>
> Daniel Kahneman

Cognitive Biases

As a group, the cognitive biases Kahneman and Tversky categorized can be defined as systematic errors in thinking that affect the decisions and judgments we make when processing and interpreting information.[47] As time has passed, mental shortcuts have evolved. Example, when we sense danger, we react quickly and employ a "fight or flight" tactic. Most cognitive biases, however, rather than clarifying, tend to cloud our judgment, creating systematic errors in our thinking process that cause us to lose objectivity.

Generally speaking, there are two types of cognitive biases: information processing and emotional biases. Information processing biases are statistical, quantitative errors of judgment that are relatively easy to fix with new information. Emotional biases are much harder to change as they are based on attitudes and feelings, conscious and unconscious.[48]

I've piloted small aircraft for many years. One of the most important lessons in aviation is the need for a calm, cool hand, particularly for individual pilots like myself. We have the same license as professional airline pilots but they are much more thoroughly trained, especially in emergency procedures. They also have one or two other trained pilots in the aircraft that can take over the controls if necessary. If you fly long enough as a single pilot, you are going to experience moments of terror. The question is, how are you going to handle those moments?

As pilots, we are instructed to "always fly the plane." What they mean by that is you can reach a point of sensory overload, oversaturation if you will, which can cause you to panic, get discombobulated and turn into a stall. A well-known problem is that under pressure, pilots sometimes freeze and let go of the controls. Seasoned pilots understand that no matter what happens and how confused you may be, you have to continue to fly the plane, right up until your last breath.

I think a similar thing happens to some investors when losses or market volatility causes them to freak out, grab their mouse and make panic-driven decisions without thinking it though. I see people with 20-30% of their portfolios overweighted in a single tech stock like Apple become terrified every time the company makes a move. Like a pilot inadvertently flying upside down in a fog, they become disoriented and do the wrong thing.

What follows is a brief examination of some of the most common cognitive biases people display when making investment decisions.

Anchoring

When you rely on an initial piece of information to make subsequent judgments, it's called an anchoring bias. Psychologists use the term to describe the human tendency to rely too heavily, or anchor, on a single piece of information when making decisions. In his best-selling book on cognitive biases and heuristics, Kahneman offers this example of anchoring: "In negotiation, many people think that you have an advantage if you go second. But actually, the advantage is going first. And the reason is in something about the way the mind works. The mind tries to make sense out of whatever you put before it. This built-in tendency that we have of trying to make sense of everything that we encounter, that is a mechanism for anchoring."[49]

The anchoring effect often occurs in negotiations. For example, the initial price offered for an automobile sets the standard for the rest of the negotiations, so that prices lower than the initial price seem more reasonable even if they are still higher than what the car is really worth. While anchoring affects negotiations, goal-setting can affect the end result. In a review of goal setting research, negotiation scholars Deborah Zetik and Alice Stuhlmacher of DePaul University found that when negotiators set specific, challenging goals, they consistently outperform those who set lower or vague goals.[50] As it relates to investing and saving, those who agree and commit to specific goals, such as retirement or college savings goals, tend to save more and are more likely to reach their goals than those who have a less-defined blueprint. We began helping our clients shift to goal-based planning many years ago in much the same way institutional investors (like pension plans) have done and found to be very productive. In other words, we set the tone of being in the goal phase.

Confirmation

Confirmation is a bias that prompts us to embrace information that supports what we already believe and ignore information that refutes our beliefs. We look for answers that justify our point of view. Confirmation bias occurs when people filter out potentially useful facts and opinions that don't coincide with their preconceived notions. Having our beliefs confirmed makes us feel validated whereas conflicting information might make us feel insecure or foolish. When we research an investment, confirmation causes us to seek out sources that reinforce our preconceived judgment about the investment.[51]

In her book, *Mistakes Were Made (but Not by Me): Why We Justify Foolish Beliefs, Bad Decisions, and Hurtful Acts*, Carol Tarvis offers a cogent description of confirmation bias:

> "If new information is consonant with our beliefs, we think it is well founded and useful: 'Just what I always said!' But if the new information is dissonant, then we consider it biased or foolish: 'What a dumb argument!' So powerful is the need for consonance that when people are forced to look at disconfirming evidence, they will find a way to criticize, distort or dismiss it so that they can maintain or even strengthen their existing belief."

Cognitive Dissonance

This is the mental conflict that occurs when we discover our beliefs are wrong. Confirmation bias occurs when we selectively collect evidence that supports our beliefs and minimizes contradictory evidence. Cognitive dissonance occurs when newly acquired information conflicts with pre-existing understandings, causing discomfort. When we make investment decisions that result in losses, we rationalize the losses in order to ease our cognitive dissonance: "I shouldn't have listened to my broker; I knew better," or "The stock kept climbing; everyone was buying it." **The bias prevents us from learning how to avoid the same mistake in the future.**[52]

Cognitive dissonance was first described by social psychologist Leon Festinger. It arose from the participant observation study of a cult which believed that the earth was going to be destroyed by a flood, and what happened to its members, many of whom had abandoned their homes and jobs to work for the cult. When the flood failed to occur, most members, recognizing that they had made fools of themselves, put it down to experience, whereas committed members tended to reinterpret the evidence to show that they were right all along, that the earth was not destroyed because of the faithfulness of the cult members.[53]

Disposition Effect

The disposition effect is the tendency of investors to sell winning positions and hold onto losing positions. This effect directly contradicts the investing adage, "Cut your losses short and let your winners run." As a result of their fear of loss, investors often hesitate to realize their losses and hold stocks for too long, hoping for a recovery. It's a reluctance to sell a stock that has lost money. By not taking a loss, investors can avoid responsibility for their mistakes.

For investors, the disposition effect is all about hoping to get even. Selling a stock at a loss is the equivalent of admitting we were wrong. Similarly, realizing a gain proves that we were right. Thus, the tendency of this bias is to avoid regret and seek gratification.

The bias is readily apparent in real estate dealings, where owners refuse to lower the price of properties that don't sell, despite common sense telling them the only reason the properties haven't moved is because their price is too high.

In discussing the irrational behavior disposition effect has on investors, Nicholas Barberis, Professor of Finance at the Yale School of Management, examines the significance of active investors regularly being outperformed by passive, longer-term investors. He asks, "Why do buyers think they know something the seller doesn't? Why do investors think the odds don't apply to them? Why do they think they are the exception to the apparently obvious rule?"[54]

Familiarity

The familiarity bias encourages us to invest in "familiar" things: companies whose names are well-known to us or whose products or services we like, or in local or regional companies we know—or think we know—more about because they are in close proximity. Beyond the geographic familiarity bias, investors also exhibit strong preferences for investing in the companies they work for or where a friend or family member is employed.

The result of buying familiar investments is that we fail to do adequate research and underestimate the level of risk in the investment. We end up with a portfolio that is overweighted in a single company, industry or geographic area and burdened with unnecessary risk.

The familiarity bias is prevalent here in the Seattle area. There are numerous Fortune 500 companies headquartered here and locals are not only cognizant of developments at these firms, they grow increasingly comfortable investing in them as a result of their being nearby. The fact that many of these companies have generated impressive stock returns over an extended period has made locals feel even more secure investing heavily in them—sometimes to the extent that their portfolio becomes overweighted in a single issue or sector. No matter how successful a company is, it is subject to competition, obsolescence, product liability, bad publicity, shareholder proxy issues, leadership turnover and other setbacks.

Fear of Regret

You've probably heard someone rationalize a questionable action or purchase by saying, "I knew if I didn't do it, I would probably regret it later."

Fear of regret refers to investors anticipating regret if they make a wrong choice and this concern becomes a factor in making decisions. Fear of regret can play a significant role in dissuading us from taking action. It impels investors to buy hot stocks for fear of missing out. It may also cause investors to hold on to losing stocks to avoid feeling regret, hoping the stocks will somehow return to the original purchase price. The fear of feeling responsible for losses is typically greater than the pain of the loss.

We sometimes think less about making a good decision and more about avoiding a bad one. This anticipation of regret over making the wrong choice is often factored into our decision-making as a form of emotional insurance. Regret aversion tends to be an even larger factor in decisions with greater or longer-lasting consequences. A diner may experience regret bias when choosing an entrée, but the ramifications are trivial when compared to the potential regret over choosing the wrong automobile or home. This makes regret aversion a consequential bias as it can impact high stakes decisions.[55]

Framing

Framing bias occurs when people make a decision based on the way the information is presented, as opposed to just on the facts themselves. Framing may cause investors willingness to tolerate risk to fall when markets are falling. Alternatively, their risk tolerance may rise when markets are rising. This often causes investors to buy-high and sell-low.

Most people prefer an outcome that is presented in a positive light as opposed to a negative light, despite the same outcome. A politician who runs on a promise to "increase employment" is likely to garner more votes than one who proposes to "reduce unemployment" merely by framing the same issue in a different light.

Another analogy would be if you were diagnosed with a serious illness, and two doctors give you different diagnoses. One says, "With proper treatment, you have an 80 percent chance of a full recovery." The other says, "There's a 20 percent chance that you'll die even after being treated." Which doctor would you choose for treatment? Even though both diagnoses are exactly the same, most people will pick the first doctor because an 80 percent chance of recovery sounds better than a 20 percent chance of death.[56]

Gambler's Fallacy

The gambler's fallacy—also known as the negative recency effect—occurs when a bettor, speculator or investor expects a reversal in luck after a prolonged run of one outcome. In other words, after a series of wins, they come to expect a loss (or vice versa). It causes people to assume that if a coin has landed "heads" six times in a row, it's more likely to land "tails" the seventh time. In fact, the odds are still 50-50.

A classic example is the roulette player who diligently records the outcome of each spin of the wheel, with the implicit belief that he or she can discern a pattern. If red numbers have been called more frequently in the recent past, gamblers often place their next bets on black, and vice versa. Assuming the wheel is not rigged, however, there is no logical support for this behavior.

The gambler's fallacy should not be confused with its opposite, the hot hand fallacy, which is the erroneous belief that the more frequently an outcome has occurred in the recent past, the greater is the likelihood of that outcome in the future. This bias in judgment was based on the perception that a basketball player had "hot hands" after sinking several consecutive shots. Fans who subscribe to this theory believe the player's chances of making the next basket to be higher than usual, even though previous successful shots have nothing to do with a player's chance of making the next basket.[57]

The human brain has difficulty understanding probability and large numbers, so we are disposed to believe that past events can somehow change or impact future probabilities. Many investors try to analyze the past performance of the stock market in order to pick future stocks that should be winners, usually with poor results, as evidenced by the fact that precious few money managers outperform the S&P 500.[58]

Herding

Herding occurs when we allow collective behavior to override our personal instincts. The combined actions of a large group convince us they must know something we don't. We assume they have better information than we do. Those susceptible to the herding bias make investment decisions they would not make as informed individuals.

There is abundant empirical evidence of the dangers of merging with the mob, from the crash of 1929, to the dot.com bubble burst in 2000, to the real estate debacle of 2008.

Humans are hard-wired to herd. Analyst recommendations are an endemic source of herd behavior, despite the fact that their opinions, often expressed on financial talk shows, are rarely questioned when they subsequently prove incorrect. To the contrary, the same analysts tend to appear regularly, whether their recommendations prove accurate or not. One could speculate that this might be an example of the show's producers falling victim to the familiarity bias.

Many people actually find it emotionally or psychologically painful to go against the crowd. If you have ever decided against doing something the rest of your friends or associates did, you likely felt at least some degree of discomfort. For contrarian investors, psychologists have found that it may actually cause physical pain. In fact, in one psychological study, they found that regularly being a contrarian investor or encouraging other people to be contrarian investors was somewhat like actually having your arm broken on a regular basis.[59]

Many investors religiously follow the advice of high-profile media types like Jim Cramer. Without question, Cramer is a hard-working, charismatic entertainer who enjoyed success as a hedge fund manager for 14 years, although his claims regarding performance have been widely debated. However, as G.E. Miller, writing in his blog, "20 Something Finance" noted:

> "He quotes his investing track record in favorable light all too often. He's also not the first to admit when he's been wrong, which is quite often. Perhaps, it is his ego which allows him to spit out buy and sell recommendations at breakneck pace. I hope someone, somewhere, is keeping track of the returns of all of his buy/sell picks. I'd love to see the results."[60]

I knew an advisor who diligently tabulated Cramer's buy and sell recommendations over an extended period of time. He reported that Cramer's record was abysmal and questioned why any knowledgeable investor would pay attention to his recommendations.

Loss Aversion

Loss aversion is where investors worry more about avoiding losses than making gains.

When choosing among several alternatives, loss aversion can cause us to avoid losses and choose what we perceive as sure wins because the pain of losing is greater than the satisfaction of an equivalent gain. Also known as the endowment effect, loss aversion can cause someone to work harder to keep something than they did to acquire it in the first place.

Investors experiencing this bias typically feel the pain of a loss at least twice as much as they enjoy equivalent gains. Loss aversion doesn't mean that people would prefer to avoid losses because that would be completely rational. Instead, loss aversion refers to having a much greater desire to avoid any risk that could bring about a loss, rather than to acquire a similar gain. A person viewing themselves as losing something places more value on the thing than someone who views a transaction as receiving the thing. As Kahneman put it, "losses loom larger than gains."

Not wishing to experience the pain of a loss, investors will avoid acknowledging the loss until it is actually realized and cannot be ignored. They will retain a losing investment, even as their losses increase, so that they can avoid facing reality as long as they haven't liquidated the investment. Subconsciously, they believe the loss doesn't "count" until the investment is closed. The effect of this is that investors continue to hold onto losing investments much longer than they should and end up suffering much bigger losses than necessary.[61]

Mental Accounting

In this behavior, investors compartmentalize their money, which affects how they will spend money differently, depending on the compartment. Tax refunds, bonuses and casino winnings are examples of mental accounting as they are often viewed as "found money" to be used for discretionary purchases rather than to pay bills or saved.

Mental accounting causes us to make bad decisions about money. It's a bias based on the fact that people do not think of value in absolute terms but rather as being relative to other factors. It's like filing money into different mental bank accounts and applying different rules, depending on how the money was acquired. Is the money regular income or an unexpected windfall? We are more likely to spend windfall gains than regular income—and are inclined to spend them on luxuries versus essentials—even though there is nothing different about the money. We feel like it's special, so we feel justified in spending it extravagantly.[62]

Overconfidence

Overconfidence bias is the assumption that we are smarter than the next guy, typically due to a fictitious sense of competence or knowledge. It prompts us to believe we can predict the outcomes of our investment decisions.

Professor Donald A. Moore calls overconfidence "the mother of all psychological biases." Professor Daniel Kahneman called it "the most significant of the cognitive biases." Among many other things, overconfidence has been blamed for the sinking of the Titanic, the nuclear accident at Chernobyl, the loss of Space Shuttles Challenger and Columbia, and the subprime mortgage crisis of 2008. Overconfidence contributes to excessive day trading, entrepreneurial failure, legal disputes, political partisanship and even war.[63]

Writing in *Psychology Today*,[64] Moore notes,

> "Yet another way overconfidence earns its title as the mother of all biases is by giving the other decision-making biases teeth. If we were appropriately humble about our psychological vulnerabilities, we would be better able to protect ourselves from the errors to which human nature makes us prone. Instead, an excessive faith in ourselves and our judgment means that we too often ignore our vulnerability to bias and error."

Putting aside my decision to list these biases in alphabetical order, it appears we should pay particular attention to the perils of overconfidence bias.

A grand example of overconfidence is the survey of students at the Harvard Business School where 86% said they were better looking than their peers. That some of these people may now be in charge of major corporations or high political office is a frightening prospect!

People who purchase lottery tickets probably suffer from overconfidence bias. It is three times more likely for a person driving 10 miles to buy a lottery ticket to be killed in a car accident than to win the jackpot (Orkin, 1991).

People tend to be unrealistically optimistic about their financial futures. When they get within a few years of their planned retirement and realize they have insufficient funds, they may resort to risky investments they hope will somehow make up for what they failed to do.[65]

Recency Bias

This is the speculative conviction that a recent trend will continue into the future. It's strikingly evident in how increasing numbers of individual investors buy stocks as a bull market lengthens. Not only do more and more investors jump in, but they tend to buy high-profile stocks after the issues have already experienced substantial appreciation and their continued outperformance is questionable, MAMAA (Meta, Amazon, Microsoft, Apple and Alphabet) stocks being a recent example. The bias is equally observable in down markets. The worse the market declined during the 2008 financial crisis, the more the trading volume intensified. Seeking to exit losing positions, many investors sold, locking in losses at or near the bottom. Then, convinced the declines would continue, many sat on the sidelines and passively watched as a decade-long bull market emerged and stocks renewed their upward rise.[66]

It's far easier for us to remember what happened most recently, a mental shortcut that can short-circuit investing decisions. Recency bias causes us to place excessive importance on what we most vividly remember. We see our investment portfolio dropping in value and recency bias convinces us that it will continue to keep on dropping.[67]

Sunk Cost Fallacy

This bias causes us to believe we are entitled to get something out if we put something in, whether it's effort, time or money. When we make an investment bet and lose, we experience a sunk cost bias—a loss that cannot be recovered. Our aversion to losing makes us irrationally cling to the idea of recoupling the loss, even though it has already disappeared. Poker players call this "chasing the pot"—making a bet and chasing after it, likely making additional bets with the hope of recovering the original bet instead of cutting our losses.[68]

People often overeat at a restaurant, ordering too much food and then having to consume all of it in order to "get their money's worth." Similarly, someone who bought a $50 concert ticket will drive through a blizzard to attend because they feel compelled to do so after having made the initial investment. If the costs outweigh the benefits, the extra costs incurred (inconvenience, time or even money) are held in a different mental account than the one associated with the ticket transaction (Thaler, 1999).

An epic example of sunk cost was the SST Concorde, a supersonic passenger jet which was a joint project between the French and British governments. After significant investment, it became apparent that the project was likely to lose money. The great amount of money already spent (and perhaps the desire to shield some government egos) prompted officials to continue, despite the obvious losses. The predictable result was ever greater losses until no one could continue to justify the project and the SST was retired amid grand pomposity. The bias was in full effect in this instance, causing catastrophic financial losses because officials found themselves unable to write off the sunk costs and accept the smaller losses.[69]

Overcoming Biases

Many of our cognitive biases are the product of human nature. Accurate beliefs have frequently mattered less for survival than the ability to cooperate and persuade. Our beliefs also tend to be self-protective.

Traditional financial theory suggests that people with money to invest tend to make consistent, rational financial decisions. This implies that when individuals receive new information, they revise their thinking, then make informed investment choices. This concept may sound perfectly logical but as we know, investors often act irrationally, leading to counterproductive results. Much of this is due to the behavioral biases discussed here. Everyone has embedded biases within their psyche. These biases can be helpful in getting us through our daily lives but be detrimental to sound investing.

Investing behavioral biases are comprised of both cognitive and emotional biases. Cognitive biases stem chiefly from information processing or memory errors, whereas emotional biases stem from impulse or intuition and results in action based on feelings instead of facts.[70]

In my experience, most people are unaware of the behavioral biases that influence their investment judgments. Most will readily agree that biases affect other people's choices but resist acknowledging behaviors that cloud their own judgment. Researchers contend that this denial is due in large part to the fact that biases often occur unconsciously. As a result, people tend to infer that they are unbiased.

Legendary investor Benjamin Graham stressed that when making investment decisions, people should "establish proper mental and emotional attitudes." Graham observed that the investor's "chief problem and even his worst enemy, is likely to be himself." Behavioral biases are often the chief culprit.

While a copious amount of time has been devoted to the study of behavioral biases, few remedies have been discovered. Even behavioral finance originator Daniel Kahneman was at a loss as to how to overcome them. When asked, he admitted that after 40 years of experience, he too continues to commit these errors. He added, "Knowing the errors is not the recipe to avoiding them."

In my career as an advisor, I've encountered behavioral biases on almost a daily basis. They are innate in all of us. The key is to recognize them and minimize their impact on our decision-making so they don't jeopardize the important task of managing our financial future.

Perhaps the most common bias I've experienced is overconfidence, likely a biproduct of where I and most of my clients live, Seattle. In addition to the awe-inspiring beauty of the Pacific Northwest, the Seattle area is the home of some of the nation's most successful and enduring companies, including Amazon, Boeing, Microsoft, Paccar, Starbucks and Weyerhaeuser.

The employees of these companies often accumulate significant wealth from their deferred 401K plans. Many times, these benefits comprise the bulk of an employee's retirement fund, and it's not unusual for them to have investment portfolios heavily overweighted in the stock of their employer. It's often very difficult to get them to diversify away some of the risk of having most of their wealth tied up in a single stock when that stock has made them wealthy and they feel an understandable loyalty to the company that has provided their retirement security.

But having so much of one's wealth invested in a single stock—regardless of how well the stock has performed historically—is inadvisable from a financial risk perspective.

An example is Renton, WA-based Paccar, a 115-year-old Fortune 500 manufacturer of Kenworth and Peterbilt trucks. I have numerous clients who work for the Paccar family, many have for decades. It is a well-run company staffed by competent people who tend to be highly skilled. Many have become wealthy from owning company stock. But even highly successful companies like Paccar are susceptible to economic caprice, which happened during the financial crisis of 2008. Paccar stock had reached a high of 59.21 in July, 2007, but the financial crisis saw it plunge to a low of 26.73, a decrease of 55% in just 19 months! Obviously, a host of companies and industries were savaged by the crisis, and millions of investors were negatively affected. However, the impact was compounded for those whose portfolios lacked adequate diversity.

For Paccar employees, it took nearly seven years for their stock to recover the loss, again reaching 59.21 on Feb 7, 2014. Losses like these can change people's lives in ways not always apparent. They can cause important plans—weddings, college, major purchases—to be postponed or jettisoned altogether. The employees at Paccar learned a hard lesson: It's easier to build wealth with a single stock than it is to maintain wealth with a single stock because of the concentration risk.

In another widespread example of behavioral bias, many people in the area invested heavily in Frontier Bank, which was headquartered in nearby Everett, WA and had been in the area for many years. Most people outside of the Pacific Northwest probably never heard of it. It was a highly successful bank that worked closely with local real estate developers, among other businesses. Investing in the bank had made some people very wealthy. The CEO, a kind and generous man, was a well-known figure and highly regarded in the community. Many of the bank's employees, including lower-level workers, had become wealthy off of Frontier Bank stock.

Frontier Bank had 47 branches in Washington and Oregon. It was one of several local community banks that failed after lending too much to developers during the real estate runup prior to the financial crisis and ensuing recession. Frontier Bank was shuttered on April 30, 2010, its assets seized by the FDIC and sold to Union Bank of San Francisco. In 2013, the FDIC filed a lawsuit seeking $46 million in damages, alleging that the bank issued 11 multimillion-dollar loans to various borrowers who later defaulted, including a $22 million loan to a borrower whose liabilities to Frontier exceeded $53 million. Another major loan supported development of Streamline Tower in Las Vegas, a 21-story luxury condominium project that subsequently lurched into foreclosure. The lawsuit said Frontier was the biggest commercial bank headquartered in Western Washington at the time of its failure, with $3.6 billion in assets and $3.1 billion in deposits. In 2016, former executives settled a professional liability lawsuit brought by the Federal Deposit Insurance Corp. for $10 million.[71]

These slow-motion financial train wrecks often cause investors to lose everything they have saved over a lifetime. It has caused me great pain to see people suffer this kind of devastation. It rarely gets reported by the media, other than some vague reference, but people endure real pain and stress when companies make these kinds of errors.

One investor (not a client) invested in the bank on the advice of a Frontier banker he knew. As the bank continued to generate profits during the real boom of the early 2000's, the investor sold off some of his business assets in order to invest further in the bank. His roughly $ 200k investment eventually burgeoned into $12 million. His lifestyle was elevated and he acquired the trappings of a wealthy investor. He became a generous benefactor of a local private school his children attended and even helped fund scholarships for other, less fortunate children. Just prior to his economic implosion, his daughter, a CPA, came to see me and implored me to talk to her father about reducing some of his investment risk by diversifying his Frontier stock. The daughter said, "Dad is enthralled with the stock and refuses to sell any of it and reduce his exposure. You may be the only person I know who can convince him to diversify."

I approached the fellow and we spoke briefly but it was obvious he had no intention of letting go any of the bank stock. It had made him rich and, being what I would call an "immature investor," he refused to consider the possibility that he could get hurt. I had to tell his concerned daughter that there was nothing I could do to change her dad's mind.

When Frontier got into trouble, the stock plunged but the investor, like many others, refused to believe the bank could fail. When the FDIC lawsuit was announced, the bank imploded and its stock sank to zero. Devastated investors lost everything. I felt sorry for them.

It's difficult to get someone to diversify their portfolio once they have become zealous about the stock that made them wealthy in the first place. It's hard for them to recognize the risk. They can't understand how the party could ever end.

Well, the party didn't end, but unfortunately it took a long pause at an inopportune time.

My aborted attempt to help the investor was one of those situations where my experience and financial knowledge were of little value. It was frustrating and I still think about what I might have said that would have convinced him to change his mind, but his overconfidence bias was impenetrable. He lost his investment and much of what he had built up over the years in his businesses. It was truly sad, and he represented just one of thousands of investors and employees who were victims of their overconfidence or familiarity bias.

Unlike those who invested in Frontier Bank, Washington Mutual, and other banks that ultimately failed, those who held Paccar stock that we were able to convince to hang on and ride out the tailspin were ultimately rewarded for their perseverance.

For those unable or unwilling to stay the course with a stock that is only temporarily in distress but issued by a fundamentally sound company, their inability to overcome their loss aversion or herding bias can be devastating.

This happened to Paccar engineers and executives who had accumulated multimillion dollar stock portfolios, only to see their value eviscerated by the recession. The stock ultimately rebounded (to 85 as of this writing) as it has through various crises. I had previously discussed a financial plan, to diversify some of the risk away, with the employees. Those that refused later came in after having lost a major portion of their stock value and said, "Okay, let's diversify," but the loss was irretrievable. What they failed to understand is that the company, despite being well-run with a huge upside profit potential over the long term, is susceptible to market volatility or an economic crisis that can momentarily splinter a company. For well-run companies, its typically a temporary situation, but people become so frightened that they panic and liquidate. We managed to talk most of the Paccar employees into riding it out but, without question, it changed the trajectory of their retirement.

Fundamentals are Important

Diversifying your portfolio risk is fundamental. Each sector within asset class has certain characteristics which, over time, are reasonably predictable. Within the stock asset class there are small cap, mid cap, large cap, value, growth and others. Each provides a specific set of traits that can complement or offset others. If a Microsoft engineer accumulates a fortune in company stock, depending on the price to earnings ratio at the time, the stock may fall into one of several categories, such as growth or mid cap. We might logically look to see if there are other stocks in that space that are attractive and use them to diversify and reduce risk.

When a stock within a portfolio does exceptionally well, over time it gradually comes to represent a larger percentage of the portfolio. It's important to rebalance in order to maintain an appropriate asset allocation. This is another instance where the appropriate thing to do becomes an obstacle for someone who has accumulated a considerable amount of wealth by buying and holding a single stock, especially if it is their company stock. If the stock is in a tax-advantaged account, selling off some of that stock and reinvesting the money into other stocks that help balance the portfolio does not trigger a taxable event. Meanwhile the client achieves better diversification and reduced portfolio risk.

I know a lot of extremely smart people who are otherwise critical thinkers but lack that ability when it comes to financial matters in general and investing in particular. It can sometimes be a challenge for them to admit they might do better by letting a financial professional help them avoid potentially damaging biases such as overconfidence, loss aversion or familiarity. That may mean creating a financial plan they can commit to and fall back on when the markets get crazy. They also may find the calm, reassuring presence of a trusted advisor can help them avoid impulsive decisions & unhelpful biases, particularly during periods of extreme volatility or uncertainty.

Investors have to learn that market trends are not all linear. Stocks that do exceptionally well cannot rise indefinitely. Google the "Nifty Fifty" stocks of the past century and notice how many of them have gone the way of the dodo bird. Even the best-performing stocks reach a point where they're no longer great performers. Witness Apple. Superior returns can be achieved by diversifying outside or inside the same asset classes by reducing the concentration risk inherent in a single issue.

Try to avoid falling in love with a single stock, regardless of how well it has performed in the past. No stock is forever. As the adage goes, "Never fall in love with something that won't love you back."

> "Never buy a stock because it has gone up or sell one because it has gone down."
>
> Benjamin Graham,
> *The Intelligent Investor*

Chapter Five

Economic Indicators, the Business Cycle and Value Investing

Savvy investors have a good understanding of the four stages of the business cycle: expansion, peak, contraction, and trough. There are economic indicators that help predict what stage of the business cycle we are in. Pilots have an array of indicators that provide information critical to safe flight, including attitude indicator, altimeter, heading, vertical speed, tachometer and fuel gauges.

Perhaps due to my personal and professional success as an investor over prolonged periods, I am frequently asked how I go about choosing investments for my clients' portfolios. Of particular interest to my more analytical clients are the economic indicators that are harbingers of the business cycle.

As a value investor, I'm what the pioneering investor Benjamin Graham would call a "bottom feeder." In his classic book, *The Intelligent Investor,*[72] Graham explains the term—and his value investing philosophy on stock picking and market fluctuations—using the parable of "Mr. Market."

Graham advises us to imagine we have a business partner named Mr. Market, an obliging fellow who shows up each day to tell us what he thinks our interest in the business is worth. Usually, the prices he quotes seem reasonable based on our business prospects, but on some days, Mr. Market displays some erratic behavior. On these days, he is overwhelmed with either limitless optimism or hopeless despair, and will quote a price that sounds rather ridiculous. As intelligent, value investors, we have to be on guard against Mr. Market's temperamental outbursts. Rather than fall prey to his pricing gyrations—we must learn to take advantage of them.

If we understand the true value of our business and its prospects, we can take advantage of Mr. Market by selling when he quotes an outrageously high price and buying when he quotes an absurdly low price. Here's the best part: Mr. Market is impervious to how many times we abuse the relationship for our own benefit. Regardless of how often we saddle him with losses or rob him of gains, he will show up the next day ready to do business with you again.

Graham's Mr. Market analogy is a delightful metaphor for investors. Each day, the stock market quotes on thousands of businesses, and we can ignore or take advantage of those prices.[73]

There are numerous definitions of value investing and as many descriptions of the analyses used to uncover undervalued stocks of companies with potential that, for one reason or another, are unpopular at the time. For Graham, a key concept was that of intrinsic value of a company or its stock. The essence of value investing is using a stock analysis method to determine the stock's real value, with an eye toward buying stocks whose current share price is below its genuine value or worth, and with the belief that the market will eventually correct the share price to a higher level that more accurately represents its true value.

While Graham managed to keep things fairly simple, determining whether a stock's current price represents a value is a complex, protracted process. The financials are obviously important but must be interpreted in light of the current economic conditions and where we are in the business cycle. There are economic indicators that help predict, from a macroeconomic view, what stage of the business cycle we are in.

The traditional definition of economic or business cycles contains four stages: expansion, peak, contraction, and trough. An expansion is characterized by increasing employment, economic growth, and upward pressure on prices. A peak is the highest point of the business cycle, when the economy is producing at maximum allowable output, employment is at or above full employment, and inflationary pressures on prices are evident. Following a peak, the economy typically enters into a correction which is characterized by a contraction where growth slows, employment declines (unemployment increases), and pricing pressures subside. The slowing ceases at the trough and at this point the economy has hit a bottom from which the next stage of expansion and contraction will emerge.[74]

A more comprehensive characterization lists six stages: expansion, peak, recession, depression, trough and recovery.

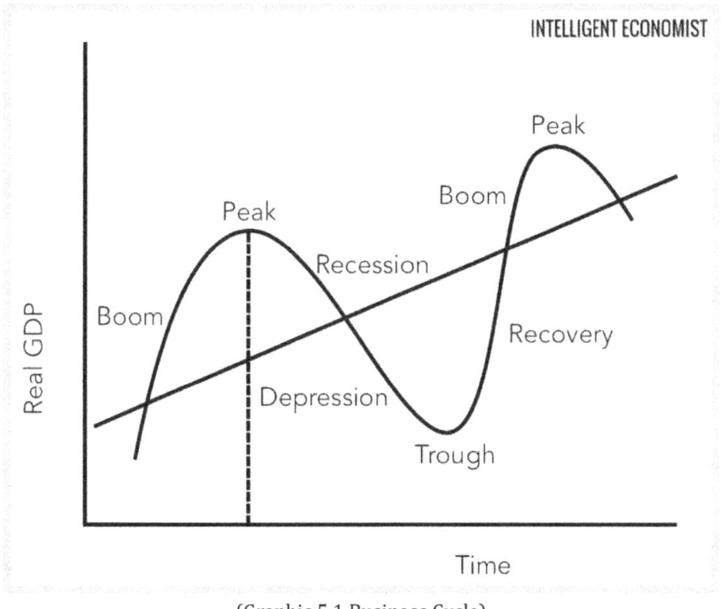

(Graphic 5.1 Business Cycle)

Expansion or Boom

In the graph above, the curve above the trend line represents the expansion phase of the business cycle. The periods of expansion (economic growth where real output increases) follow a period of recessions.

The booms characterize fast economic growth, which tends to be inflationary and unsustainable. During this expansion period, employment, investment income, wages, profits, demand, and supply are high. The movement of the money supply is typically continuous and uninterrupted.

Peak

The peak is the second stage of the trade cycle. This stage is the maximum growth the economy can achieve, and there are no further signs of economic growth according to economic indicators. At this point, prices also hit their maximum level. The end of the peak marks the beginning of the contraction of the economy.

Recession

The recession stage is often characterized by high unemployment, negative economic growth, low sales due to reduced consumer demand, income stagnation or even deflation, and real output falling. Cyclical unemployment typically increases during a recession. If rapid expansion takes place, then the economy can heat up, and the rate of inflation could rise.

Depression

If the recession becomes more severe, and the economy continues to fall below the trend line, then the economy enters a depression period. Economic activity and growth continue to decline. Additionally, unemployment increases, production decreases further, consumer confidence falls, and both trade and investment decline. There are more bankruptcies, and both businesses and consumers alike find themselves struggling to receive credit.

Trough

The trough is the lowest point in the economy. All indicators of good economic health are at their lowest now. The economic growth rate is negative. This should be the end of the recession or depression and the beginning of the recovery phase.

Recovery

The recovery phase of the business cycle marks the beginning of improvement in the economy. Economic activity starts to pick up again. Investment, employment, confidence, spending, and prices begin to increase as the economy begins to grow. This happens as low prices help to fuel higher levels of demand and concurrently production and employment levels begin to increase. Lending also increases at this time, further contributing to economic revitalization. The recovery phase is the final stage of a single business cycle.[75]

Business cycles are dated according to when the direction of economic activity changes. The peak of the cycle refers to the last month before several key economic indicators—such as employment, output, and retail sales— begin to fall. The trough of the cycle refers to the last month before the same economic indicators begin to rise. Because key economic indicators often change direction at slightly different times, the dating of peaks and troughs is necessarily somewhat subjective. In many ways, the term "business cycle" is misleading. "Cycle" seems to imply that there is some regularity in the timing and duration of upswings and downswings in economic activity. Most economists, however, do not think there is.[76]

Economic cycles have been classified depending on their periodicity. The most common are:

- **Very short cycles**, with duration of 30-40 months; also known as Kitchin cycles, based on Joseph Kitchin's 1923 article, "Review of Economic Statistics," published in the Harvard University Press.

- **Short cycles**, with duration of 9-11 years; also known as Juglar cycles, based on the research of French economist Clement Juglar.

- **Long cycles** with duration of 15-25 years; commonly known as Kuznets cycles, whose analysis placed the origin of cycles in demographic factors such as birth rates or migrations;

- **Exceptionally long**, or **Kondratiev cycles**, with durations of 50-60 years. These cycles originate with breakthroughs in capital goods, such as the steam engine or the Internet.

Many papers and works have been written on business cycles and different points of view have taken form. Keynesian economics[77] tries to deal with the economic fluctuation to minimize their impact. Business cycles are seen as a proof of market failure, and justify government intervention in order to assure the correct level of economic activity. Until the optimum level of employment has been reached, the economy will not be readjusted. Depending on the cycle phase, expansionary or contractionary economic policies may be used.

New Classical Macroeconomics supporters have also dealt with economic cycles, and as a result the Real business cycle theory arises as an alternative view to Keynes, Kydland and Prescott, and in general the Chicago School, are mostly related with the development of this theory. For them, cycles are explained by technological shocks. The fluctuations in the economy are seen to be produced by shifts in the supply curve, as a result of changes in productivity levels. These shocks can be caused by different factors: technology innovation, unusual weather conditions, changes in raw material prices, new policies and regulatory measures, etc. What is basic for these shocks to occur is an alteration in the effectiveness of either capital or labor factors, and therefore changing productivity. As a result, in changes in the production quantity, the supply curve shifts, implying a new equilibrium point in the supply and demand model. Thus, they believe that the economy will reach its new equilibrium point, through the forces of demand and supply, without the need for a government intervention. In fact, from their view, government intervention will only worsen the situation.[78]

In his seminal 1986 book, "Stabilizing an Unstable Economy,"[79] Nobel Laureate Hyman Minsky offers his definition of the five stages in a financial bubble: displacement, boom, euphoria, profit taking and panic.

1. **Displacement**: A displacement occurs when investors get enamored by a new paradigm, such as an innovative new technology or interest rates that are historically low. A classic example of displacement is the decline in the federal funds rate from 6.5% in May 2000 to 1% in June 2003. Over this three-year period, the interest rate on 30-year fixed-rate mortgages fell by 2.5 percentage points to a historic low of 5.21%, sowing the seeds for the housing bubble.

2. **Boom**: Prices rise slowly at first, following a displacement, but then gain momentum as more and more participants enter the market, setting the stage for the boom phase. During this phase, the asset in question attracts widespread media coverage. Fear of missing out on what could be a once-in-a-lifetime opportunity spurs more speculation, drawing an increasing number of participants into the fold.

3. **Euphoria**: During this phase, caution is thrown to the wind, as asset prices skyrocket. The "greater fool" theory plays out everywhere. Valuations reach extreme levels during this phase. For example, at the peak of the Japanese real estate bubble in 1989, land in Tokyo sold for as much as $139,000 per square foot, or more than 350-times the value of Manhattan property. After the bubble burst, real estate lost approximately 80% of its inflated value, while stock prices declined by 70%. Similarly, at the height of the Internet bubble in March 2000, the combined value of all technology stocks on the Nasdaq was higher than the GDP of most nations.

During the euphoric phase, new valuation measures and metrics are touted to justify the relentless rise in asset prices.

4. **Profit Taking**: By this time, the smart money--heeding the warning signs--is generally selling out positions and taking profits. But estimating the exact time when a bubble is due to collapse can be a difficult exercise and extremely hazardous to one's financial health, because, as John Maynard Keynes put it, "the markets can stay irrational longer than you can stay solvent."

Note that it only takes a relatively minor event to prick a bubble, but once it is pricked, the bubble cannot "inflate" again. In August 2007, for example, French bank BNP Paribas halted withdrawals from three investment funds with substantial exposure to U.S. subprime mortgages because it could not value their holdings. While this development initially rattled financial markets, it was brushed aside over the next couple months, as global equity markets reached new highs. In retrospect, this relatively minor event was indeed a warning sign of the turbulent times to come.

5. **Panic**: In the panic stage, asset prices reverse course and descend as rapidly as they had ascended. Investors and speculators, faced with margin calls and plunging values of their holdings, now want to liquidate them at any price. As supply overwhelms demand, asset prices slide sharply.

One of the most vivid examples of global panic in financial markets occurred in October 2008, weeks after Lehman Brothers declared bankruptcy and Fannie Mae, Freddie Mac and AIG almost collapsed. The S&P 500 plunged almost 17% that month, its ninth-worst monthly performance. In that single month, global equity markets lost a staggering $9.3 trillion of 22% of their combined market capitalization.

As Minsky and a number of other experts opine, speculative bubbles in some asset or the other are inevitable in a free-market economy. However, becoming familiar with the steps involved in bubble formation may help you to spot the next one and avoid becoming an unwitting participant in it.[80]

In the United States, there have been 14 boom and bust cycles since 1929. The average boom has lasted about two years and three months, while the average bust period has lasted about one year and five months. While the averages are worth noting since they highlight the shorter nature of busts, they should not be taken as the typical length. To show just how much booms and busts can vary depending on the cycle, let's look at the shortest and longest booms and busts. Since 1929, the most prolonged economic contraction (bust) lasted 43 months. This specific economic contraction is also known as the Great Depression. The shortest economic contraction occurred in 1980 and lasted for only six months. In contrast, the most extended period of economic expansion (boom) was previously 120 months, lasting from March of 1991 to March of 2001. However, the most recent economic expansion exceeded this, lasting from July of 2009 until March of 2020 (128 months). The shortest economic expansion lasted for 12 months, from July of 1981 to November of 1982.[81]

Interest Rates

Interest rates play a huge part in determining business cycles. Short-term interest rates are adjusted by the Federal Reserve (Fed), which operates under a mandate to promote employment and price stability. This mandate has changed considerably over the decades since the Fed was established in 1913. If economic growth stagnates and unemployment rises, the Fed can lower interest rates to make it cheaper to borrow, which tends to stimulate the economy as it spurs hiring, investing and consumer spending. Conversely, when the economy is growing fast, inflation may become a concern, in which case the Fed can employ a fiscal strategy by raising interest rates to make borrowing more expensive and discourage spending.

An article published by the Federal Reserve Bank of St Louis provides a memorable example of the Fed taking action against inflation:

> "On Oct. 6, 1979, Fed Chairman Paul Volcker took dramatic steps to rein in the runaway inflation that had been sapping the strength of our economy since the mid-1960s. Without his bold change in monetary policy and his determination to stick with it through

several painful years, the U.S. economy would have continued its downward spiral. By reversing the misguided policies of his predecessors, Volcker set the table for the long economic expansions of the 1980s and 1990s.

How bad was the period of the Great Inflation? The inflation rate, a mere 1 percent in 1965, hit 14 percent by 1980. Unemployment trended up from a low of 3.5 percent (annual average) in 1969 to 9.7 percent in 1982. The stock market was in the dumps. Oil prices jumped off the charts. Presidents Richard Nixon and Jimmy Carter became desperate enough to tinker with price controls, the results being disastrous.

Volcker, in office only two months, took the radical step of switching Fed policy from targeting interest rates to targeting the money supply. The days of "easy credit" turned into the days of "very expensive credit." The prime lending rate exceeded 21 percent. Unemployment reached double digits in some months. The dollar depreciated significantly in world foreign exchange markets. Volcker's tough medicine led to not one, but two, recessions before prices finally stabilized."[82]

While interest rate changes typically do not directly affect the stock market, Fed actions can have a trickle-down effect that impact stock prices. When the Fed raises interest rates, banks increase their rates for consumer loans. In theory, this means there's less money available for consumer spending. Higher rates for business loans can sometimes cause companies to slow or cease hiring and expansion. Reduced consumer and business spending can impair the value of a company's stock.[83]

Whenever interest rates are rising or falling, you commonly hear about the federal funds rate. This is the rate that banks use to lend each other money. It can change daily, and because this rate's movement affects all other loan rates, it is used as an indicator to show whether interest rates are rising or falling. A good example of this occurred between 1980 and 1981. Inflation was at 14% and the Fed raised interest rates to 19%.[84] This caused a severe recession, but it did put an end to the spiraling inflation that the country was seeing. Conversely, falling interest rates can cause recessions to end. When the Fed lowers the federal funds rate, borrowing money becomes cheaper; this entices people to start spending again.

As an example of how interest rates can affect the growth of a business, let's take the case of a successful business growing at 10-12% annually in a 4% interest rate environment. Borrowing to grow the business at 4% and allowing for, let's say, 3% annual inflation, you can see that going to the debt market can be a smart move for a company like this. A company can increase profits if it is able to borrow money at a cost significantly lower than its growth rate. That's one reason why low interest rates are good for the stock market. Companies can leverage debt to increase growth and consequently, their stock price.

A fascinating example of the impact of low interest rates involves the country's most highly valued company, Apple. When I first saw that Apple, a company awash in cash reserves, was borrowing $14 billion in early 2021, I questioned why. After some thought, Apple's rationale became clear to me. The company borrowed the money to buy back stock rather than tapping into its roughly $200 billion of reserves because the interest rate on the debt is historically low. The after-tax interest cost on the $2.5 billion of five-year notes, for example, is less than the after-tax cost of the cash dividend Apple pays its stockholders.[85]

Rising or falling interest rates also affect consumer and business psychology. When interest rates are rising, both businesses and consumers will cut back on spending. This will cause earnings to fall and stock prices to drop. On the other hand, when interest rates have fallen significantly, consumers and businesses will increase spending, causing stock prices to rise. Interest rates also affect bond prices. There is an inverse relationship between bond prices and interest rates, meaning that as interest rates rise, bond prices fall, and as interest rates fall, bond prices rise. The longer the maturity of the bond, the more it will fluctuate in relation to interest rates.[86] In 2022, decades of noncorrelation between equities and fixed income investments reversed itself, with the two moving in tandem, responding to rampant inflation and rising Treasury yields.

The interest rate cycle is closely related to the economic or trade cycle. In theory, movements in interest rates should mirror the economic cycle. If the economy is growing strongly and inflationary pressures increasing, central banks will increase interest rates to slow down the economy and prevent inflation. If the economy enters into recession with falling inflation and rising unemployment, central banks will cut interest rates to provide an economic stimulus to try and increase the rate of economic growth.[87]

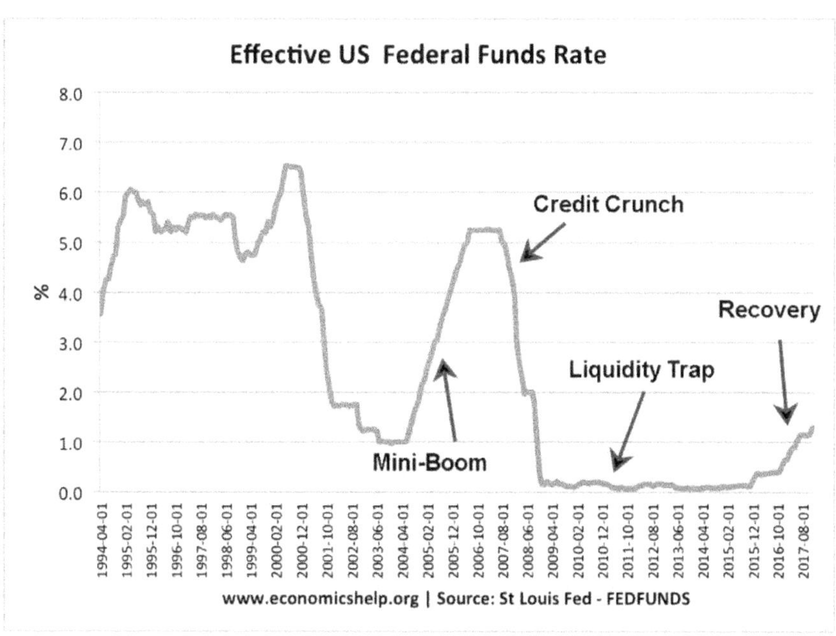

(Graphic 5.2 Int Rates 94-2017)

Inflation

Inflation is the decline of purchasing power of a given currency over time. The rise in the general level of prices, often expressed as a percentage, means that a unit of currency effectively buys less than it did in prior periods. Inflation can be contrasted with deflation, which occurs when the purchasing power of money increases and prices decline.[88]

One source of inflationary concerns is the widely held view that the rate of inflation is a cyclical phenomenon, falling during recessions and rising as the economy approaches a cyclical peak. According to this explanation, inflation is influenced by the degree of slack in markets for goods, services, and resources. When there are ample supplies of unused resources available, price pressures are presumed to diminish. Alternatively, the inflation rate is believed to accelerate as high employment conditions arise. During such periods, resource availability becomes more limited and firms, competing for scarce resources to meet growing demand for their products, bid up resource prices and consequently product prices. Such an explanation has considerable appeal since it appears to be based upon standard supply-demand considerations, but the analysis is incomplete and its use for explaining inflation is limited. The explanation obscures the nature of the inflationary process, fostering confusion about the cause of inflation and, more importantly, confusion over appropriate government policies. An alternative view contends that inflation results from a sustained rate of growth in the money stock which exceeds the growth rate of the quantity of money demanded by the nation's wealth owners.[89]

The impetus for the business cycle may have changed during the past few decades. The typical post-World War II business cycle was pretty straight-forward:

1) An economy growing beyond its productive potential starts to generate inflationary pressures;

2) The central bank raises interest rates to curtail price pressures;

3) The economy goes into recession, excesses are wrung out of the system, inflation abates;

4) The central bank lowers interest rates, the economy bounces back. Rinse and repeat.

There was no big debt hangover to constrain the recovery. Hence, deep downturns were almost always followed by sharp rebounds. The normal response once the Fed lowers interest rates is for the public to borrow and spend. That's how monetary policy works: by changing the incentive to spend versus save.[90]

Today's pattern is different. The last three recessions — the downturns of 1990-1991, 2001 and 2007-2009 — all featured a financial component, that, if it wasn't the proximate cause of the recession, acted as a driver. Starting in 2007, the financial crisis was the force accelerating, deepening and prolonging the downturn.

According to BIS economists, whether it was the savings and loan crisis in the late 1980s, the internet and technology stock bubble in the late 1990s, or the subprime housing bubble in the early 2000s, "the nature of recessions has changed from inflation-induced to financial cycle-induced recessions." The term "financial cycle" refers to the self-reinforcing interactions between perceptions of value and risk, risk-taking, and financing constraints. Typically, rapid increases in credit drive up property and asset prices, which in turn increase collateral values and thus the amount of credit the private sector can obtain until, at some point, the process goes into reverse. Historically, this mutually reinforcing interaction between financing constraints and perceptions of value and risks has tended to cause serious macroeconomic dislocations.

Research by noted economists like Drehmann (2012), Claessens (2012) and Aikman (2015) identified two important features of the financial cycle. First, financial cycle peaks tend to coincide with banking crises or considerable financial stress. This is not surprising. During expansions, the self-reinforcing interaction between financing constraints, asset prices and risk-taking can overstretch balance sheets, making them more fragile and sowing the seeds of the subsequent financial contraction. This, in turn, can drag down the economy and put further stress on the financial system.

Second, the financial cycle can be much longer than the business cycle. Business cycles as traditionally measured have tended to last up to eight years, and financial cycles around 15–20 years since the early 1980s. The difference in length means that a financial cycle can span more than one business cycle. As a result, while financial cycle peaks tend to usher in recessions, not all recessions are preceded by such peaks.[91]

Approximately twelve years after the financial crisis, Federal Reserve Chairman Jay Powell explained the new strategy at the annual monetary policy conference, usually held in Jackson Hole but conducted online in 2020 due to the pandemic. Powell's speech noted four major changes in the economy in recent years. First, estimates of long-run potential growth of the economy have declined. Second, interest rates have fallen. Third, our long expansion after the Great Recession led to a strong labor market, which especially helped disadvantaged people. And fourth, the strong labor market did not lead to higher inflation.

The Fed is afraid of inflation running too low. This fear is the basis of the new strategy. Powell explained that if inflation is sometimes less than the Fed's two percent target and sometimes at the target but seldom above target, then the average will be below the target. That will drive expectations of lower inflation, which will pull interest rates even lower. When a recession comes and the Fed wants to stimulate the economy, it will have little room to cut interest rates. Higher average interest rates provide more flexibility, in the Fed's opinion. Not everyone will agree with that, especially those who believe quantitative easing has power beyond pulling interest rates down.[92] More on this later in this chapter.

Stock Market

It is well known that stock prices are an imperfect leading indicator of recessions and recoveries. As the economist Paul Samuelson famously quipped, "The stock market has predicted nine out of the last five recessions." But in reality, the relationship between economic cycles and stock prices is less erratic than such a comment might imply. Historically, cyclical upswings and downswings in stock prices have almost a one-to-one correspondence with upturns and downturns in economic growth.

Stock prices and yields have the additional advantage of being available immediately. As you might expect if you've ever taken a finance course, asset prices tend to incorporate "the market's" best guess of future events and, by and large, they are as good predictors of the economy as we have. Maybe the best of these is the stock market. In Figure 2 I've plotted the annual growth rate of real GDP with the annual growth rate of the S&P 500 composite stock index. What you might expect is that the stock market anticipates movements in the economy: in recessions profits and earnings are down so stock prices should fall as soon as a recession is anticipated by the market. That's pretty much what you see. In the figure we see that every post-war downturn in the economy has been at least matched, if not anticipated, by the stock market. The problem is that there have been several downturns in the stock market that didn't turn into recessions---so-called false signals. A classic case is the October 1987 crash, which was followed by several years of continued growth.[93]

Yield Curve

A yield curve is a visual representation of the yield relationship between bonds of the same credit quality and different maturities—i.e., the time remaining until a bond's principal amount is repaid—at a single point in time. The resulting curve is a key bond market benchmark and a leading economic indicator. While investors plot yield curves for various types of bonds, the one that's most often referenced is the U.S. Treasury yield curve, reflecting the relationship between short, intermediate and long-maturity Treasuries.[94]

The curve helps to forecast interest rates in the future and analyze risk in the investment. It gives a trade-off between maturity and yield. The curve helps investors understand that the securities are temporarily underpriced or overpriced. Most importantly it helps in the prediction of an upcoming recession. An inverted yield curve appears when long-term yields fall below short-term yields. It also indicates that people want money now and not later because during a recession, demands fall. It is when long term investors realize that the short-term bonds are more lucrative and the government might not be able to repay the said amount and therefore, they invest in short-term bonds. This type of yield curve is an indicator of an economic downturn and indicates an upcoming recession.[95]

The difference between long-term and short-term interest rates ("the slope of the yield curve" or "the term spread") has borne a consistent negative relationship with subsequent real economic activity in the United States, with a lead time of about four to six quarters. The yield curve has predicted essentially every U.S. recession since 1950 with only one "false" signal, which preceded the credit crunch and slowdown in production in 1967.[96]

GDP

While GDP is an important component in inflation, it is also important as an economic indicator in its own right. When compared to the previous year's reading, it tells you how fast the economy is growing (or contracting). GDP is the dollar value of all goods and services produced by a given country during a certain period. It is measured by either adding all of the income earned in an economy, or by all the spending in an economy. Both measures should be roughly equal.

Gross domestic income includes wages and salaries, corporate profits, interest collected by lenders, and taxes collected by governments. GDP domestic expenditures includes consumer spending, housing investment, government spending, business spending (investment in factories, equipment, and inventory), as well as foreign spending on our exports minus our spending on their imports. With so many individual components affecting GDP (and through the output gap, inflation) you can see how easy it is for the number of economic reports to mushroom.

GDP affects the stock market through its effect on inflation, as well as through its use as a key indicator of economic activity and future economic prospects by investors. Any significant change in the GDP, either up or down, can have a big effect on investing sentiment. If investors believe the economy is improving (and corporate earnings along with it) they are likely to be willing to pay more for any given stock. If there is a decline in GDP (or investors expect a decline) they would only be willing to buy a given stock for less, leading to a decline in the stock market.

On top of this effect, there is also an economic theory that suggests the stock market itself exerts a reverse effect on economic activity, usually called the "wealth effect". This theory says that a fall in the stock market makes an individual's personal wealth (or perceived wealth) fall. They consequently stop spending as much. Since consumer spending represents around two-thirds of GDP, a small change in consumption exerts a significant effect on GDP. This means that as the stock market falls, it causes GDP to fall even further, which intensifies the downward pressure on the stock market.[97]

Oil

There are different aspects to different boom and bust cycles. One example is the significant role played by the oil crisis that created the 1970's recession. While oil is not as big a factor today, it remains a major indicator.

How do high oil prices affect the economy on a "micro" level? As a consumer, you may already understand the microeconomic implications of higher oil prices. When observing higher oil prices, most of us are likely to think about the price of gasoline, a necessary purchase for most households. When gasoline prices increase, a larger share of households' budgets is likely to be spent on it, which leaves less to spend on other goods and services. The same goes for businesses whose goods must be shipped from place to place or that use fuel as a major input (such as the airline industry). Higher oil prices tend to make production more expensive for businesses, just as they make it more expensive for households to do the things they normally do.

It is not a far leap to understand how oil prices affect the macroeconomy. Oil price increases are generally thought to increase inflation and reduce economic growth. In terms of inflation, oil prices directly affect the prices of goods made with petroleum products. As mentioned above, oil prices indirectly affect costs such as transportation, manufacturing, and heating. The increase in these costs can in turn affect the prices of a variety of goods and services, as producers may pass production costs on to consumers. The extent to which oil price increases lead to consumption price increases depends on how important oil is for the production of a given type of good or service. Oil price increases can also stifle the growth of the economy through their effect on the supply and demand for goods other than oil. Increases in oil prices can depress the supply of other goods because they increase the costs of producing them. In economics terminology, high oil prices can shift up the supply curve for the goods and services for which oil is an input.[98]

It's true that every recession since the 1950s has been preceded by an inversion in the part of the yield curve that measures the gap between the 90-day Treasury Rate and 10-year Treasury Note yields. But there's also no shortage of market participants who say years of extraordinary monetary policy measures by the Federal Reserve and other central banks around the world have distorted the bond markets, rendering the yield curve less useful as a recession gauge. If so, then maybe other market measures—like oil prices—serve as better indicators of whether a downturn is or isn't on the horizon.[99]

Money Supply

The M1 money supply includes coins and currency in circulation—the coins and bills that circulate in an economy that the U.S. Treasury does not hold at the Federal Reserve Bank, or in bank vaults. Closely related to currency are checkable deposits, also known as demand deposits. These are the amounts held in checking accounts. They are called demand deposits or checkable deposits because the banking institution must give the deposit holder his money "on demand" when the customer writes a check or uses a debit card. These items together—currency, and checking accounts in banks—comprise the definition of money known as M1, which the Federal Reserve System measures daily.[100] M2 includes M1 and adds on forms of savings, including money market deposits, savings deposits, and retail time deposits (under $100,000).

Holding all else equal, any increase in M that is effective in boosting spending beyond the market's embedded expectations is bearish for bonds (inflation increases, eating into yields) and bullish for stocks (companies can generally pass off higher costs by increasing the prices of goods and services). Accordingly, any indication of where the money supply is going, and how the formation of credit might be impacted in conjunction, can lead to an understanding of where the economy and financial markets might go.[101]

The prevailing view seems to be that the Federal Reserve, as the nation's monetary authority, pursues an activist, countercyclical monetary policy. In economic parlance, this is referred to as "leaning against the wind." Countercyclical monetary policy can be thought of in the following manner: When the Fed perceives economic activity to be waning, it attempts to boost output and employment by increasing the supply of money, thereby putting downward pressure on interest rates and stimulating growth in such interest-sensitive sectors as housing and consumer durables. When the Fed perceives inflation to be accelerating, it does just the opposite—it restricts the growth of money, which tends to put upward pressure on interest rates and ease inflationary pressures. Thus, by altering the money supply, the Fed attempts to sufficiently influence interest rates to affect overall economic activity and inflation.

This policy prescription, of course, is overly simplistic and subject to numerous caveats. For instance, should the Fed concern itself with short-term disturbances to output, employment or changes to the price level? Many economists believe that by attempting to offset these short-term disturbances—instead of adhering to the Fed's traditional goal of long-run price stability ("wringing inflation out of the economy over time")—the Fed merely adds to the instability of an already uncertain situation.[102]

In his outstanding book on economic indicators, *Business Cycles*,[103] Lars Tvede provides insights into the importance of the money supply. He notes that the leading indicator and "prime mover" cited by the US Conference Board's index is the expansion of the money supply, and that all other indicators within the index are moving mainly as a result of what happens to money supply.

> "Government is the only institution that can take a valuable commodity like paper and make it worthless by applying ink."
>
> Ludwig von Mises

Value Investing Metrics

Value investing seeks to take advantage of these economic indicators, combined with intensive analysis of a number of financial metrics. The first and most obvious metric is the price to earnings (PE) ratio, the measure of the share price relative to the annual net income earned by the firm per share. The PE ratio— often referred to as a "multiple" because it demonstrates how much an investor is willing to pay for one dollar of earnings—shows current investor demand for a company share. A high PE ratio generally indicates increased demand because investors anticipate earnings growth in the future. The PE ratio uses units of years, which can be interpreted as the number of years of earnings to pay back purchase price.[104] The average PE ratio over the previous decade is something always worth investigating.

Next, I would look at a company's relative PE ratio—the ratio of its PE to the PE of the market—which tells me how a company's stock has performed versus other issues in its asset class.

A higher relative P/E multiple is an indication of higher risk than the P/E, since P/E ratios can vary widely, depending on the amount of money invested in the stock markets. A stock with a high relative P/E multiple must outperform the market to maintain its multiple. Of this writing in 2023, the current S&P 500 10-year P/E Ratio is 27.7, which represents 37.1% above the modern-era market average of 20.2.

Typically, the next assessment is a company's earnings per share (EPS), a ratio calculated by dividing the company's net profit by its number of outstanding shares of common stock. The EPS formula indicates a company's ability to produce net profits for common shareholders. A "diluted" EPS in a financial report includes options, convertible securities and warrants that can affect total shares outstanding when exercised.[105]

The EPS is important for investors because it is used to assess company performance, predict future earnings and estimate the value of the company's shares. The higher the EPS, the more profitable the company is deemed to be.[106]

Another metric is the company's price to book ratio (P/B ratio), which refers to a company's fundamental worth—the difference between its assets and its expenses and debts. The P/B ratio is another way—besides relative P/E—to compare the price of a stock with other, similar stocks in the same industry, sector or asset class. As a value investor, I also want to determine how much the company reinvests in itself each year, preferably a minimum of 5%.

A company's long-term debt (LTD) is yet another important consideration. The LTD refers to money owed that is not expected to be repaid within a year, usually in the form of corporate bonds. Debts expected to be repaid within 12 months are classified as current liabilities. The interest expense on a company's debt is an important point. How much is the company paying out relative to its share price? What is the ratio of debt to assets? Does the company have any long-term pension liabilities?

Another interesting point is stock buybacks—open market repurchases of shares by the issuing corporation. On the balance sheet, these have the same effect as paying out shareholder dividends. Companies that repurchase shares, such as Berkshire Hathaway, Apple and recently, major oil companies, can be important economic indicators, particularly if they are not issuing a dividend.

A 2020 article in the *Harvard Business Review* takes the position that stock buybacks are dangerous for the economy because of the soaring corporate debt they have helped create. It suggests that companies doing buybacks diminish the liquidity they might need in an economic downturn, and that they would be better off leveraging earnings in productive ways that might yield revenues and profits versus taking on debt to finance buybacks.

The article contrasts buybacks with dividends, which provide shareholders with a reward for holding shares. But it warns that excessive dividend payouts can undercut investment in productive capabilities in the same way that buybacks can.[107]

A complex but vital piece of knowledge is a company's expected return on its equities. The expected return is an unknown variable with numerous probabilities. It's calculated by multiplying potential outcomes (returns) by the chances of each outcome occurring, and then calculating the sum of those results. The expected return is based on historical data, which may or may not provide reliable forecasting of future returns. Hence, the outcome is not guaranteed. Expected return is simply a measure of probabilities intended to show the likelihood that a given investment will generate a positive return, and what the likely return will be.[108]

As I said, it's a complex process, and its application can produce a wide variety of results.

Indicators And Investment Decisions

Business as a whole tends to lag one or more cycles behind stock prices. On the 5th of September 1929, economist and entrepreneur Roger Babson predicted—for the third consecutive year—that a market crash was imminent. His warning was clear:

> "A crash is coming, and it may be terrific. The vicious circle will get in full swing and the result will be a serious business depression. There may be a

> stampede for selling which will exceed anything that the Stock Exchange has ever witnessed. Wise are those investors who now get out of debt."

In response to his comments, the market dropped about three percent that day, a loss which came to be known as the "Babson Break."

An article in *International Man* describes what happened next. Rather than taking a cautious approach, Wall Street vilified Babson. Virtually every economist and business leader spurned his comments. Even his patriotism was called into question. Economists of the day, such as Professor Irving Fisher, repeatedly reassured investors that nothing in the nature of a crash was remotely possible and that a resumption in the boom was imminent. Financier Bernard Baruch cabled Winston Churchill to say, 'Financial storm definitely passed.' President Herbert Hoover assured Americans that the market was sound.

Less than two months later, however, the market suddenly went into freefall. But unlike what most people today have come to believe, the market did not collapse in a single day; it did so in stages, not reaching its bottom of 89% losses until July 1932.[109]

Babson subsequently ran an unsuccessful presidential campaign as a Prohibitionist in 1940. When he died in 1967, he was worth in excess of 50 million dollars. One of Babson's secrets was that traders knew it would be better to forecast economic movements through the stock market and leading indicators than to forecast stock market movements through economic studies.

That aside, bonds may be an even better economic indicator than equities. The National Bureau of Economic Research analyzed the cyclical behavior of interest rates all the way back to 1802 and found significant evidence that stock market boom and bust cycles are closely linked to and can often be determined in advance by the movement of interest rates and other indicators.

Credit quality is another indicator in the business cycle. Describing the financial conditions that might precede a depression in a 1955 speech for the American Finance Association, business cycle specialist Geoffrey Moore cited a rapid increase in the volume of credit and debt, escalating speculative increases in the prices of investment, such as stocks, commodities and real estate, vigorous competition among lenders for new business, relaxation of credit terms and lending standards, and reductions in the risk premiums obtained by lenders. If this sounds a lot like 2006, you are paying attention.

A great 2000 book by Yale University professor Robert Shiller, titled *Irrational Exuberance*, examines economic bubbles in the 1990s and early 2000s. Shiller sent questionnaires to 2000 private investors and another 1000 to institutional investors asking what motivated them to sell. He received 889 responses, among which only a handful cited specific economic or political news that compelled them to sell. The vast majority of respondents said they sold because markets were falling, and that no other factors were as important. That this response was from supposedly knowledgeable institutional investors supports Hadady's theory that investors can collectively act quite irrationally, and the advantage of trading against popular opinion.

> **"A recession is when your neighbor loses his job: a depression is when you lose yours."**
> President Harry Truman

In the years following the 2008 financial crisis, a combination of productivity gains, low interest rates and low inflation has grown earnings and substantially higher equity prices. Further fueling the economic boom has been a demographic of middle-aged people saving for their pensions that provided access to an abundance of capital for new investment projects. There is no lack of positive feedback loops in this capital investment boom, reminiscent of the 1990s. There were a host of late investors who jumped on the bandwagon just as things got out of control, leading to the bursting of the dot.com bubble.

Investors like me enter the game early because we recognize value. Investors who do not understand value tend to get in the game late, typically after a significant price movement catches their attention. Late Tesla buyers are an example. They see the continuing price climb and their emotional accelerators kick in the turbo charger, but only after a trend has been clearly established and going on for some time. This is a prime example of the cognitive dissonance discussed in chapter five. The latter stage of the market we saw in 2021 may be a classic example of investors getting in on the tail end of a protracted market upswing

> "There is nothing so disturbing to one's well-being and judgment as to see a friend get rich."
> Charles P. Kindleberger

Chapter Six

Managing Risk

The number one reason why flights get into trouble is pilot error. It's the same reason most investors underperform the market.

Similar factors contribute to these failures. For example, fatigue. Flying requires concentration and sound judgment. Tired or distracted pilots are candidates for accidents. Lifelong financial management requires ongoing planning and commitment.

Pilots unable to manage stress when something goes wrong are susceptible to errors in judgment. Individuals lacking investment composure overreact to market gyrations and make poor choices. Pilots are required to make quick decisions based on information relayed by their instruments. Misreading that information can jeopardize flight safety. Unsophisticated investors can misread market signals and make hasty decisions that jeopardize their portfolios. Pilots lacking adequate training may pick up bad habits that lead to serious errors. Inexperienced investors easily fall prey to bad habits in the form of cognitive biases.

There's a tendency for investors to focus on the most common risk, market risk, but there are other risks that should be considered. Virtually all investment-related risks fall into one of two categories: systematic risks and unsystematic risks.

Systematic risk is inherent to the market and unmanageable for investors. It's apt to cause fluctuations in investments and potentially erode their value. It is sometimes referred to as market risk or volatility, is endemic to all investments and securities, and can only be reduced by diversification or by holding a greater number of shares. Interest rate risk, purchasing power risk (inflation), political risk, economic risk, and exchange rate (currency risk) are examples. It affects the entire market or market segment as opposed to individual securities or companies.[110] The 1929 market crash and the 2008-09 Great Recession are macroeconomic examples.

Systematic risk is represented by the Greek letter β (Beta). The Beta of a stock is a measurement of its volatility. A Beta of 1.0 represents similar fluctuations to that of the overall market increases or decreases.

Unsystematic risk is primarily industry or company specific, such as business, credit, operational or liquidity risk. Examples include the failure of an individual company like Lehman Brothers or Enron. Unsystematic risk is controllable and can be avoided through diversification and other intelligible strategies. Because investors can easily diversify away from Unsystematic risk, increasing it offers no additional return.

Systematic Risk

> "The four most expensive words in the English language: 'This time it's different.'"
>
> John Templeton
>
> *The Four Pillars of Investing*

Systematic risk is often referred to as market risk, perhaps because it is the most prominent source of risk in securities. When the market declines, even share prices of solid, stable companies can fall, primarily as the result of investors' herd mentality, which is one of the destructive behaviors I discussed in chapter four.

A classic example is the dotcom bubble. Some of the tech companies negatively affected were well-managed firms, but many lacked sound business models. Despite this, investors bought into them because everyone else was buying into them and people find it emotionally difficult, even painful, to go against the crowd. Today, we see a potentially similar situation with the FANG stocks—Facebook, Amazon, Netflix and Google.

Analyst recommendations can have a major impact on investor herd mentality. Like investors, analysts can find it hard to ignore what the crowd is doing. If the herd is buying into Apple stock, it's hard for an analyst to recommend selling Apple stock because being wrong can not only cause clients pain, it can be a career-threatening mistake.[111] Investors often opt to recreate the decisions of those they believe are "better-informed" investors.

Renowned economist John Maynard Keynes observed that it is better to be conventionally wrong than unconventionally right and that following others may help individuals to maintain good reputations, i.e., it makes sense to follow the crowd because there is safety in numbers. Scharfstein & Stein (1990) incorporated this insight about social influence into their analysis of herding in fund managers' decisions. Fund managers have to convince people that they are investing wisely and, as short-term performance is not a good indicator of skill, they rely for their reputations on comparisons with peers. This provides an incentive to follow others and disregard private information.[112]

> "There are two kinds of forecasters: those who don't know, and those who don't know they don't know."
>
> John Kenneth Galbraith

Unsystematic Risk

Unsystematic risk is more specific and focused, and typically represented by things that affect individual stocks or industries. Unsystematic risk is usually due to internal factors and therefore can be controlled or reduced. Examples include regulatory changes that affect an industry, competitive issues, recalls, CEO firings, earnings reports, fraud, legal actions and labor issues.

Suppose you have a diversified portfolio of 30 stocks, five of which are pharmaceutical companies. Now suppose an Unsystematic risk occurs: A Congressional investigation determines that major drug companies have been guilty of fixing prices. Penalties, fines and stricter regulations on the industry follow, causing stock prices to suddenly plummet. Your portfolio is negatively affected but not severely damaged because the harm is limited to a single industry representing a small portion of your holdings.

On the other hand, an event like Black Monday in 1987 is systematic risk that affects virtually the entire market. Having a diversified portfolio is not going to help you avoid losses because the event pulls down everything.[113]

Unsystematic risks affect the stock of a specific company or industry whereas systematic risks impact almost all securities in the market.

A portfolio's risk, both systematic and unsystematic, is measured by standard deviation, represented by the Greek letter σ (Sigma), the variation of the mean non-annualized average return. Graphic 6.1 illustrates how quickly unsystematic risk is reduced by adding a modest number of stocks to a single-stock portfolio. Most unsystematic risk can be eliminated, ensuring the portfolio is comprised of 20 or more stocks from different sectors. A portfolio's systematic risk cannot be circumvented or eradicated by diversification but it may be reduced by hedging.[114]

Stock Portfolio: Standard Deviations of Annual Returns

[how risk is reduced when stocks from different industries are added]

Number of Stocks	Standard Deviation	Risk Reduced	Number of Stocks	Standard Deviation	Risk Reduced
1	49.2%	0%	30	20.9%	58%
2	37.4%	24%	50	20.2%	59%
4	29.7%	40%	100	19.7%	60%
6	26.6%	46%	200	19.4%	61%
8	25.0%	49%	500	19.3%	61%
10	23.9%	51%	1,000	19.2%	61%
20	21.7%	56%			

Source: E.J. Elton and M. J. Gruber, published in the Journal of Business, Oct 1977.

(Graphic 6.1: Standard Deviations)

A classic 1968 study by Evans and Archer, *Diversification and the Reduction of Dispersion*, concluded an investor owning 15 randomly chosen stocks would have a portfolio no riskier than the overall stock market. This research confirmed earlier advice from Benjamin Graham in his 1949 book, *The Intelligent Investor*. Graham recommended owning 10-30 stocks for proper diversification.[115]

Currency Risk

Currency or exchange rate risk is the risk that a decrease in the underlying value of a nation's currency will reduce the purchasing power of income or investment paid in that currency.

In today's globalized economy most, companies have exposure to foreign currency. This type of risk affects only the securities of companies with foreign exchange transactions or exposures such as companies that export or import raw material or products.[116]

Whenever companies or investors possess assets or business operations across national boundaries, they experience currency risk if their positions are not hedged. Simply put, currency risk is the possibility that currency depreciation will cause a negative effect on the value of assets, investments, and their related interest and dividend payment streams, specifically, those securities that are denominated in foreign currency.[117]

A currency's value relative to other currencies vacillates in response to demand on the currency exchanges and for the assets traded in that currency on global markets. A currency's strength, over time, tends to reflect the perceived health of an economy as well as its future prospects. When that perspective changes, currency movements can be abrupt and fierce. In the short term, various other factors drive the financial markets' perception of the health of an economy and its currency's value.

An example would be a reduction in the purchasing power of a country's currency as a result of inflation, resulting in consumers getting less goods and services for each unit of currency. Central banks might attempt to curb inflation by raising interest rates, which typically stimulates demand for a currency as investors in international markets seek out higher yielding currencies.[118]

Moneyzine offers another example: "An investor purchases foreign bonds and at the time of purchase the investor would receive 100 units of their domestic currency annually, resulting in a 10% return on investment. At the time of purchase, 100 units of domestic currency were worth 50 units of the foreign currency. Over time, the foreign currency weakens against the investor's domestic currency and now 50 units of the foreign currency are worth 70 units of the domestic currency. Payment on the bond is still fixed at 50 units of foreign currency. However, that currency now provides the investor with only 70 units of their domestic currency. In this example, the investor's return has now declined to 7% from the original 10% RIO."[119]

Interest Rate Risk

Interest rate risk is the risk that interest rates will rise or fall. Interest rate risks contain two components—price risk and reinvestment risk—which work in opposite directions.

Price risk is a change in the price of a security due to changes in interest rates. It is often referred to as maturity risk since the greater a bond's duration, the greater the change in price for a given change in interest rates. A bond's interest rate duration is a measure of its price sensitivity to changes in interest rates. If a bond has a duration of five years, every 1% move in interest rates will cause its price to move about 5%. If, for example, interest rates were to rise by 4%, the value of the bond would fall by around 20%.[120]

When interest rates rise, the market price of bonds will fall, reflecting investors' ability to get a higher interest rate on their money elsewhere. When interest rates fall, bond prices increase, and there is less price risk.[121] This has often been the case during steep equity selloffs when investors, seeking more security, turn to bonds.

Reinvestment risk is associated with reinvesting interest/dividend income. It refers to the likelihood an investor won't be able to duplicate their current rate of return on their next investment, such as coupon payments on a bond. A *bond coupon* is a term for the interest payments made on a bond. While reinvestment risk is most common in bond investing, any investment producing cash flow exposes investors to some level of reinvestment risk.[122] Bond funds and exchange-traded funds, however, are continuously reinvesting into new bonds as the bond portfolio matures. I also prefer actively managed bond funds as opposed to passive bond funds, which is one reason why I prefer these to individual bond investments.

Some interest rate considerations for bond investments:

1) Because of the inverse relationship between bond prices and their yields, interest rate increases cause a bond's price to fall or drop, known as being at a discount. Conversely, if interest rates drop, a bond's price rises or is considered at a premium. Market fluctuations represent an interest rate risk that must be accounted for when equity selloffs in a single day can have dramatic results, prompting investors to panic and flee to safer investments like bonds.

2) The longer a bond's maturity, the greater its sensitivity to interest rate changes. As a bond approaches its maturity, its price fluctuates less from changes in the market, so shorter-term securities have less interest rate risk.

3) Interest rate increases trigger larger changes in a bond's price than a comparable interest rate decrease. This means that a bond can lose more overall value in price than it can gain or sell at a premium.

4) Prices of low coupon bonds are much less sensitive to market yield changes than the prices of higher coupon bonds.

If an investor plans to hold a bond or debt instrument to maturity, none of the above factors matter much. Holding a bond to maturity makes interest rate fluctuations virtually irrelevant because all bonds pay the face value at maturity.[123]

Suppose you buy a 10-year, $1,000 bond with a four percent coupon rate and interest rates rise to 6 percent. If you need to liquidate that bond prior to maturity, you must compete with newer bonds carrying higher coupon rates. The newer bonds shrink the market for older bonds paying less interest. The decreased demand depresses the price of older bonds in the secondary market, which likely means you will receive a lower price for your bond than you paid for it. This is one reason why interest rate risk is a form of market risk.

In a rising interest rate environment or when interest rates are historically low, bonds with a longer term or higher coupon represent what's known as opportunity risk—the risk that a better opportunity will occur. The longer the term of a bond, the greater the chance a more attractive investment opportunity will become available. Likewise, the longer term of a bond means that any number of other factors may occur that might negatively affect the investment. Remember the inverse relationship between bond prices and interest rates: when interest rates go up, the price of a bond will go down (think of a seesaw). Known as holding-period risk, this is the risk that not only might a better opportunity be missed, but there is more time for something to happen during the time you hold a bond to negatively affect your investment.[124]

> "Managing risk is very different from managing strategy.
> Risk management focuses on the negative-threats and failures rather than opportunities and successes."
> Robert S. Kaplan

Concentration Risk

The risk that overweighting of investments in a particular stock, bond or market segment could result in a large loss of portfolio value is known as concentration risk. Concentration can occur for various reasons:

1) Believing an investment or sector will outperform its benchmark or an index, you invest more heavily.

2) If a particular investment has outperformed relative to the rest of your portfolio, it may now represent a much higher percentage of your portfolio than before. This happens frequently in bull markets where a stock or sector does well and distorts the intended balance between equities and bonds in your portfolio.

3) Loyalty to one's company causes many people to overweight their company stock in a 401k or other retirement savings plan account. This can also work in reverse, when disgruntled ex or retired employees of a company sell off all of their company stock or other form of deferred compensation because of hard feelings.

4) Investments of the same type or within the same sector or industry can cause concentration risk due to high correlation, that is, what affects one investment is likely to happen to the others.

5) Too many illiquid investments can cause concentration risk. Investments such as private equity placements and non-traded REITS may be difficult to liquidate quickly.

6) Fees are another concentration risk issue. Investments such as variable annuities typically impose a significant surrender charge if you sell before a specified time. (We will discuss this in detail in a later chapter.) High-cost mutual funds are another source of excessive fees—not merely management fees, but turnover ratios inside of these funds can trigger trading costs and taxes.

Should an emergency or other event trigger a sudden need for cash and you are heavily invested in illiquid securities, you may not be able to access the money you need when you need it, or at least not without paying a stiff premium.[125]

Longevity Risk

> **"Age gives you an excuse for not being very good at things that you were not very good at when you were young."**
> Thomas Sowell

The risk of outliving your income or suffering the loss of purchasing power due to longer life expectancies is called longevity risk. People 90 and older now comprise 4.7 percent of the population age 65 and older, as compared with only 2.8 percent in 1980.[126] It's not nearly as uncommon for people to live into triple digits anymore.

One element of longevity risk is uncertainty over how long someone might live. In a defined-contribution plan such as a 401k, individual retirees are subject to both longevity risk and investment risk—uncertainty about investment returns. Defined-pension plans provide assurance that plan participants will receive a specified income throughout retirement. Their retirement income is therefore not affected by lifespan uncertainty, nor is it sensitive to market fluctuations. Thus, retirees are shielded from both market risk and longevity risk. However, they are not protected against upsurges in the cost of living, so their income is vulnerable to inflationary pressures. Also, unless backed by the Pension Benefit Guaranty Corporation (PBGC), their retirement benefits are contingent upon the ability of their plan to meet its obligations.[127]

PBGC is a federal agency created by the Employee Retirement Income Security Act of 1974 (ERISA) to protect pension benefits in private-sector defined benefit plans. If a plan ends—known as plan termination—without sufficient money to pay all benefits, PBGC's insurance program will pay the benefit provided by the terminated pension plan up to the limits set by law.[128]

Shortfall risk is closely related to longevity risk, also resulting from insufficient savings, weak portfolio returns and/or inflation.[129] A common example is lacking sufficient funds for four years of college funding.

Economic Risk

Economic risk is the risk that the economic environment will shrink the value of an investment or source of income. Economic risk should never become an issue if income withdrawals come from safe/fixed income investments, such as bonds and money market funds.

The biggest global economic risk factor is unemployment, designated as the top potential cause for economic crisis in 31 countries by the World Economic Forum (WEF). Even short periods of unemployment can have severe implications, especially for low-income families or those who fail to establish an emergency fund. Elevated levels of joblessness can propel increased government benefits spending that can strain the nation's budget allocation. Prolonged periods of unemployment can negatively impact productivity and the country's ability to pull itself out of economic malaise.

An example is the prolonged high unemployment rate for prime age workers in Italy during the past two decades. In 2020, it was 30% for 15–24-year-olds and 14% for 25–34-year-old workers. Spain has suffered chronic high unemployment for the past three decades, soaring as high as 25% during 2015.[130]

Cyber-attacks are now the second-most significant economic risk factor. The WEF estimates that data breaches and various other kinds of cyber incidents are the greatest threat to the economy of 19 countries. There's also the question of whose responsibility it is to bail out customers if they face monetary loss as a result of a cyber-attack. Without establishing it, if a government is unable to offer any aid in doing so, the burden will fall on the private sector.[131]

Another facet of economic risk stems from the gross domestic product (GDP). When the GDP moves higher, it tends to spur optimism about the economy which in turn tends to boost stock prices. The increased consumer spending that results due to this optimism continues to boost GDP. Conversely, a lower than anticipated GDP can be a harbinger of lower confidence, even pessimism about the economy. When confidence drops, the stock market often does the same. This cycle may repeat itself as the lower stock market prompts actions that in turn impact GDP.

In my opinion, the wealth effect is a major economic driver as consumers are willing to spend more due to increasing investment portfolios and home values.

On August 1st of 2019, The Dow Jones Industrial Average lost more than 300 points when new tariffs on China took effect, then lost another 750 points on August 5th as the trade war intensified. Tariffs and trade wars typically make doing business more expensive for US companies because they must now pay higher taxes on imported items. Depending on how long the tariffs last, companies must decide whether to pass the cost on to their customers. High consumer costs can lead to slower buying and economic growth. This usually involves a "double whammy" when a country's currency drops sufficiently to cause the cost of imported goods to rise sharply. Companies that choose not to pass the increased costs on to their customers take a profit margin hit. While the impact of trade wars might not be long-lasting, they send ripples through the economy, and can affect stock prices.[132]

The US federal deficit is another element of economic risk. As the federal debt mounts, the government must spend more of its budget on interest costs, increasingly crowding out private investments. Over the next 10 years, the Congressional Budget Office (CBO) estimates that interest costs will total $4.6 trillion under current law. Currently, the United States spends over $800 million per day on interest payments. As more federal resources are diverted to interest payments, there will be less available to invest in areas important for economic growth. While less importantly, there will also be less opportunity to stimulate the economy by lowering interest rates. Continuing low interest rates will surely help the economy recover from the current pandemic, but as history tells us, a low interest rate environment eventually comes to an end. When it does and interest rates rise, the federal government's borrowing costs will increase incrementally.

> *Within 30 years, CBO projects that interest costs would be the largest federal spending "program" and would be more than three times what the federal government has historically spent on R&D, non-defense infrastructure and education combined.*

Federal borrowing competes for funds in the nation's capital markets, thereby raising interest rates and crowding out new investment in business equipment and structures. Innovation is therefore inhibited and things like life-saving healthcare advancements are delayed. Additionally, at some point, investors might begin to doubt the government's ability to repay debt and could demand even higher interest rates, further raising the cost of borrowing for businesses and consumers. Once investors lose confidence in the nation's fiscal policies, interest rates on federal borrowing could rise as higher yields would be demanded to purchase such securities. A rapid increase in Treasury rates could also lead to higher rates of inflation, which would reduce the value of outstanding government securities and result in losses by holders of those securities.[133]

Inflation Risk

> **"If inflation continues to soar, you're going to have to work like a dog just to live like one."**
> George Gobel

Inflation is the persistent and sustained increase in price levels. It erodes the purchasing power of money. The price increases mean the same amount of money buys fewer goods and services. Barring an increase in your income during times of rising inflation, you are effectively getting less income in real terms.

Fixed income securities like bonds and annuities are susceptible to purchasing power risk because their income is stabilized. For bondholders, the threat of inflation risk is that the yield will not keep pace with purchasing power. For instance, if you buy a five-year bond with a coupon rate of 5 percent and the rate of inflation jumps to 8 percent, the purchasing power of your bond interest has declined. All bonds except those that adjust for inflation, such as Treasury Inflation-Protected Securities (TIPS), have exposure to some degree of inflation risk.[134]

TIPS are a security issued by the US government and are indexed to inflation in order to protect investors from a decline in the purchasing power of their money. As inflation rises, TIPS adjust in price to maintain their real value.[135]

The inability to easily find a buyer for a bond you need to sell is closely related and called liquidity risk. Bonds that trade more frequently are more liquid. Some bonds, like US Treasury securities, are easier to sell because there is almost always a ready market. Some bonds turn out to be "no bid," meaning no buying interest and thus, are highly illiquid.[136]

A client of mine purchased a CD back in 1983 from her banker. The CD promised 10% interest for life, but at the time, US Treasuries were paying about 13%, making the 10% offer not such a good deal at the time. However, interest rates plummeted to around 6% by 2000, so overall, she did quite well.

After an extended period of extremely low inflation, the general expectation is that at least a moderate rise in inflation will occur over the next few years. The large increase in money supply, the Fed's determination not to stifle a recovery from the pandemic and a potential post-pandemic consumer spending portend inflationary pressure. Factors that have held inflation at bay like technological efficiencies, globalization and cheap labor in China and other Asian countries that have kept price growth low for decades are fading.

Inflation-linked bonds are an option that offers protection from rising prices. Their outstanding principal and interest rates are adjusted in response to inflation. This means their purchase price coupon gains value when inflation is rising. But, if inflation stays low, investors can lose ground by holding them if regular bond yields increase. If expectations for increasing inflation develop, these bonds become more expensive. As such, their main attraction is for investors who think the risks of inflation are higher than the market is currently pricing in.[137]

The Impact of Inflation

Widow, Age 50
30-Year Life Expectancy
5% Certificate of Deposit Interest Rate
4% Average Inflation Rate
$1,000,000 Available for Investment

Years	(A) Capital Purchasing Power	(B) CD Interest Rate	(C) Real Yield
Now	$1,000,000	5%	$50,000
10	675,564	5%	33,778
20	456,387	5%	22,819
30	308,319	5%	15,416

Assume that she never touches a penny's worth of principal but fully uses the interest income for her living expenses. Over the next decade the cost of living will advance nearly 50 percent, reducing the purchasing power of her $1,000,000 by almost one third, to $675,564. Her $50,000 income stream likewise loses nearly one-third of its value and can purchase only $33,778 worth of goods and services. Continuing in this same manner over the remaining two decades of her life expectancy, the purchasing power of her initial $1,000,000 drops to only $308,319, with an annual income stream capable of purchasing only $15,416 worth of goods and services!

(Graphic: 6.2 Impact of Inflation)

Political Risk

> "Politicians are people who, when they see light at the end of the tunnel, go out and buy some more tunnel."
> John Quinton

Of course, when politicians "buy more tunnel," they never use their own money!

Political risk is the threat that the political climate will produce changes in regulations and laws that impact the economy, tax laws and government programs like Social Security benefits.

A common example of political risk is countries that are in political upheaval. The number of countries that rated "extreme risk" in the Civil Unrest Index jumped by 67% in just one year, from 12 in 2019 to 20 in 2020. You may recall when Communists overthrew regimes in Cuba, China and Russia, many investors lost the value of their properties, stock and savings as the result of nationalization.

As various countries continue to experience dramatic changes in social attitudes and opinions, unrest that disrupts economies ensues. According to data from the Civil Unrest Index provided by global risk analysis consultant Verisk Maplecroft, 75 countries are projected to likely experience an increase in protests by late 2022. Of these, 34—predominantly in Europe and the Americas—are expected to see a particularly significant deterioration. During 2020, the US plunged from the 91st riskiest jurisdiction in the Index to the 34th. The firm anticipates unrest to remain significantly elevated compared to historic trends over the next two years. The increase is pinned primarily to the erosion of mechanisms that have historically defused tensions, such as freedoms of assembly and the press and an independent judiciary. The post-pandemic period is also expected to inflame public dissatisfaction with government.[138]

Political risks can be sudden and fluid. Unfounded rumors can undo years of competent corporate management and policy. Technology is now contributing to political risk. The rise in cell phone ownership allows everyone with a phone to be a photographer or news reporter. An online video can erode confidence in a company and its stock within minutes.[139] I do, however, believe transparency and honesty are attributes that provide a clearer picture for investors, which is always better.

The risks prompted by the pandemic promise to be long-lasting and profound. There is concern that further lockdowns or vaccine delays may occur, triggering more market volatility. Economies of countries around world are struggling with unemployment caused by the pandemic. In the US, unemployment rose to 8.9% in 2020, according to the International Monetary Fund (IMF), ending a decade of jobs expansion. IMF estimated that the global economy shrunk by 4.4% in 2020, describing the decline as the worst since the Great Depression of the 1930s.[140]

Assuming developed markets eventually get the effects of the pandemic under control, the virus will likely remain a threat in emerging markets, where weak health systems, dense urban slums and poverty magnify the challenges of fighting the pandemic. In a few countries there are already early signs of political instability and civil unrest; in others the political effects will become clearer as the virus and government responses unfold.[141] These recent market disruptions are significant and are just one example of how outliers like the coronavirus can add uncertainty and should be a consideration for every generation as history has a way of repeating itself.

Tax Risk

> "The crime of taxation is not in the taking it, it's in the way that it's spent."
>
> Will Rogers

There is a risk that changes in the tax laws will render particular investments less beneficial.

The 2020 Coronavirus Aid, Relief and Economic Security (CARES) Act effectively tripled the federal budget deficit and ballooned the national debt by nearly 60 percent. Should the economy fail to grow at an accelerated pace, the government will be forced to raise revenue, which usually means changes to the tax code, which in turn affects stock prices.

In addition to the passage of the CARES Act (March 27, 2020), there were three other government stimulus spending packages prior to the 2020 presidential election:

1) Coronavirus Preparedness and Response Supplemental Appropriations Act (March 6, 2020)

2) Families First Coronavirus Response Act (March 18, 2020)

3) Paycheck Protection Program and Health Care Enhancement Act (April 24, 2020)

Overall, roughly $3.5 trillion was authorized by these and other measures during 2020.[142]

The newly-elected Biden Administration promptly adopted a $1.9 trillion stimulus bill, then allocated an additional $10 billion to expand vaccine access, $1.7 billion to track COVID-19 variants and $2 trillion for the "American Jobs Plan", among other proposed expenditures. How to pay for these programs? Tax increases, of course. The other, not so obvious way is inflation. By creating inflation, the current debt carried forward looks smaller. Current proposals include raising the corporate tax rate from 21% to 28%, imposing a 15% levy on profitable firms that previously paid no taxes and a minimum tax on global profits. In total, the increases are aimed at raising $2.5 trillion in revenue over 15 years to help offset the cost of the infrastructure plan.[143]

Personal income tax rate boosts are also currently being proposed. Details remain a bit sketchy but initially, the hikes appear to be limited to those earning in excess of $400,000 annually—although the Administration's press secretary clarified that the $400,000 threshold applied to families, not individuals, likely meaning individuals making $200,000 could be affected as well.[144]

Changes in personal income tax rates alter consumer behavior. Tax cuts increase people's disposable income, which spurs spending; tax increases tend to have the opposite effect. As the government takes a larger percentage of their income, workers have less to spend on discretionary items, such as concert/sporting event tickets, dining out, new car purchases, a second home, RV, boat, etc.

Changes in tax policy change consumption and investment, and as a result, they influence stock prices. According to the Tax Policy Center, changes in tax rates can have a substantial impact on these items, particularly when the economy is weak. Nevertheless, the effects are typically short-term. Tax policy changes that increase deficits, however, can slow the economy in the long run.[145]

A simplified explanation of the relationship between tax rates and government revenues is that at a tax rate of 0%, the government collects zero revenue. It can increase revenue by increasing tax rates, but only up to a certain point—the "revenue maximizing point"—beyond which increasing tax rates further damages the economy sufficiently to cause revenue to decrease. Taken to its extreme, at a tax rate of 100%, the incentive to work is effectively eliminated.[146]

The relationship between tax rates set by a government and tax revenues collected is best depicted by The Laffer Curve, introduced by American economist, Arthur Laffer. In 1974, Laffer explained the concept to lawmakers who had advocated raising taxes to fund increased government spending designed to stimulate demand. The policy was proving ineffective, however, and Laffer contended that the problem was due not because of too little demand but because of the burden heavy taxes and regulations imposed on producers, who were left without incentive to produce more.

Tax rate cuts tend to decrease government revenue but they simultaneously put more money in the hands of taxpayers, increasing their disposable income. Over time, business activity increases, companies hire more employees, who in turn spend more, leading to economic growth. The growth, in turn, creates a larger tax base and generates higher total tax revenue. Conversely, higher tax rates increase the financial burden on taxpayers. Revenues to the government may increase marginally in the short term, but higher tax rates reduce taxpayers' disposable income and spending. Demand falls and producers respond by creating less, leading to higher unemployment. The tax base for the government falls and so does its tax revenue.[147]

One of the changes currently proposed by the Biden administration is raising taxes on long-term capital gains and qualified dividends to the level of the ordinary income tax rate of 39.6 percent from the existing 20% on income above $1 million. A 2010 study by the Congressional Research Service examined what it called "behavioral responses" to changes in capital gains taxes. The capital gains tax discourages capital gains realizations because capital gains are taxed only when realized. Because of this, "investors may be encouraged to hold suboptimal portfolios or forego investment opportunities with higher pre-tax returns." In other words, when capital gains taxes are high, investors will likely respond by holding on to stocks rather than selling, which in theory makes the market less efficient.[148]

Risk Mitigation Strategies

> "A major lesson in risk management is that a 'receding sea' is not a lucky offer of an extra piece of free beach, but the warning sign of an upcoming tsunami."
>
> Jos Berkemeijer

Systematic risks can be mitigated through asset allocation by owning different asset categories with little or no correlation to one another. Asset allocation can also be adjusted based on changing valuations. Investments deemed to be overpriced can be reduced or liquidated, if possible.

Hedging can be used to reduce systematic risk. Investors can purchase puts on their securities. Puts are a risk-management strategy that help guard against the loss of unrealized gains. A put option gives the buyer the right to sell the underlying asset at a set price at any time up to the expiration date. Put value will rise if securities value drops.[149]

There are two versions of the put: married and protective. A married put is purchased at the same time a stock position is acquired. A protective put is purchased for holdings already in the portfolio. We sometimes consider this for clients with significant risks from large positions in stocks such as Microsoft (MSFT). A put strategy is best utilized as a form of insurance rather than speculation. Think of it as buying insurance to protect a highly concentrated equity position, particularly if the position represents a significant amount of one's net worth.

The difference between diversification and hedging is subtle, but important. With diversification, when the number of assets in a portfolio increases, the risk of the portfolio tends to decrease. Diversification relies on a tenuous connection between the returns of the assets in the portfolio. For example, if you hold 20 stocks in your portfolio, a poor business decision by one of those companies which results in a decrease in that stock's price is unlikely to impact the investment returns of the remaining nineteen companies.

With hedging, assets that are negatively correlated can be joined together in a portfolio to reduce systematic risk. For example, while stock prices tend to drop in value 6-12 months before a recession, bond prices rise. This negative correlation means that certain investments can serve as a hedge against volatility and stock losses. Thus, diversification relates to similar assets with uncorrelated returns. Hedging relates to dissimilar assets with returns that are negatively correlated.[150]

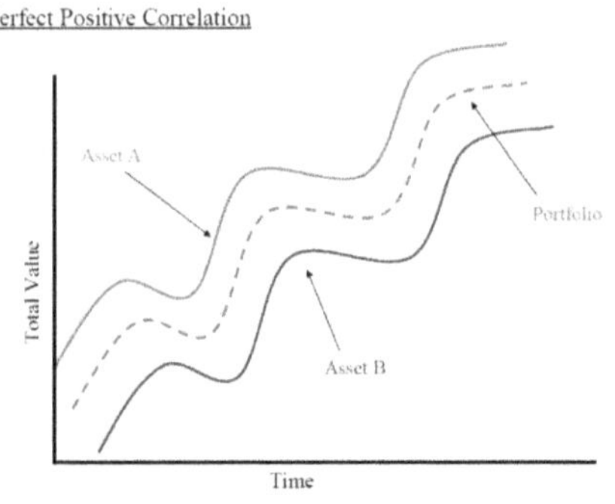

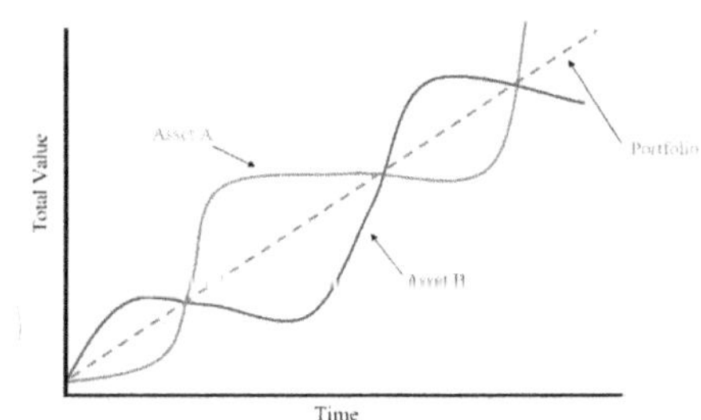

Graphic 6.3 illustrates the difference between perfect positive correlation and perfect negative correlation.
(Graphic 6.3: Positive & Negative Correlation)

The rationale behind diversification is simple and remains as valid as it was when professor Harry Markowitz first postulated what became known as Modern Portfolio Theory 70 years ago, that is, most market returns are driven by a small percentage of stocks, but there's no way to know in advance which ones will move ahead, or when. Rather than trying to pick those winners by timing the market, applying a diversified strategy reduces risk and volatility by spreading out the bets. When one investment performs poorly, others can offset the losses. Certain asset classes do show common attributes, but not always on your schedule.

Imperfect Correlation

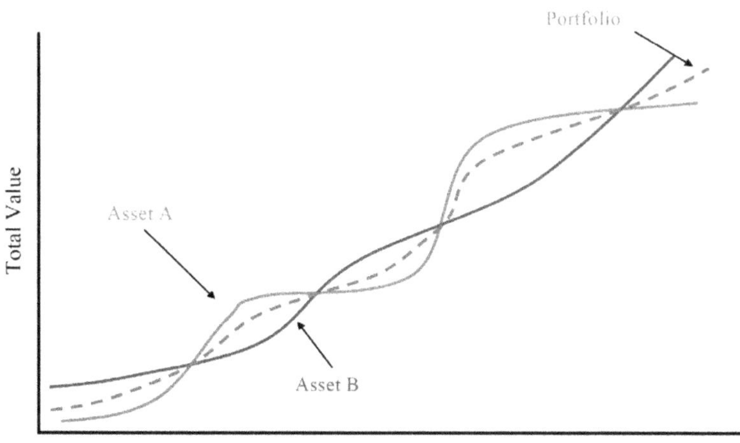

Graphic 6.4 depicts the value of imperfect correlation over time.
(Graphic 6.4: Imperfect Correlation)

Here's the problem: there is no universal definition of diversification. Some believe adequate diversification requires holding a certain number of components—stocks, or funds that track a certain index, such as the S&P 500. Indexes that assign weights to components based on size have become exceedingly top-heavy in recent times as a small group of stocks have grown exceedingly large. A decade ago, the five largest US stocks made up just over 10% of the market as represented by the S&P 500. In 2020, the five largest companies—Apple, Microsoft, Amazon, Facebook and Alphabet accounted for roughly a quarter of the index, the highest percentage over 20 years. Diversification is a risk strategy, and can be an effective one, but like any tactic designed to reduce risk, there is a likelihood it will also limit performance. A diversified stock fund or index, by definition, will own less of Apple, Amazon, Facebook, and the like, which means it could underperform the S&P 500 when those stocks have big years.[151]

Another often overlooked point is that these indexes are not always equally weighted. This means that currency risk might be reduced through diversification using international assets, provided the foreign securities are issued in US dollars. Alternatives available to manage currency risk for investing internationally include currency futures, forwards and options or currency-hedged funds. These are complex and typically expensive instruments, however. A simpler and more liquid alternative to hedge against currency risk are currency-hedged ETFs, which have built-in hedges against currency fluctuations relative to the US dollar.[152] As a practice, I seldom hedge client's foreign investments as it's usually not worth the additional cost.

One way to lessen interest rate risk while pursuing higher yields and reducing illiquidity is a portfolio laddering strategy using bonds or other fixed income securities that mature at differing intervals. As the bonds closest to maturity expire, the investments are rolled over in order to maintain the position of holding bonds with equally spaced maturities. This strategy is used to attain higher average yields while reducing illiquidity and interest rate risk.[153] I have not seen the benefit of this, however, for over a decade now.

As we see a more traditional yield curve with yield increases over time, there will likely become a more practical strategy for some investors. Shorter-term bonds are less sensitive to rising interest rates than longer-term bonds but the lower sensitivity is offset by the fact that the shorter the duration, the lower the yield. A strategy to address this issue is investing in floating-rate securities—such as bank loans and TIPS—which have adjustable interest rates that make them less sensitive to rate increases.

Another approach to offset the impact of rising rates is to invest in bond market segments that aren't as interest-rate sensitive, such as securities that fall on the lower end of investment grade, like high-yield bonds and convertible bonds. Like all strategies, however, these securities come with a caveat: the investor trades credit risk for interest-rate risk.

When it comes to investing in bonds, I believe in buying low-cost actively managed bond funds, such as Vanguard's Core Bond Fund, but there are many great options to choose from and I typically choose from several sources to further increase diversification. I do not buy bonds with the expectation of meaningful returns. I buy bonds to mitigate risk, principally to offset equity risk.

As to concentration risk, the debate between advocates of concentration or diversification in an investment portfolio will likely continue into the next millennium. Warren Buffet is exceptionally good at picking stocks, a talent lacking in the majority of active investors. His famous adage that "diversification may preserve wealth, but concentration builds wealth" is a highly respected investment mantra.

Buffet built a portfolio buying low when most investors lost interest in stock ownership in the 1970s. Through Berkshire Hathaway, Buffet was able to buy major stakes in corporations, giving him a significant advantage not available to most investors.

A 2020 *Fortune* article described how he laid the groundwork for his strategy:

> *"Buffett didn't close the last Berkshire mill until 1985, but by the late 1960s it was clear that the company's future lay not in the textile business but in the capital-allocation game. Those who wanted to remain invested with him took Berkshire shares in lieu of cash, and the modern-day Berkshire Hathaway was born. Buffett began using Berkshire's assets to buy cheap stocks, and the proceeds from those winners to buy still more. The Berkshire machine really got going, however, when Buffett began buying insurance companies—not as shares in the open market but as wholly owned Berkshire subsidiaries. As a pure profit proposition, an insurance company faces prospects no rosier than a textile company. Both industries are characterized by commoditization, low barriers to entry and high capital requirements. However, Buffett understood*

something important about the industry before nearly anyone else did: Until the claims come due, insurers can invest the premiums they've taken in. With so-called long-tailed business, there can be decades between taking in the cash and paying out the claims. The resulting "float," as it's called—the cash generated by premiums yet to be paid out—can prove exceedingly valuable in the hands of a good capital allocator. Every year an insurance company must pay out claims, but every year it takes in new premiums, thus ensuring a sort of perpetual-motion machine of cash flow. For more than 50 years now, Buffett has invested this float with uncanny acumen, growing and changing as an investor in a remarkably fluid way."[154]

During 2019, the S&P 500 Index posted an absolute return of 31.5%, the second-highest annual return since 2001. The S&P MidCap 400 Index also did well, growing 26.2% and the S&P SmallCap 600 returned 22.8%. It was truly a banner year for equities and while active fund managers posted excellent returns, 70% of equity funds were unable to beat their benchmarks. It was the ninth consecutive year that the majority of large-cap funds failed to outperform the S&P 500.[155]

The disagreement about the efficiency of markets is reflected in the fact that so many among the investment community continue to devote time and resources to identifying mispriced stocks. A definitive expression of the dangers of diversification comes from the great investment thinker, John Maynard Keynes, who wrote to a friend in 1934:

"As times goes on, I get more and more convinced that the right method of investment is to put large sums into enterprises which one thinks one knows something about and in the management of which one thoroughly believes. It is a mistake to think one limits one's risk by spreading too much between enterprises about which

one knows little and has no reason for special confidence."

Done correctly, balancing concentration and diversification is a precise practice that typically should be left to experienced professionals.[156]

Inflation risk can jeopardize a portfolio because of the way inflation eviscerates purchasing power over time. Fixed-income securities are especially susceptible to inflation risk because their rate of return is, as the name implies, fixed. If you hold bonds paying a 5% fixed rate of return and inflation rears up while you own the bonds, your purchasing power represented by those securities declines. On the other hand, owning equities provides greater flexibility as companies can defend themselves against inflation by simply raising the prices of their goods and services. Think of companies such as General Mills, Costco, Proctor & Gamble, etc.[157]

Any fixed rate investment—bonds, annuities, money-market funds, CD's, bank deposits and the like—lack the ability to effectively abate inflationary risks. Investments that ostensibly lessen inflationary pressures include stocks, funds, inflation-indexed bonds, real estate rental property and inflation-resistant commodities, such as oil. These types of investments, which can be fairly immune to inflation, carry other, economic-related risks. Finally, diversifying across a variety of asset classes can also help minimize inflation risk.[158]

The issue of tax risk has been pushed to the forefront of planning as a result of the 2020 elections. Minimizing taxes should never be a part of your investment strategy but, being aware of tax ramifications and incorporating strategies to address the impact of taxes on your investment returns just makes sense. In other words, don't let the tax tail wag the financial dog.

Summary

Investment risk cannot be eliminated, but it can be mitigated. All investments carry some degree of risk. Even the most conservative investments, like bank certificates of deposit or US Treasuries, come with inflation risk. Typically, an investment's level of risk correlates with the potential level of return. Historically, a diversified portfolio of stocks, held for the long term, substantially reduces the risk of loss. That does not mean, however, that there is no risk in investing in stocks over a long period of time.

Investment strategies that help reduce both systematic and unsystematic risk include asset allocation and diversification. Hedging can also help reduce potential loss, but it can add significantly to investment cost.

While there is no way to completely avoid investment risk, the counsel of an experienced financial advisor can help ensure prudent planning that minimizes risk and helps you avoid the destructive behaviors that jeopardize portfolio returns.

> "The essence of risk management lies in maximizing the areas where we have some control over the outcome while minimizing the areas where we have absolutely no control over the outcome."
>
> Peter L. Bernstein

Chapter Seven

Business Owners and Pilots

Many small businesses die a premature—and often unnecessary—death because the owner failed to understand what it would take to be successful. Those who fly for fun or as a hobby often make the same mistakes. New business owners that formerly worked as employees likely enjoyed the support of other employees when encountering problems. Running their own business requires they acquire additional competencies, but being anxious to get started, many fail to fulfill this vital step. I've encountered numerous new pilots who exhibit the same failings. Fresh from flight school, they can't wait to get up into the air and experience the exhilaration and serenity. But the majority of aviation accidents are caused by pilot error, and too often, an inexperienced pilot, unable to handle an unexpected difficulty, was the culprit.

My heart goes out to the self-employed. They are in a very different situation than someone working at a large Fortune 500 company such as Boeing or Microsoft. Too many of them die with their boots on.

Business owners must understand that their business is an appointment for them. It's either a job or it's a business. If it's a job, the owner must ensure a satisfactory retirement with benefits comparable to what would be received as an employee working for a large company. If it's a business, the primary issue becomes viability as a going concern so it can be sold and hopefully continue meaningful employment to employees for an equitable price at the owner's chosen retirement date.

According to data from the Bureau of Labor Statistics, approximately 20 percent of small businesses fail within the first year and roughly half by year five. And the end of a decade, only 30 percent of businesses remain—a 70 percent failure rate.[159]

There are many reasons why a small business fails. The original *Saturday Night Live* show had a sketch that featured a store called "The Scotch Tape Boutique," a mall shop that sold nothing but tape and whose owner had a difficult time understanding why business was always bad. Have you ever passed a retail store that sells something equally specific and wondered, "who put up the money for that business and what were they thinking?"

Many go into business with the wind in their face instead of at their backs. Business failures are not always a case of poor management. Some people simply follow their dream, ignoring or failing to get professional advice about its practicality. Markets change in response to a variety of factors, causing some to fail. Others fall prey to insufficient capital, lack of expertise, inability to manage employees, cashflow issues, poor location, an outlier event like the pandemic or simply poor planning.[160]

Even when the business is successful, the owner may not be able to convert its value into money for retirement. Virtually every year, we have two or three successful, self-employed professionals or people in service industries who decide it's time to retire. The bulk of their net worth is tied up in their businesses and now they are in their sixties and tired of the daily grind. They want to call it quits and cash out but they don't have a transfer strategy. They don't have anyone in the firm able to buy the business. Those capable of taking over are too old to do so and are planning their own retirement. Attracting a buyer is difficult because the value in the business is primarily tied to the client relationships the owner has built over the years. Once the owner leaves, much of the value evaporates.

In one instance, the owner of an equipment leasing company suffered a heart attack and was advised by his doctors to retire. His was a well-established company with over 20 employees. He asked for our help in formulating a retirement strategy but it was like asking for a miracle. The problem was he had continuously funneled profits back into the business over the years but had taken very little money out for retirement. He and his wife combined had less than a hundred thousand dollars in their IRAs. He had an inventory of specialized equipment but it was susceptible to wear and tear. Every time a piece broke down, he was forced to spend 50 to 100 thousand dollars to repair or replace the equipment. The couple was anxious to find some way to quickly save enough to retire, but they were also demoralized and too tired to put in the extra time and effort to earn the necessary money. There wasn't much we could do to help.

One of the problems that plague the self-employed is thinking their business is worth more than it actually is. They must try to extract as much as they can for their retirement from their business. They need to plan ahead as to what their last day at work will look like so they don't wind up presiding over the destruction of their business because they lacked the resources to retire comfortably or were unable to attract a buyer willing to adequately reimburse them for their years of labor.

I've recently had consultations with several small business owners about planning for retirement. I offered them all the same advice. You must pay yourself out of your business. Set up a 401k and contribute to it religiously, because you will die with your boots on if you don't. You have to understand that this business is your conduit for your future financial freedom, so that you can do whatever you want in retirement. I hope they take the advice because most wind up working into their 70s because they haven't taken enough out of the business for themselves. They didn't get enough out of the business from day one, which is a tragic mistake.

Some of the self-employed will eventually run their businesses into the ground as a result of treating them like a "lifestyle job." By that I mean the business is intentionally kept going at a bare minimum, generating just enough profit to allow the owner to maintain a lifestyle. This usually occurs in the service industry where the business is composed of a single person or perhaps a married couple. These may be accountants, attorneys, consultants or similar occupations. They are typically inadequately staffed, so when the owners take a vacation or simply don't feel like working, clients suffer the consequences.

We've had clients tell us about their frustrating experiences with lifestyle business owners. One client ran afoul of the tax laws when acting on advice from a lifestyle accountant. We tried to help but couldn't get anyone to answer the phone, later learning the owner couple was in Hawaii on extended vacation and had left no way for clients to reach them. In another instance, an attorney who worked from her home and frequently disappeared for days on end was unavailable to help a client arrested in a mistaken identity case.

People often start businesses without thinking through the longer-term outcomes. They are literally babes in the woods when it comes to comprehending the hours, overhead and other issues that running a business entails. Most worked as an employee prior to becoming their own boss and probably focused on a single activity, able to ignore the many issues every business encounters because there were other employees and support staff handling them. They may know little about marketing or balancing books. But they are excited and eager to begin their new career. This is known as the Wonder Stage.

After being in business for a while and not making as much in the way of profits as they had hoped, they wrestle with cashflow, employment, pricing and other issues. They struggle to grow volume, believing that will lead to more profitability. They are now working considerably longer hours than they did as an employee, dealing with the myriad tasks and bookkeeping requirements of a single entity business. Perhaps they hired an employee or two and now feel the pressure of meeting payroll. There is always something the business needs that has to be bought, usually on credit with finance charges adding to their overhead. They start to feel stressed. They are overworked and forget to do things. They make mistakes. And they still haven't managed to save anything for retirement. This is the Blunder Stage.

I sometimes have to tell a small business owner, "You're in the *Blunder Stage*. You're working like crazy but seemingly not getting anywhere. You take a small salary and everything else goes back into the business. You're not taking care of your future." When this continues for an extended period, the business frequently becomes a lifestyle job, where the exhausted owner has no time for marketing because of the time spent trying to keep current clients happy. There's no exit strategy and no chance to find a ready buyer. Eventually, the dream is abandoned and the only remaining option is exercised: the business becomes a lifestyle job and the owner hangs on.

Business owners have to keep their focus on their eventual retirement needs, particularly those who reinvest most of their profits back into the business or those who treat their business as a job. This means setting up an individual 401k, which offers distinct advantages for self-employed individuals because they can contribute as both employee and employer, giving them a higher limit than other tax-advantaged plans.[161] The self-employed can contribute up to $58,000 in 2021, $64,000 for those age 50 or older.[162] Spouses who work for the business can make the same employer contributions and the owner can then match those.

The 401k and other employer-based retirement plans are a virtual necessity for accumulating enough retirement savings. A SIMPLE IRA, another of the savings plans available to those self-employed, only allows a maximum of $15,500 in 2023, plus an additional $3,500 for those 50 and older. As you can see, the IRA won't allow enough contributions to fully fund a retirement. Those who build a successful business may be able to set up a defined benefit contribution plan with annual contribution limits as high as $160,000.

Owners must be highly disciplined in making plan contributions. The old saw of starting early certainly applies to the self-employed. Unlike those working for large companies, there's no HR Department to advise the self-employed when it comes to retirement savings. They must make the commitment to pay themselves. I know this sounds basic but unfortunately, the majority of small business owners fail to achieve financial independence.

Taxes

Even when a business becomes successful and the owner is able to attract a buyer, there are significant tax issues to be considered.

Profits received from the sale of a business are taxed as either ordinary income or capital gains. There's a big difference. The tax rate on long-term capital gains for noncorporate taxpayers is much lower than the highest maximum individual tax rate. Given that most small business owners who are successful in selling their company are in high tax brackets, this rate differential is very important in reducing tax liability. The sale of the business assets will likely be taxed at capital gains rates, whereas money received as part of a consulting agreement will be taxed as ordinary income. Because what is good for the seller is bad for the buyer and vice versa, negotiating the price of each asset category can be contentious, something sellers are often unprepared for.[163]

There are two approaches to a business sale: asset or stock. An asset transaction sale involves the capital assets. A capital asset is tangible property, such as the building and equipment. By definition, a capital asset must be something that has value going forward of more than a year.[164] A stock sale is the sale of all or a majority share of stock to the buyer. This method is typically used by S and C corporations.[165]

According to the IRS, "The sale of a trade or business for a lump sum is considered a sale of each individual asset rather than of a single asset."[166]

Taxation treatment also varies based on the type of business. For example, in the sale of a business that is a sole proprietorship, each asset is treated separately. Most are taxed as capital gains, but some assets, such as real estate, equipment and inventory, are typically taxed as ordinary income.

Selling a corporation provides a choice of whether to sell stock or specify the transaction as a sale of assets. Sellers tend to prefer to sell the stock and pay capital gains whereas buyers prefer an asset sale which creates a higher basis for the depreciable assets they are acquiring.[167]

The owner of a corporation is a shareholder that has capital gains or losses when selling their shares, not necessarily when the business is sold. In the sale of a corporation or partnership, the interest or investment of an owner is treated as a capital asset. The capital gain of a partner is the gain to the owner, not the capital gain of the business.[168]

Have a Business Plan

It's critical for owners to build and operate a viable business that represents a going concern for a buyer. Whatever the reason someone decides to be self-employed or own their own business, it's prudent to have a formal business plan, something few entrepreneurs can do objectively on their own. An experienced accountant can certainly be helpful, as could a business consultant or local college that has adult education courses in business or a business incubator program. The local Chamber of Commerce is another option where the prospective business owner can sit down with somebody qualified to work out a business plan to determine if the idea is viable.

Here in Washington state, Everett Community College, where I teach adult education classes, has an excellent incubator program. It's a two-year course taught by successful business people who are retired consultants. They take adult students through the hard work necessary to formulate a business plan and a strategy to get the nascent business off on the right track so that it evolves into a going business and not just a job. There's a big difference. I've seen a lot of self-employed people merely create a job for themselves to support a lifestyle. That's fine if that's their goal, but in most cases, their expectation is that they are building a viable business, in which case they must think differently than someone who is simply an employee. For example, what must they do to ensure they can take a vacation every year and get away from the stress of the business?

Small business owners often fail to give enough thought to their fee structure. Those just starting out may be so anxious to get business that they accept reduced fees. Whatever the fee structure, owners must make sure they are charging enough to put 15 or 20 percent of their salary aside for retirement. It's not unusual for a small business owner to take an equally small salary—perhaps 60 or 70 thousand a year—while the business is generating 150 thousand a year in profits. Even though the husband-and-wife owners may already be in their 50s, there still may be time for them to increase their Social Security (SS) wage base. If one spouse hasn't been part of the business, the other should find something for them to do and get on the payroll. I often see married couples in business where the wife is helping or even working full time but not taking any wages. It's usually well worth paying the FICA to get her on payroll, creating SS benefits for her and qualifying her for 401k contributions. They need to do this before they grow weary of running the business and find they don't have enough to retire comfortably.

Debt

Another issue for the self-employed—especially in the early stages of their business—is taking on too much debt. Banks are rarely eager to loan new businesses money so owners are forced to find other means of financing their operations, from credit cards to home equity lines of credit. Clients sometimes send their friends or children to me for advice on starting a business and one of the first things I caution them about is funding the business with credit or loans before the business has earned it. Keeping expenses manageable is the first rule of staying out of debt. Whether its buying office furniture, a computer, signing a lease or other expense, I advise new owners to "earn it before you spend it."

Another tidbit of advice I offer is to get a referral for a good accountant, preferably a CPA that will take the time to teach you the ropes. Learn about things like federal withholding taxes. Here in Washington state, we have the infamous E&O tax that consumes roughly 2% of gross revenue. There are constantly evolving regulations and new laws that nascent business owners must be aware of. The cost of hiring a trained professional to help navigate that minefield is money well spent.

Disability Insurance

Disability insurance for self-employed business owners can be a problem. Depending on where they live, it can either be prohibitively expensive, difficult to acquire or both.

Insurance carriers typically market to physicians, dentists, attorneys and other professionals while they are still in medical or law school. It's rare for me to encounter a professional person without disability insurance because companies like Northwestern Mutual, Mass Mutual and New York Life go after medical professionals and sell them disability insurance before they ever open their practice. My partner's brother is a dental surgeon who bought a policy and later broke his ankle on a curb outside of his office. He is now retired but while he continued to practice, he collected on that policy for his entire career because that ankle fracture prevented him from standing on his feet all day to do surgery.

I've had clients who are surgeons tell me they are considering dropping their disability policy because "it's costing me $1,200 a month!" I told one of them who has a hobby of building furniture in his garage, "If you slice your finger on that table saw, you may not be able to do surgery anymore. You're the family's breadwinner making $600 thousand a year, but you don't have enough financial resources yet to be able to take that risk. You'll need that insurance income if something happens."

But for other self-employed people, like those in construction and the trades, there's no one advising them during their twenties about what can happen if they are injured and unable to work. I remember once reading a statistic that the majority of home foreclosures was due to disability.

There is not a lot of competition among carriers here in Washington state. The self-employed can't get the advantages of group disability policies like larger employers. We have a group disability policy for our employees and get some pricing advantages that someone with less than ten employees cannot. It's one more issue the self-employed have to do for themselves as opposed to having it provided by an employer.

The challenge for many self-employed people in Washington State is that they don't want to pay the cost of the state's Department of Labor and Industries (L&I) coverage, a quasi-insurance system covering workers hurt on the job. L&I pays benefits out of an insurance pool called the Washington State Fund, which is financed by premiums paid by employers and employees.

The Department of Labor and Industries determines the Washington L&I tax rates, which are based on factors such as the type of business, its claim history, the job's risk classification and the industry's accident and illness rates. The level of the job's risk is a major factor in determining rates. For example, rates in the construction industry are higher than rates for retail workers. The more likely it is for an employee to get hurt or sick on the job, the higher the rate.[169]

The problem with L&I is if you are a tradesman or contractor, it's really expensive— four to six dollars an hour for someone like a carpenter or roofer— and so a lot of self-employed contractors opt out of it. Washington is one of the few states in the U.S. where small businesspeople are required to purchase disability income insurance through the state mandated labor and industries (L&I) plan. Businesses over 500 employees can opt out. Claims are handled by a select few state-appointed physicians and are very difficult for victims of work-related accidents to receive compensation. In other words, the so-called benefits are woefully inadequate.

Washington recently also passed the Long-Term Care Act, ostensibly to lessen the state's Medicare burden. It's a payroll tax that began January 1, 2022 and is funded by a 0.58% tax on every employee's wage, regardless of age. This tax is permanent and applies to all residents, even for those whose employer is located outside of the state. There is no cap on the tax and all forms of remuneration—including stock-based compensation, bonuses, paid time off and severance pay—are subject to the tax.

Benefits are not vested for workers until they have paid into the pool for a minimum of ten years and are not payable until January 2025, nor are they payable to workers that have moved and reside outside of Washington state when they need benefits. The maximum benefit is $36,000. According to the 2020 Genworth Cost of Care survey for Washington State, the average long-term care claim lasts for 2.5 years. The average cost per month for nursing home care is $11,954 in a private room, $6,750 for assisted living and $6,670 for home health care.[170]

This isn't meant to be a gripe against the state government. I don't sell long-term disability insurance but it is an unfortunate fact of life that small businesses in our state are required to buy state-sponsored disability and medical accident coverage as it is very expensive and leaves them exposed to significant financial risk due to unacceptable terms of coverage. If possible, a small business owner is advised to opt out of state sponsored coverage and buy on the private insurance market from a knowledgeable insurance broker at a reasonable cost. Most go without it and risk everything they've worked for.

Large business owners often retire well off. The self-employed or those working for smaller employers tend to do less well. There are a lot of professionals that fail to save an adequate amount for retirement. There are just as many non-professionals who are injured or get sick and suffer a similar fate.

Summary

As a business owner, you have to decide whether your business is a job or an actual business. If the latter, you have to provide yourself with retirement benefits comparable to those you would have enjoyed as a corporate employee. Neglecting to do so is one of the major omissions of the self-employed.

You should carefully build a business that will command an equitable price when you are ready to retire and want to cash in. I've seen so many people with the preponderance of their net worth tied up in their business and lacking an exit strategy for when they want out. There's no one to transfer the business to and little opportunity to find a ready buyer.

Finally, you must have a formal business plan. Without a business "road map," you are unlikely to get where you hope to go. Find a competent professional to help you do this; it's too important to risk doing it yourself. Also, find a good accountant, ideally a CPA and/or CFP willing to take a personal interest and teach you what you need to know about taxes.

CHAPTER EIGHT

INFLATION & RETIREMENT INCOME PLANNING

Pilots flying private jets have the flexibility to change flight plans mid-flight, if weather conditions, air traffic control instructions or other factors occur that imperil the safety of the flight. Retirement plans also need the flexibility to make changes when necessary. One reason might be rampant inflation, which we have all experienced the past couple of years.

One of the most corrosive factors in planning for retirement income is inflation. Over time, inflation can be volatile and unpredictable, and its effect can significantly diminish your buying power. A low inflation rate today doesn't guarantee a low or even moderate inflation rate over the next 20–30 years

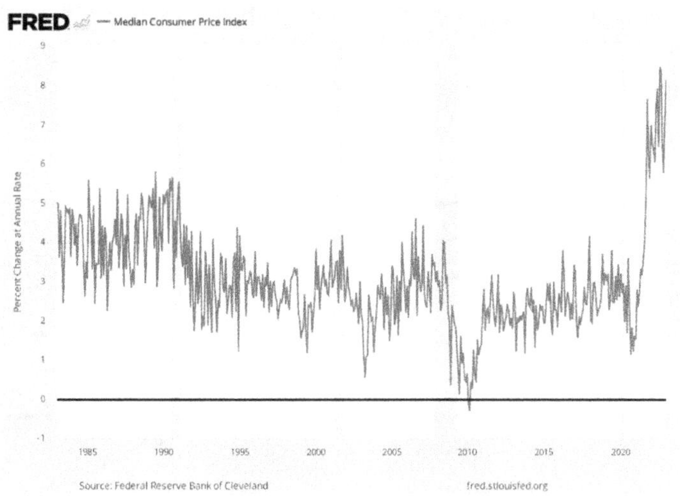

(Graphic 8.1: Historical Rates of Inflation)

Inflation erodes the purchasing power of dollars in the future and compounds in a negative direction. This is an important planning consideration, especially for anyone retiring on a fixed income.

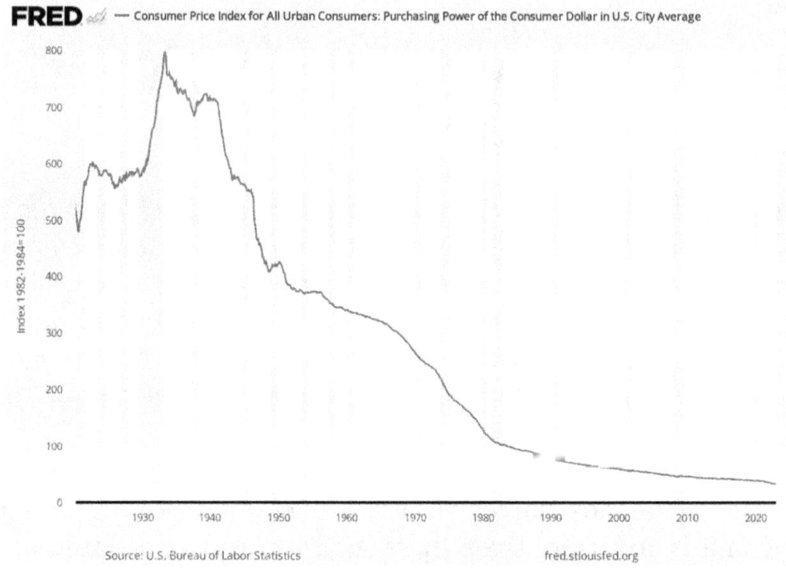

(Graphic 8.2: Inflation & Purchasing Power)

As an example of the impact of inflation on future purchasing power, let's assume a widow, age 50, with a life expectancy of another 30 years. She has one million dollars saved and invested in a 5% certificate of deposit. Now let's assume an average inflation rate of 4% over those 30 years. (See graphic 8.3)

	(A)	(B)	(C)
Years:	*Capital Purchasing Power*	*CD Interest Rate*	*Real Yield*
Now	$ 1,000,000.00	5%	$ 50,000.00
10	$ 675,564.00	5%	$ 33,778.00
20	$ 456,387.00	5%	$ 22,819.00
30	$ 308,319.00	5%	$ 15,416.00

(Graphic 8.3: Impact of Inflation)

Assuming she never touches the principal but uses the interest income for her living expenses, her cost of living will increase nearly 50 percent, reducing the purchasing power of her $1,000,000 by almost one third, to $675,564. Her $50,000 income stream likewise loses nearly one-third of its value and can purchase only $33,778 worth of goods and services. Continuing in this same manner over the remaining two decades of her life expectancy, the purchasing power of her initial $1,000,000 drops to only $308,319, with an annual income stream capable of purchasing only $15,416 worth of goods and services.

For another example of the effect of inflation during retirement, see graphic 8.4. Here, let's assume a married couple, both the same age, both expect to retire at age 65 and live for another 20 years. Let's now assume the inflation rate continues at a steady 3% annually over their 20-year retirement and their living expenses remain the same. As you can see from the graphic, their current expenses of $5,500 a month (or $66,000 a year) may total more than two million dollars over the course of their 20-year retirement.

Average Inflation	***3%***
Today	$ 1.00
5 Years	$ 1.16
10 Years	$ 1.34
15 Years	$ 1.56

Monthly Expenses *Today*	$ 5,500.00
Annual Expenses *Today*	$ 66,000.00
Monthly Retirement Income (80% reduction)	$ 4,400.00
Monthly Expenses *in 15 Years*	$ 6,855.20
Annual Expenses *in 15 Years*	$ 82,262.40

(Graphic 8.4: Inflation and Retirement Yearly Living Expenses)

Debt Management

It's important for those who need debt counselling to get help when planning for retirement income.

Seniors are carrying unprecedented levels of debt. According to a 2019 Congressional Research Service report, the percentage of households led by people aged 65 and older with any type of debt increased from 38% in 1989 to 61% in 2016. The amount owed jumped from about $7,500 to more than $31,000 in 2016 dollars. Carrying high levels of debt can cause stress and jeopardize retirement income planning.[171]

The escalation of home prices and resulting longer-term mortgages can have seniors making monthly mortgage payments well into retirement. Medical debt can also be an issue for retirees. While Medicare covers many healthcare costs, not every procedure is included and retirees can spend thousands—or tens of thousands—on medical bills over the course of their retirement.[172]

Credit card interest is another problem. With interest rates on most cards at 20% or more, users pay a dollar in interest for every five they borrow. High interest rates like this threaten finances at any stage of life, let alone retirees living on a fixed income. It's vital for retirees to pay down as much high-interest debt as possible and avoid accruing any new credit card debt prior to retirement. Eliminating credit card debt before retiring should be a high priority.[173]

Tax Planning

One way for investors to maximize tax savings is called *asset locations*, which refers to holding investments and funds in the appropriate type of account. Stocks and stock funds, for example, should generally be held in taxable accounts or Roth's because most of their return is taxed at a capital gains rate that's lower than the tax rate for ordinary income. Bonds and bond funds, on the other hand, should generally be held in non-Roth retirement accounts as they are less tax-efficient and most of their returns are yields taxed as ordinary income.

Using a sequencing strategy for withdrawals is advisable as it can reduce tax costs over the long run. The prevailing wisdom is to withdraw from taxable accounts first, then from tax-deferred 401k and IRA accounts and from Roth accounts last. While that tends to be good advice, there are situations where it can cause problems down the road. For example, delaying withdrawals from an IRA account permits it to continue to compound and grow, which could exacerbate required minimum distributions. (You may recall our discussion in chapter two about potential future tax bombs.)

One factor to be aware of is the current marginal income tax rates. For 2021, single taxpayers will be pushed from a 12% to a 22% tax rate after $40,525 of taxable income. A retiree who withdraws that amount from either taxable or tax-deferred accounts could withdraw additional funds for the year from Roth accounts to prevent jumping into the higher tax bracket. Since taxes on a Roth account have already been paid, the withdrawal would not increase the retiree's taxable income and could remain in the lower 12% bracket.[174]

It's a good idea to diversify retirement savings, based on how the money will be taxed. In estimating how much of your income will be taxed in retirement, you should consider not only your savings but also other sources of income, including Social Security and pensions. While current tax rates are relatively low by historical standards, politicians have a penchant for raising rates when they want to spend money to garner votes, which happens with depressing regularity. It's the wise investor who assumes tax rates will be higher in the coming years. If you're wrong, no harm done.

There are four types of savings accounts available for retirement, each having a different tax profile: taxable, tax deferred, Roth and healthcare savings (HSA).

Taxable savings in bank and brokerage accounts are funded with after-tax dollars. You can sell securities in your brokerage account and contribute or withdraw money at any time and for any reason without penalty. Any taxable investment income is taxed in the year it's earned, and investments sold for a profit are subject to capital gains taxes. If you sell an investment for a loss, you may be able to use it to offset any gains or ordinary income up to the current threshold. These accounts are also exempt from RMDs.

Contributions to tax-deferred accounts, such as 401k, 403b and traditional IRAs, reduce taxable income dollar for dollar in the year of contribution. Pretax contributions and gains are usually not taxed until retirement, when withdrawals are taxed as ordinary income rates. Keep in mind that you must begin taking RMDs from tax-deferred savings accounts at age 72.

As previously mentioned, contributions to Roth accounts are made with after-tax dollars, so while they don't reduce current taxable income, there's no taxes owed on income or appreciation when withdrawals are made in retirement. Important note: a Roth IRA is exempt from RMDs but a Roth 401k is not. Rolling a Roth 401k into a Roth IRA during retirement avoids RMDs however.

Health savings accounts (HSAs) can be an effective savings vehicle (if your employer offers one and you're covered by an eligible high-deductible health plan). Contributions reduce your taxable income up to annual limits; investments grow tax-free and there are no taxes due on withdrawals for qualified medical expenses. Once you reach age 65, withdrawals for nonmedical purposes will be taxed as ordinary income. HSAs are also exempt from RMDs.[175] I highly recommend these in the right situations.

Social Security Decisions

The Transamerica Center for Retirement Research report on the self-employed and retirement found that only 55% of the self-employed indicate they consistently save for retirement, while 30% save from time to time, and, shockingly, 15% say they never save. Of those who are saving for retirement, relatively few are saving in tax-advantaged retirement accounts. Only 31% are saving in a traditional or Roth IRA, according to the report. And only 40% expect retirement income from typical retirement accounts such as 401(k), 403(b), or IRA plans. Only 31% of the self-employed in our report have a backup plan in the event they are unable to work before their planned retirement.

Only about 4% make the optimum claiming decision, according to a study released a couple of years ago by financial services firm United Capital. The researchers had access to data from a long-term health study of Americans and were able to match that information with the Social Security (SS) claiming decisions of the individuals. The data allowed the researchers to use hindsight to determine the claiming decision that would have maximized lifetime benefits for the individuals. They concluded that most Americans claim their benefits too early and over their lifetimes shortchange themselves of $100,000 or more of benefits.

Social Security Benefits

The most an individual who files a claim for SS retirement benefits in 2021 can receive per month is: $3,895 for someone who files at age 70. $3,148 for someone who files at full retirement age (FRA)—currently 66 and 2 months. $2,324 for someone who files at 62.

For anyone born in 1954 or later, The Bipartisan Budget Act of 2015 changed the rules applying to spousal benefits. They are now capped at 50% of the benefits the other spouse would receive at their FRA. Also, the applying spouse does not qualify for benefits unless their spouse is already receiving SS.[176]

SS benefits are reduced for those who claim them before their FRA, currently 66 or 67, depending on year of birth. Similarly, benefits grow higher—8% annually until age 70—for those who claim benefits after their FRA. The earliest age for filing is 62.

It's important to understand that early filing impacts spousal benefits, regardless of whether the husband or wife claimed early, at FRA or later. The earlier one claims, the greater the spousal benefit. Also, an individual cannot receive both their own benefit and a spousal benefit: they would receive the greater of the two benefits.[177] The longer the higher earner can delay taking benefits, the more money there will be for the surviving spouse.

Aside from worries about the solvency of SS, personal financial issues, inability to continue working or the expectation of a shortened lifespan, there is another reason to consider taking early SS benefits. If you can't wait to stop working so you can travel extensively, join a country club, buy a second home or other bucket list item—what's known as the go-go phase of retirement—and then anticipate slowing down and spending less after a few years, taking early benefits might make financial sense.[178]

The self-employed that claim early SS benefits—anytime between age 62 and full retirement age (FRA)—will see their benefits reduced. Individuals who continue to work after starting SS benefits may also see a reduction. Until reaching FRA, SS will reduce benefits for those who exceed a certain amount of earned income for the year. For the year 2021, the limit is $18,960. So, for someone collecting SS benefits before FRA, those benefits are reduced by $1 for every $2 earned over the limit. Once individuals reach FRA, there is no limit on the amount of money they may earn and still receive their full SS benefit. The amounts of early retirement benefits lost are not necessarily gone. When the person reaches FRA, SS recalculates their benefit and partially makes up for the amounts lost because of the earned income rule, a little bit each year. It typically takes up to 15 years to completely recoup lost benefits. Importantly, the readjustment does not change the permanent percentage reduction in benefits as a result of taking early retirement benefits.[179]

The SS tax rate for 2023 is 12.4% on self-employment income up to $160,200. There are no SS taxes on earnings above that amount. There is no such cap for Medicare contributions, however, the 2.9% Medicare tax must be paid on self-employment income. Self-employment income could lower an individual's benefit if they claimed SS before reaching full retirement age (currently 66 and 2 months and gradually rising over the next several years to 67).[180]

Rollovers

Withdrawals (or distributions) from a traditional IRA or 401k are subject to pro rata rules. The pro-rata rule affects taxation of distributions and comes into play when a traditional IRA or 401k consists of both pre-tax and after-tax monies. These after-tax dollars can come from non-deductible IRA contributions or rollovers of after-tax funds from employer plans. Either way, once those monies are in the account, subsequent distributions or conversions are subject to the pro-rata rule. Roth IRA distributions are not subject to the pro-rata rule but do have their own rules.[181]

With a 401k the pro-rata rule applies only to single plans with mixed taxation. With an IRA it applies to the aggregation of all a person's traditional IRA accounts. So once a mixed 401K is rolled separately to both a Roth IRA and a Traditional IRA, the conversions—and subsequent distributions—become needlessly complicated.[182]

Once retirement savings are moved from a 401k into an IRA, it's best to avoid receiving a check made out directly to the account owner. It should instead be made out to the IRA custodian for the owner's benefit. Doing this avoids tax withholding. If the check is payable directly to the owner, it is considered a distribution and the 401k is required to withhold 20% for taxes.[183]

Many times, people avoid or delay rolling their 401k into an IRA because they've done well with their 401k and don't understand the ramifications of taking distributions. Sometimes, they don't know who to trust so they do nothing, or they take distributions from the 401k when the market has gone down and they don't realize the forces working against them. If they roll it to an IRA, they can determine how much money they want for monthly or quarterly distributions. For example, if they want $1000 a month, that's $12,000 a year or $60,000 over five years; they might want to put that money into short term treasury bonds, a mutual fund, index fund or money market fund that suffers little fluctuation. Then, they can chop off that $12,000 once a year and put it into a high-yield money market, and have that self-liquidate via their monthly reduction. Selective re-balancing on a timely basis to replenish the ongoing monthly, quarterly, and annual income needs without market volatility as we've isolated our cashflow needs in a fixed asset class.

CHAPTER NINE

INSURANCE: A RISK-TRANSFER STRATEGY

Responsible pilots know they need insurance designed to protect them from financial loss in the event of an accident or other occurrence resulting in damage to their aircraft or injuries to passengers. Like life, health or liability insurance for individuals, pilot insurance varies greatly, depending on the type of aircraft, pilot experience and related factors.[184]

In my experience working with affluent clients, I find they are best served by effective financial planning and money management that delivers expected rates of return.

Having accumulated significant financial assets, their focus—particularly in retirement— changes from making money to protecting their income and lifestyle. This means gaining a better understanding of the major components of planning, such as tax management, long-term care, income planning and risk management.

Despite their financial comfort and being only 5-10 years away from retirement, few people in their fifties have even a cursory understanding of Medicare supplements, let alone Medicare Advantage. When I ask them their expectations for health care in terms of future adjusted dollars, few have little more than a notion about the actual out-of-pocket costs.

Long-Term Insurance

As a result of this limited knowledge, the public (even highly successful, intelligent people) are easily misled when it comes to late life healthcare. For a long time, I have known that long-term care insurance is not a complete answer to the missing gaps in coverage for someone suffering from Alzheimer's, dementia or other terminal illnesses.

Insurers have been raising rates on their long-term care insurance policies for over a decade. Having originated in the 1990s, long-term care is a relatively new product as compared to more traditional insurance offerings. Early policies have proved to be dramatically underpriced due to insurers underestimating claims costs and misjudging the number of people that would cancel their policy for one reason or another. The result is that insurers have had to increase premiums in order to compensate for their earlier inaccurate pricing assumptions in order to have enough reserves to pay claims. It's a balancing act that has resulted in some policyholders seeing their rates doubled during just the past ten years.[185] The increases leave less affluent policyholders with few palatable choices, such as reducing their daily benefit at a time when the daily cost of care is rapidly increasing or reducing the duration period of their benefits, potentially leaving them without coverage as their illness reaches its peak and care is needed most.[186]

It's important to understand that insurance is fundamentally a risk-transfer strategy. From that perspective, I believe long-term care policies are an insufficient response, especially for those saving for retirement or still working to reduce debt. For example, if a couple nearing or in retirement is still carrying significant mortgage or credit card debt, they would generally be better off paying down those debts versus taking on the cost of a long-term care policy.

The perception that healthcare costs are likely to devour a major chunk of retiree's finances was given widespread credence by a series of unnecessarily alarming reports emanating from Fidelity Investments and other major brokerage firms. The primary culprit was a Fidelity report, "Planning for Income to Last," that estimated a 65-year-old couple retiring in 2010 would need approximately $250,000 to $430,000 to cover medical costs in retirement.[187] The estimate did not include "other health-related expenses, such as over-the-counter medications, most dental services and long-term care."

Data like this tends to strike fear in the hearts of retirees, which may be exactly what it is intended to do. People hear that they need hundreds of thousands of dollars for expected out-of-pocket medical costs, even though there is no upper dollar limit on Medicare benefits. There are limits to some individual Medicare benefits, for example,

Medicare Part A covers a hospital stay for any single spell of illness or injury for 100 days. This is known as a benefit period, and there's no limit to the number of benefit periods a person on Medicare can have.[188]

Medicare Advantage, or Part C plans, are required to provide an out-of-pocket limit for services covered under Parts A and B. In 2021, the out-of-pocket limit may not exceed $7,550 for in-network services and $11,300 for in-network and out-of-network services combined.[189]

Despite that, a good deal of confusion and fear exists about actual costs, perpetrated predominantly by one of the largest mutual fund companies in America. I sense many middle-class couples that have done a good job of saving for retirement are now too frightened to spend money on the things in life they might otherwise be doing. Many people need some professional analysis that is easily done through an independent review we call a financial strategy. We use this term versus a financial plan because the word "strategy" implies taking action, which entails change. What we have found is that most people we talk to have enough resources to be doing more—and enjoying life more—than they believe, because they have been fed so much fear.

For years, my now-retired partner and I conducted financial literacy classes for adults in or approaching retirement at Everett Community College and others. He would pass out copies of healthcare cost reports Fidelity had posted on their website for retail do-it-yourself investors. The reports predicted couples would need almost $500,000 in savings to cover retirement healthcare costs and I could see the wide-eyed, frightened look those predictions triggered in the attendees.

In reality, even if one accepts the costs quoted in the reports as accurate, the costs are typically spread out over a 20-year span and adjusted for inflation. It was difficult for those attending the classes to grasp the fact that on an annual basis, the costs would be manageable for most people with a decent-sized tax-deferred savings account, as well as the fact that their future incomes would also be inflation-adjusted to some degree. So, while the estimated costs of healthcare were a piece of the spending puzzle, they did not accurately depict the entire financial picture. That's the problem with the fear caused by companies selling insurance or financial products: when consumers are fed a small piece of disturbing information, their imagination tends to run wild before they have a chance to acquire the full picture.

The Fidelity reports were given widespread publicity by other investment firms, insurers and the major media. The campaigns ran for a long time and likely caused unnecessary stress for a lot of people by taking advantage of one of the two basic emotions: fear.

I am skeptical of the financial industry's penchant for employing fear tactics when it comes to health costs in retirement. Even a quarter million dollars amortized over 20-25 years is not an insurmountable sum for most people. That roughly $15-18,000 annual expenditure for healthcare is very much in line with the 18% of the U.S. gross domestic product (GDP) spent on healthcare in 2020,[190] for a couple retiring in 2023, while also assuming a great deal of utilization.

I remember attending a seminar some 30 years ago where the speaker talked about how healthcare costs would consume 13% of U.S. GDP by the year 2000. I was aghast at that figure and surmised if it happened, it might well destroy our economy. Well, it's 2023 and we are well north of that figure and still surviving as a country. So, while several hundred thousand dollars is a substantial sum, it is less imposing when viewed over a period of two decades, roughly the expected lifespan of the average retiree. In financial circles, we refer to this as "the time value of money."

While Fidelity was the primary culprit inciting fear in retirees, most everyone in the financial services industry jumped on the fear bandwagon. Over the years, when I would bring up the topic of healthcare in retirement, most people's first reaction was that the expenses had the potential to consume everything they had accumulated during their working years.

I recall the ongoing political debates about how, as a nation, the U.S. was going to handle the cost of medical coverage for retirees. It may be as much a soft spot for retirees today as it was 30 years ago. People still think healthcare will be their largest expense in retirement. That conviction is usually based on speculation driven by marketing and misperception, not hard data. People tend to make subconscious estimates versus putting together a financial plan and dealing with hard numbers where they can take into consideration things like the imputed cost of time, inflation and other relevant factors. Even with a solid plan, healthcare will likely be a considerable expense because we have to budget roughly $1000 monthly for a married couple's Medicare Part B and supplemental coverage. Given an annual retirement income of say $70,000,

$12,000 in Medicare cost plus perhaps another $3,000-5,000 in out-of-pocket healthcare cost represents roughly 17% of the average budget. That's a significant figure but not the all-consuming one-third or more of income monster people have been led to believe it is by the financial products industry. It's simply not the case for most people.

I reluctantly recommended three long-term care policies early in my career. The premiums on one have gone up so much that the client had to cut coverage and reduce benefits to make it palatable to continue to pay the premium. Another client saw their premium more than double over 30 months. I don't know of a single case of someone who hasn't had a significant rate increase. I rarely find a reason to refer someone to a long-term care insurance specialist. The premium increases alone preclude them from being a viable healthcare coverage solution for all but the most affluent.

What we have preached over the years is the importance of money compounding inside an IRA, 401k or other tax-deferred account. Since no one knows exactly when we're going to take our last breath, we need to maintain an adequate reserve inside of our tax-deferred accounts to carry us through old age. Unfortunately, there is no perfect income planning template that guarantees we can bounce the last check at the funeral home. What we do know is that we need to have sufficient reserves to cover contingencies like prolonged Alzheimer's or dementia care.

According to Alzheimer's Association's data, the average lifetime cost of care for an Alzheimer patient was $358,000. On average, about 70% of that cost fell to the patient's family acting as caregivers. A 2021 Genworth Financial study suggested:

- The average cost of a semi-private room in a nursing home is $7,513 per month, or $90,156 per year.
- The average cost of a private room in a nursing home is $8,517 per month, or $102,204 per year.
- The average cost of a home health aide is $4,385 per month, or $52,620 per year.
- The average cost of adult day healthcare services is $1,625 per month, or $19,500 per year.[191]

These costs typically come late in life when we are often taking only the RMD distributions from our IRA accounts. Social Security income helps offset some of that, of course, so it may not be as distressingly bleak of a picture for most middle-class retirees.

Statistics indicate that on average, a person with Alzheimer's lives four to eight years after diagnosis.[192] According to the latest U.S. Department of Health and Human Services Administration on Aging (AOA) research, the average woman needs long-term care services for 3.7 years, and the average man for 2.2 years. These numbers typically include some combination of home care provided by family members or paid caregivers, care in an assisted living community and care in a skilled nursing facility. A report jointly prepared by the American Health Care Association and National Center for Assisted Living found that the average length of stay for residents in an assisted living facility is about 28 months with the median being 22 months.

If planning is done early and correctly, the need for long-term insurance is unlikely as there will be sufficient assets available to cover that contingency. It's difficult to make this clear to individuals without actually conducting a formal financial analysis. Once done, clients usually can see that even with conservative estimates of growth within their IRA, they will have more than sufficient resources, and far more than what a long-term policy would provide.

According to an article in *Investment News,* Genworth, the largest long-term care insurer by number of policyholders, received approval in the first quarter (of 2019) to increase premiums an average 62% among policyholders cumulatively paying $241 million in premiums. That level is elevated from prior years. Genworth, which spun off from General Electric in 2006, raised costs an average 45% in 2018, affecting $875 million in annual premiums. In 2016 and 2017, the insurer raised premiums an average of 28% each year. Some 40 plus states approved policy premium increases in excess of 200%. Some especially expensive policies—such as those with unlimited years of coverage and 5% compound annual inflation protection saw 300% increases![193]

Subsequently, Genworth Life Insurance Company in 2020 agreed to pay up to $24.5 million to end a class action lawsuit alleging the company withheld information about rate increases from long-term care policyholders.[194]

Long-term care insurance is rarely a practical solution for most people. If they create a plan that includes workable income strategies, they're usually going to have sufficient resources remaining from their tax-deferred savings accounts and investable assets to cover the risk of dementia, Alzheimer's and other progressive diseases. If they were to buy an insurance policy, the limitations—typically a couple hundred thousand dollars—would provide less coverage than by merely not exceeding distribution limits from an optimum asset allocation in their investments to satisfy that risk. Plus, if they never have need for this type of care, the money continues compounding.

Self-Insuring

For many, we recommend self-insuring the small stuff over time. If you regard insurance as a risk transfer strategy, the concept of absorbing more of the risk with higher deductibles and not trading dollars with the insurance companies can make sense, especially over extended periods. Automobile insurance is a prime example, although one problem with financing at low interest rates is you typically have to accept a deductible no higher than $500 and purchase full coverage. On the other hand, consumers like me who buy inexpensive cars can be comfortable with a high deductible and liability-only coverage.

I haven't purchased comprehensive coverage for any of my cars for so long, I can't remember the last time I bought it. The key question to ask is, "What am I comfortable with in terms of risk transfer?" Obviously, you don't want to take a risk that could potentially wipe you out financially, but if you avoid low deductibles and self-insure the smaller stuff versus exchanging dollars with insurance companies, you can realize surprising savings over extended periods. The reason banks and insurance companies usually own the biggest buildings in town is that they have the advantage of winning over time if their customers choose to completely insure every little thing.

In addition to self-insuring the little stuff, it can be profitable to extend waiting periods for benefits to begin, such as periods for filing claims for disability income insurance. For most, three months of disability will not be catastrophic, whereas a longer period, such as twelve months or more might wipe them out. Again, the concept of self-insuring what you can afford to handle on your own.

Over the past few decades, we have developed spreadsheets that run the numbers related to self-insuring and inevitably conclude that for someone with a middle-class income, even assuming their premiums never increase, is financially better off self-insuring using the time value of money compounding in an investment account. Graphic 9.1 illustrates this point.

	LTC Policy Benefits	
Benefit Age 55	$	165,000.00
Benefit Age 85	**$**	**388,833.31**

	Taxable Account Contribution	
Value Age 55	$	5,025.00
Value Age 85	$	506,859.53
Capital Gains (15%)	$	53,416.43
Net Benefits	**$**	**453,443.10**

Benefit Increase	
3%	
Total Premiums Paid	
$	150,750.00
Average Return (Balanced Portfolio)	
7.00%	

https://www.aaltci.org/long-term-care-insurance/learning-center/ltcfacts-2022.php#2022costs

55-year old couple in US can expect to pay $5,025 per year on average (2022) 165,000 Starting benefit, 3% annual increase

(Graphic 9.1: Self Insuring)

Term Life Insurance

Occasionally, situations arise when it may be advantageous to convert a term policy into whole life, provided the policy permits it without proof of insurability. It's an uncommon circumstance but over the years, I have encountered situations where somebody has a 10-year term and they've been diagnosed with late-stage cancer or other terminal illness. In those instances, they may own a term policy that allows conversion to whole life insurance. They might outlive the term guarantees and then have the insurance company terminate the policy whereas if they took advantage of their right to convert, it would be worth it to pay the higher premium, knowing that their probability of living past a few years is unlikely.

I have a client that suffers from an autoimmune disorder. The damage it's caused to his heart is irreparable and he is not going to recover from it. At age 57, he has less than 10 years to live. His term life insurance policy was due to expire in two years. I examined it and found it has a conversion clause. The policy also will pay up to 75% of the proceeds if his cardiologist confirms he cannot live beyond a decade because it contains an accelerated death benefit rider. Things like this happily don't occur very often, but when they do and an individual is destined to die prematurely, it may be worthwhile to convert the policy, as we did in this case. In any event, it's worth having a policy examined by an expert to determine the best options for the policyholder.

The probability of cancer or other debilitating illnesses increases as people age, I probably encounter one or two situations a year where someone has a term policy and has been diagnosed with a terminal illness and by converting, their spouse could collect on the policy as opposed to allowing the term limit to expire.

On the other hand, some people are emotionally attached to life insurance despite having sufficient financial reserves to permit the surviving spouse to maintain his or her established lifestyle.

Life insurance—especially term insurance—is essential for couples in their working years, especially if they are raising children. For the majority of clients we see—people with substantial assets in or approaching retirement—the need for life insurance as it applies to retirement income planning is typically nonexistent. The exception would be those whose net worth is north of the federal exemption amount, currently $11.7 million for individuals and $23.4 million for married couples, in which case the use of life insurance can be successfully argued. Pay the premiums to an insurance company and let them pay the estate tax, via an ILIT[195] for example.

Disability

While disability insurance is not a critical element of the life planning work, I do for clients approaching retirement, it is an important consideration for those in their working years. I've never been without it. It would terrify me to be in my working years, have a debilitating accident or contract a life-threatening ailment, not be able to earn an income anymore and put all that financial pressure on my wife.

While I do not sell disability insurance, I always address the subject when working with younger people. In my earlier career I did recommend it because I believe in it, possibly because of my dad, who was an apple rancher and had a serious accident when I was still young. He had disability income insurance of $500 a week and his policy enabled our family to maintain our lifestyle.

It was that incident that convinced me to never be without disability coverage. At age 22 and fresh out of the Coast Guard, I bought income disability insurance on myself, even though I was working and putting myself through school selling mutual funds. I have never been without it since. I include all of my employees in an employer-paid, long-term group disability income policy.

A few months back, a 53-year-old woman who had been disabled virtually all of her adult life came to see us about managing her money. She was earning about $150k annually as a financial analyst when she developed a cranial disorder that made it impossible for her to continue working.

Fortunately, she owned a long-term disability policy that now paid her $5k monthly. In addition, her employer maintained a disability policy that paid her an additional $2500 monthly, although that income is subject to tax while the income from her personal policy is tax-free. She had saved $400k in her 401k but still owed over $100k on her condo mortgage. This is an example of someone a decade away from retirement who made a sound decision regarding protecting her income.

Taxation of disability benefits depends on who is paying the premiums. Benefits are taxable if premiums are paid by the employer or paid by the individual with pre-tax dollars. If paid by the individual with after-tax dollars, disability income payments are free from federal taxation.

Another person 10 years from retirement with more substantial savings and no debt may be just fine without disability coverage. That's the case with perhaps two-thirds of the people we see. The other one-third, like much of the population that is 5-10 years from retirement, could find themselves in financial trouble without disability protection. For those nearing retirement, if an illness or accident could cause them to lose assets and start going backwards financially, they should put a price tag on that and decide if that's a risk they're willing to take. The biggest financial risk people a decade out from retirement have is the risk of loss of income. In other words, your ability to earn an income is possibly your greatest asset.

Umbrella Liability

Attorneys love it when judges make new exceptions for lawsuits. It opens the door for more and more litigation and attorney fees. During a recent visit with family members living in Europe, I was subjected to an embarrassing barrage of comments about the U.S. legal system and how we are all so "sue happy."

If someone holds significant assets inside of their retail brokerage or savings accounts, they are susceptible to claims against those assets. If, for example, they are deemed to be the cause of an automobile accident and their comprehensive coverage has a typical limit of 300,000 and through discovery, a claimant's attorney finds they have unprotected assets in a retail, brokerage or savings account, they could be subject to a lawsuit.

We encourage clients with substantial assets outside of their IRAs, 401ks and other retirement accounts (which are fully protected against creditors in most but not all states) to secure umbrella liability insurance. Additionally, they may wish to create an asset protection trust, an irrevocable trust that can make it much more difficult for someone to gain access to their assets through civil litigation. The latter can be quite expensive, however: as much as ten thousand dollars or more to establish plus maintenance fees.[196]

I recently watched a documentary reporting on the corruption of the legal system in the U.S. The number of lawsuits filed against individuals in America over the last decade has skyrocketed and continues to grow year after year because the system has been rigged for the benefit of attorneys and the politicians they fund, and it's become a form of hidden tax on all of us.

Not long ago, we reviewed the plan for a retired client and learned that despite not having been a high-income earner during his career, over the years, he had accumulated almost a million dollars in his personal savings account, outside of his tax-deferred accounts. We recommended he immediately purchase an umbrella liability policy to protect those assets. Had he seriously injured someone at a cross section on the drive home that day, his automobile liability coverage of $300,000 would have left him exposed to a lawsuit that could have cleaned out a lifetime of savings. The umbrella policy he subsequently purchased guaranteed he would have an army of lawyers to protect him from such a contingency.

For clients who have the overwhelming bulk of their assets in tax-deferred accounts protected from lawsuits, and for those with modest amounts in their savings and brokerage accounts, umbrella policies are usually an unnecessary expense as their comprehensive insurance will cover most situations. Where people become targets is when they have significant resources in assets like real estate, most of which is paid for. In these instances, it sometimes makes sense to move those assets inside an LLC and buy a corresponding amount of umbrella coverage.

Chapter Ten

Choosing Advisory Help

Just as Certified Financial Planners (CFP®) must complete a rigorous program at an accredited institution of higher learning, flight instructors must go through a regimen of training that meets a number of specific standards, as well as pass two written exams and a practical test given by the FAA or other aviation authority. Individuals seeking to become private pilots should review several instructors and ask questions. Do they use a syllabus and assign study material? Are they prepared for every flight? Do they conduct preflight and post-flight briefings?[197]

Depending on where you are in life, financial planning may not be a priority. If you are young, without children, and have avoided significant debt by responsibly managing your money, you might only need an advisor to help with retirement planning.

But anyone with more complex needs will likely benefit from some level of professional financial assistance. A 2019 study by Vanguard concluded that investors who receive investment advice from a financial professional may see a 3% higher net portfolio return over time. Their conclusion was reached by comparing self-directed investor accounts to those receiving financial coaching.

The key is to find the right advisor for your needs and, judging by the number of people who make inappropriate advisory choices, it's obviously a more difficult task than it appears.

Knowing how each type of advisory firm is structured is one of the first steps. Fee-only financial advisors, most of whom are fiduciaries, are reimbursed for the services by the fees their clients pay—either an hourly or flat rate or as a percentage of managed assets.[198]

A fiduciary is an individual or financial advisory firm that has the responsibility of acting in the best interests of another—typically their clients or beneficiaries—in situations requiring total trust, good faith and honesty.

Clients give fiduciaries discretionary authority over the management of their assets. A fiduciary financial advisor can buy and sell securities on behalf of their clients without asking for consent prior to each transaction. As such, fiduciaries are held to a higher standard than nonfiduciary advisors.[199]

Registered Investment Advisors (RIAs) are individuals or financial firms that are bound by fiduciary duty. They may be fee-only or fee-based and many have earned the Certified Financial Planner (CFP®) designation.[200]

The fiduciary standard "requires an advisor to act solely in the client's best interest when offering personalized financial advice," according to the Certified Financial Planning Board. Most people tend to believe all financial professionals act as fiduciaries. The majority of financial advisers are not held to a fiduciary standard, however, but rather to the lower suitability standard, which only requires advisers to ensure that investments they recommend are suitable, but not necessarily the best available, given the client's circumstances.[201]

Advisors who receive commissions from financial product manufacturers or other third parties are, in effect, salespeople for investment and insurance brokerages, and are held to a lower standard than fiduciaries. This is known as the suitability standard. Commission-only advisors are not fiduciaries. They are not bound to act in the best interest of their clients.

Understanding the Conflicts

Before sitting down with potential advisors, you should be versed in the various potential conflicts of interest you are likely to encounter. Some conflicts arise from advisors' compensation arrangements, which some—but not all—advisors have a legal obligation to disclose. A good way to uncover compensation conflicts is to review the firm's legal documents describing its practices. These documents, typically available via a link at the bottom of the firm's website, provide detailed information about the firm's services, fee structures, investment strategies and disclosures.[202]

A document to look for is Form ADV, which all advisory firms registered with the SEC must complete. Firms with less than 100M must register with their respective state. Part one outlines the firm's assets under management (AUM), fees and disclosures, among other items. Part two contains a brochure prepared by the advisory firm that outlines its services, investment strategies, affiliations, fee schedules and conflicts of interest.[203]

According to the SEC, "An adviser must look to both its general disclosure obligations as a fiduciary and to the specific disclosure requirements in Form ADV. In particular, in seeking to meet its duty of loyalty as a fiduciary, an adviser must make full and fair disclosure to its clients of all material facts relating to the advisory relationship.[204]

A conflict for brokers is that that their licenses limit them to selling commissioned investment products; they are not permitted to provide financial advice or services. They instead substitute sales recommendations disguised as financial advice, causing investors to mistakenly believe they are receiving sound financial advice.

Advisors working for companies selling proprietary financial products make more money when they sell their company's products. They may actually be limited to selling the proprietary products in order to maximize company profits, which limits investor choices.[205]

Advice from stockbrokers and others selling financial products should be considered peripheral to the sale of products. That is, broker-dealer firms exist to facilitate transactions on behalf of their customers—with the focus on the transaction and not the advice. Some advisors are registered as both advisors and brokers. In addition, they may also be insurance licensed. Providing objective advice to clients is exceptionally difficult for the salespeople employed at these firms.[206]

The most common method of obtaining financial advice for those with a low net worth is the commission-based advisor. Here, the conflicts of interest are obvious. An adviser paid by commissions is an investment salesperson, not a dedicated advisor. Each investment recommendation creates a conflict of interest: does the adviser recommend the product most likely to be in the client's best interests or the product with higher fees that allow the adviser to be paid more?[207]

> "It's amazing how difficult it is for a man to understand something if he's paid a small fortune not to understand it."
>
> John Bogle
> Vanguard Founder

The fiduciary duty of an RIA involves more than the duty to be honest and avoid negligence. RIAs also have a duty of loyalty: always putting their clients' interests ahead of their own. This includes the following duties:

- To give advice unaffected by self-interest;
- To provide disclosures of potential or actual conflicts of interest;

- To maintain strict confidentiality; and
- To refrain from engaging in fraud and other misconduct.

RIAs are also urged—but not required—to implement business continuity plans to protect clients from harm if an event occurs that will disrupt services, either temporarily or permanently. Succession planning is one strategy to keep the firm operational if a key member of the RIA dies or becomes incapacitated.[208]

There are no completely conflict-free advisors, whether they're charging you commissions, by the hour or by a percentage of your assets under management. Fiduciaries typically choose a fee-only model in order to reduce any potential conflicts of interest. But that doesn't mean there are no implicit conflicts. For instance, like most business professionals, fee-only advisors want to retain their clients for as long as possible while reducing their workload as much as possible.

A Process

One of the first things to ask in your advisor interview is whether they have an organizational process. If they are not sure what you mean, ask questions such as, what happens when I need help? How often will my investments and income sources be reviewed? How often should I expect to meet with you each year? What will those meetings consist of and what will be discussed? How do you ensure my accounts are rebalanced? What methods do you use to make investment selections?

Meetings don't have to be a complicated agenda but they should cover what's most important to you. Will meetings include a review of your income relative to your account values? Do you just want the meetings to exclusively be about investment performance? If so, there's no need to meet in person because you can probably do that online. If the meetings include rebalancing strategies, that can likely be done with an email. If there's only going to be a single annual comprehensive review, there's no need for you to get in your car and drive to the advisor's office three or four times a year.

At some point, you may want to discuss buying a second home or other major purchase. Maybe you will want to upsize or downsize. Maybe you will want to start gifting to the kids. Those are all potential planning questions and you want to have an established working relationship in place for those discussions to be the most valuable. After all, if you're going to be handing over your financial resources to someone to help manage, you want to know that the person you're giving those assets to is going to provide you with advice that, over time, proves to be consistently valuable.

If you have a substantial portfolio with more expansive planning and investment needs, you want a relationship that assures you will have a lifeline thrown to you when the market plummets and your emotions run high.

Our firm maintains an ongoing process for scheduling client meetings. Each client has a different schedule and we're not here to waste their time. We expect their meetings to be meaningful. So, when you're interviewing an advisor, you want to question what will be covered in meetings, how often they should be held and what else you can expect from them.

Ongoing Financial Planning

The importance and value of personal financial planning can hardly be overstated, regardless of whether you need help with a single issue or a comprehensive financial plan for life. An experienced financial planner should be able to help you plan for college saving, tax planning, insurance, retirement and estate planning. The planner should be educated, but more importantly, committed to continuing education. You should choose someone with a certification that is accredited and devoted to strict ethical standards, such as the CFP® designation. You ought to research the planner's history and determine whether there has ever been disciplinary action against the individual. This is important because as a rule, financial planners are not required to register with state or federal regulators unless they are also investment advisers or broker-dealers, or sell insurance products.[209]

Once a plan is in place, a competent advisor will monitor the ongoing process, making minor adjustments as needed and helping guide clients through major events, such as the death of a spouse. We've never had a client couple where both spouses passed away at the same time, but it seems that we experience a spousal decease nearly every month. It can be invaluable to have an advisor who helps with the many necessary activities associated with the unfortunate event, including account consolidation, legal documentation, beneficiary changes and the like. The death of a spouse inevitably entails some level of confusion. It's reassuring to have an experienced advisor at these times, when life throws a curve at you.

Complementary Investment Philosophy

The advisor you choose should be closely aligned with your personal investment philosophy. If you believe passive investing is the best approach in the long run, you don't want to hire an advisor who prefers an aggressive approach of picking stocks or timing the market.

Have a frank discussion early on with your advisor regarding the firm's investment philosophy. Do they believe that markets are efficient, therefore you should index most or all of your portfolio? Do they believe your assets should be actively or passively managed? Do they believe that they can successfully time the market? If so, does that belief apply across the board for all asset classes or specific investment niches? Are they dogmatic about their philosophy or are they strong in one asset class and weaker in others?

This discussion should not take a long time. I have found that someone can gain a clear understanding of a person's investment belief system in just a few minutes, including their major viewpoints regarding overall market efficiency and level of risk tolerance. Whatever their perspective, it's important to agree on the appropriateness of the investment approach, given their goals and circumstances.

You want to make sure the advisory firm's investment approach also matches your personal objectives and risk tolerance. Many advisors claim to be independent, but when it comes to investment management, you need to make sure that the advisory firm's actions match its rhetoric. Bear markets don't care if your portfolio contains index funds or growth stocks. That's when you will rely most strongly on the trust you placed in your advisor and your choice of investment strategies. Knowing your advisor has experienced market declines—ideally multiple economic cycles—and knows how to prepare for and manage volatility will be psychologically invaluable when the next downturn occurs.

Equally important is that the advisor can clarify portfolio decisions made on your behalf, and that those decisions were not only made in your best interest, but that they were consistent with your investment philosophy. You protect yourself during difficult markets by being candid at the start of your advisory relationship. Don't tell the advisor you are comfortable with risking 25% of your portfolio in pursuit of higher returns if you know you will panic and want to move to cash if your portfolio suffers as little as a 10% reduction. There are numerous accounts of advisor-client relationships that went sour despite a solid rapport and good intentions. Getting clarity on how your advisor's investment process works goes a long way toward preventing misunderstandings.[210]

Too many people focus their advisor selection on past performance.

> "Being told that historical returns don't ensure future success seems to make the typical investor rely on them even more. It's as if the phrase 'past performance is no guarantee of future results' makes people think, 'Well, if it's no guarantee, then that must mean it's just pretty close to a sure thing.'"
>
> Jason Zweig

One of the mistakes investors repeatedly make is in the decision-making process. A Harvard study[211] on the selection of index funds by individuals made an interesting observation:

> *"Highlighting misleading long-horizon historical returns by providing the returns summary sheet caused students to allocate more money to the fund with the highest long-horizon historical return."*

The point is that evaluating an investment exclusively from a historical performance perspective will inevitably result in a misleading assumption of potential future performance. In other words, if the investment returned 10% annually over the past 10 years, one might think it should produce similar returns over the next ten years. What is often overlooked in that misguided assumption is the difference between starting periods. The graphic 10.1, a chart of the Vanguard S&P 500 Index fund over a quarter century illustrates this point. (The index is total return with dividends reinvested.) If an investor started investing in 1987, the fund generated a 713% annualized return over the next 13-years. Therefore, an investor would look at the performance and assume they would experience the same rate of return if they bought the fund.

(Graphic 10.1: S&P 500 1987-2013)

Unfortunately, such was not the case over the following 13-years as the fund returned just 22% on a total return basis. What was the difference between the two starting periods? Valuations.[212]

That leads to the question: exactly what defines an investment philosophy? Essentially, it is a reasoned way of forming an opinion about the markets, a set of core beliefs that help prevent you from wavering during down markets and making poor or inappropriate investment decisions. Not to be confused with investment strategy—which is how your investment philosophy is put into practice—your investment philosophy, if well thought out and aligned with your time horizon, tax status, risk aversion and goals, gives you a foundation to create a revised investment strategy should your existing strategy prove ineffective.[213]

Types of Investment Strategies

As to the types of investment strategies available to implement an investment philosophy, the principal designations include:

- Passive
- Active
- Growth
- Value
- Contrarian
- Socially Responsible
- Income

Passive Investing is a long-term strategy that buys and holds a diversified mix of assets in an effort to produce an average market return. It is not a strategy designed to beat the market. An example would be buying an index fund or ETF, whose holdings mirror a particular segment of the market.[214] Passive investors don't try to predict market movements or stock winners and losers; they sit back, ignore what the market is doing, and rely on a broad asset allocation to mimic the market. Passive investors tend to pay less in taxes because there is less trading going on than in an actively-managed account.[215]

Active Investing involves buying and selling stocks in an attempt to beat the market by taking advantage of short-term price fluctuations. Active managers can construct diversified portfolios that spread the risk among different asset classes and attempt to minimize losses during a market downturn by adjusting the investment mix. Unlike passive investment managers, active managers are not required to hold specific assets, so they are free to choose those that they believe will yield above-average returns. In addition, active managers can use strategies such as short sales and put options to protect against losses. Active investing tends to generate higher taxes than passive investing because of the more active buying and selling. Realized gains trigger capital gains taxes.[216] Active strategies also tend to result in higher fees over time.

Growth Investing pursues companies, industries or sectors that are growing faster than others and expected to continue to do so over an extended period. It is offensive investing, an active attempt to build portfolio value and generate higher returns. In contrast, defensive investing tends more towards investments that generate passive income and work to protect investment capital, such as bonds or blue-chip stocks that offer steady dividends.[217]

Value Investing is a strategy that seeks to buy stocks, bonds or other assets for less than they are worth. Essentially, value investors probe the markets for assets they believe are "on sale," that is, priced below their intrinsic value. Warren Buffett defines intrinsic value as "the discounted value of the cash that can be taken out of a business during its remaining life." Intrinsic value is rarely a single number but rather a range, due to the many assumptions that go into valuing a business.[218]

In his book, *The Little Book That Beats the Market*, Joel Greenblatt describes the value investing formula as searching for companies with a great combination of quality (reflected by a high return on capital) and a bargain price (reflected by a low price-earnings ratio). He holds that "Value investing strategies work because it's hard for people to do, for two main reasons. First, the companies that show up on value screens can be scary and not doing so well, so people find them hard to buy. Second, there can be several consecutive years when the strategy doesn't work. Most people aren't capable of sticking it out through hat."[219]

Warren Buffett argues that the concepts of growth and value investing are basically the same. In his 2000 annual letter to Berkshire Hathaway shareholders, Mr. Buffett wrote:

"Market commentators and investment managers who glibly refer to 'growth' and 'value' styles as contrasting approaches to investment are displaying their ignorance, not their sophistication."[220]

While proponents believe value strategies produce superior returns, the interpretation of why they believe so is controversial. Value strategies might produce higher returns because they are contrary to strategies followed by less sophisticated investors, such as extrapolating past earnings growth too far into the future, assuming a trend in stock prices, overreacting to good or bad news or simply equating a good investment with a well-run company irrespective of price. Regardless of the reason, some investors tend to get overly excited about stocks that have done very well in the past and buy them up, causing them to become overpriced. Similarly, they overreact to stocks that have done very badly and liquidate them, creating out-of-favor value stocks that are underpriced. Contrarian investors bet against such investors.

An alternative explanation of why value strategies have produced superior returns, argued most forcefully by Fama and French, is that they are fundamentally riskier. Investors in value stocks, such as high book-to-market stocks, tend to bear higher fundamental risk and their higher average returns are simply compensation for the risk.[221]

Contrarian Investing is based on a belief that certain investor crowd behavior can lead to mispricing in the securities markets that can be exploited. A contrarian investor is someone who trades against prevailing market sentiments. When the market buys, the contrarian sells, and vice-versa. Contrarian investors look for opportunities to buy in a bear market and opportunities to sell in a bull market, sometimes based on investor behavioral biases during large swings in the market. Exaggerated optimism or pessimism can drive stock prices to extremes by overstating or understating risk and return. Contrarian investing is similar to value investing, as both methods look for companies mispriced by the market.[222]

Socially Responsible Investing (SRI) is a strategy that aims to generate both social change and financial returns. SRI investments can include companies making a positive sustainable or social impact and exclude those making a negative impact. SRI has also come to stand for sustainable, responsible and impact investing. Environmental, Social and Governance investing (ESG) is a form of sustainable investing that considers the three factors in judging an investment's financial returns and its overall impact.[223]

Companies with strong ESG credentials represent a specific group of investment attributes, much the same as factors like company size, stock momentum or profit growth. Whether any of these factors outperform over the long run is debatable. Like other strategies, however, they are susceptible to extended periods of underperformance.[224]

Income Investing is a strategy designed to generate income rather than long-term growth. Investment income can take the form of dividends, interest and capital gains. Interest is paid by debt securities, like bonds, financial institution accounts and money market accounts. Dividends are paid by stocks. Capital gains can be generated by any investment if sold for more money than was paid for the investment.[225]

Generally, fixed income investing entails lower risk than equity investing because fixed income assets tend to be less sensitive to macroeconomic risks, such as economic downturns and geopolitical events. The risks associated with this strategy include interest rate risk, inflation risk, credit risk and liquidity risk.[226]

Individual vs Team Approach

In the advisory business, people leave their jobs for new opportunities. That can be disruptive when a long-standing advisory relationship is aborted as the result of an advisor retiring or leaving without notice. The departed advisor might be restricted from contacting clients at their new firm because of a contractual agreement. The accounts at the vacated firm are likely to be handed over to another advisor who may not be familiar with the account holders.[227]

Another potential disruption in the advisor/client relationship can occur if a client needs immediate assistance with an investment opportunity or emergency and the advisor is unavailable, perhaps vacationing. A real estate investment opportunity or a bargain price on a second home may emerge, for example, and require a quick decision. Worse, the advisor may have passed away and the client was unaware of the death. Who does the client turn to in the case of an opportunity or emergency if the departed advisor was the client's sole source of contact with the financial firm?

Recently, a local advisor who was a sole practitioner committed suicide, leaving nearly one hundred clients in limbo for an extended period. Another advisor died in a car accident a few years ago, not far from our office; his clients suffering the same deserted fate.

Early on in my career, I decided it was critical to institute a team approach. When we accept new clients, depending on their needs, they may first meet with one of our team for a financial plan review, then meet with another advisor to review their investments, and possibly a separate interview with another member of our team who specializes in account transition to gather the necessary paperwork and documentation. At many firms, one person does all of that. With the team approach, one advisor will most frequently handle financial planning, another investment management, still another administrative responsibility, and so forth. The concept is to create account oversight for multiple members of the team, as well as individual and collective team perspective. If an advisor leaves, dies or becomes incapacitated, there is no interruption of client service or need to scramble to review client histories to piece together continuing planning and investment strategies. Obviously, this is beneficial to both client and advisory firm.

The team approach has been a growing trend over the past decade, particularly for professional service firms. It's now ubiquitous among accounting and law firms because of the difficulty for one person to continue to be highly proficient in any industry subject to economic, regulatory and fiscal evolution. As an example, changes in Social Security income laws and tax rates are occurring as a result of the new administration. Here in the state of Washington where we are located, we saw a few significant tax law changes. Reforms like this can be almost impossible for a single practitioner to stay abreast of while simultaneously serving clients and managing day-to-day operations. Clients receive far better quality of advice when a firm has a deeper bench of multiple Certified Financial Planners®.

Inevitably, some people within an organization are more proficient than others at certain services. Someone at a financial advisory may not be expert at estate planning but is an extremely gifted financial tax planner. Being part of a team is extremely valuable in terms of sharing knowledge and experience with one another. I certainly don't have all the answers all the time. When a client asks me about something I may not spend a lot of time keeping up on or is beyond my expertise, I can zip down the hall and ask one of our team members who is more familiar with the issue and has the specific knowledge to answer the question or offer appropriate advice. The next best thing to knowing something is knowing where to find out.

Compensation

It's vital to understand how an advisor is compensated. It can have a significant impact on the investment recommendations you receive.

A fee-only advisor gets paid solely for their time, strategy and money management. The fee could be hourly, a flat retainer or a percentage of managed assets. A benefit is that fee-only advisors have no inherent conflicts of interest relating to compensation and usually provide more comprehensive advice as they are typically fiduciaries.

A fee-based advisor tends to be compensated by both fees for advice and commissions on the sale of investment products. The advisor may have an incentive to recommend investment products that pay high commissions, and may prioritize selling product over other important considerations, such as debt reduction, tax or retirement planning.

Fee-based advisors do not have a duty to disclose their method of compensation to clients, which can add to the general confusion relating to advisor compensation. Clients often do not realize their fee-based advisors receive commissions.[228]

There are significant differences between the advice offered by various financial firms, including brokers at warehouses, insurance agents, advisors working for broker-dealers, and independent registered investment advisors, among others. Some salespeople position themselves as advisors, especially those working for companies where the emphasis is on sales versus advice. This is prevalent among insurance companies and fund management firms, where the "advisor" is often merely selling the company's products and services.[229]

Some financial firms offer more than one type of compensation structure. Clients may pay for services differently, depending on the type of services chosen. Examples include:

- An hourly fee for advisory services;
- A flat fee for a financial plan or annual portfolio review;
- A commission on the securities;
- A load fee based on the amount invested in a mutual fund or variable annuity;
- A mark-up on the purchase of certain investments, such as bonds, and a mark-down when sold;
- A bundled or wrap fee that may cover investment advice, brokerage services, administrative expenses and other fees and expenses.

Costs and fees vary widely, depending on the firm and the kinds of services it offers. Even if the investment professional is not paid directly, such as through an annual fee, that person is still getting paid by someone else, like the company responsible for the investment products being recommended. That reimbursement may be built into the price clients pay for the financial product.[230]

> "Performance comes, performance goes. Fees never falter."
> Warren Buffett

Advisor Career and Finances

A consideration in choosing an advisor is education background. It does you no good if an advisor has a PhD but spurns continuing education or fails to keep abreast of tax and regulatory changes that affect your investments. On the other hand, I don't think you want to hire someone who never considered becoming a financial advisor until later in life. The reason I feel that way is that it takes many years of experience to accumulate the knowledge necessary to do this work effectively. You really want someone who has worked through several market cycles, both good and bad. I've seen several examples of people who made a late career change into financial services and few of them fared very well. I suspect the reason is they did not have a sufficient depth of knowledge, or were fixed in their thinking at a later time of life and were not equipped to deal with the volatility and turmoil that can and does occur in the financial markets.

I view being a financial advisor as a calling. Some people have a natural affinity for financial counselling. Those who "practice what they preach" also have a considerable net worth because their personal financial discipline mirrors their professional advice to clients. They're just good at it. They either fell into a career that they're naturally inclined to do well at or they may have studied business or finance in college because they knew at an early age what their career path was going to be. For those that have been financial advisors for three, four or five decades like myself, the experience of being around that long and living through recessions and boom times is invaluable.

Another consideration is how an advisor handles his or her personal finances. As an investor, I'd want to deal with somebody in finance that was giving me advice they could demonstrate in their own finances. I have a couple of acquaintances who are Certified Financial Planners but are inept at handling their own finances. As a client, whether you are reroofing your home, need surgery or seeking financial advice, you want the best you can find. I know several financial advisors that have an impressive presence but lack the competence to be advising others on financial matters.

What's it Cost to Fire You?

A survey of 1,400 individuals conducted by *Financial Advisor* magazine revealed that the main reason clients fire their financial advisor is poor communication, or a failure to communicate on a timely basis.

Breaking up with a financial advisor is not a decision made lightly. After years of relying on a person for financial planning and advice, it's a tough decision to leave and start over with someone new. Advisors sometimes take their clients for granted and take advantage of their client's lack of scrutiny regarding the investments being chosen. In July 2019, FINRA awarded six investors a total of $1.16 million because an investment company had inappropriately put their money into complex, high-risk investment products. Clients may not recognize the fact that their advisor isn't listening to them or is actually abusing the faith placed in them. It took the investors in the FINRA case more than five years to recognize the exploitation.[231]

Questions rarely asked during advisor interviews that should be:

- What will it cost to fire you if I am unhappy?
- Are there any penalties for leaving?
- What if I simply want to make a change and part as friends? Will that be a problem?

One of the keys to a good relationship is not having codependency on one another. A fulfilling relationship should provide mutual satisfaction and value to each of you. For the client, it's gaining account value growth over time and often more importantly, the added value of getting professional guidance in making sound financial decisions that save money, reduce stress and improve the quality of life.

Final Thoughts

Countless individuals engage an advisor as a result of financial seminars conducted after "free" dinners or other enticements. The true purpose of these inducements is not to offer valuable financial advice but rather to sell financial products. Given the widespread publicity about the surreptitious ambitions of these events, thousands of people continue to respond to invitations of something for nothing. If someone in the financial industry offers to give you something, be assured they expect something in return. Avoid these types of thinly-disguised marketing ploys. In exchange for a free meal, you can expect to be pressured into making a hurried investment decision that can cause you more pain than the indigestion from the bad food.[232]

Clarify your goals and expectations during your advisor interviews. Make certain they understand what you value most. A 2018 article in *Advisor Perspectives*[233] described a survey of both affluent people and financial advisors that revealed a startling disconnect between what wealthy clients want and what advisors think they want.

When asked what they believed clients expected, advisors responded with things like being a good listener, having trust in the advisor's ability, competence, ethical approach, someone to tell them what to do rather than present options, to wind up with more money than they would without the advisor and a relationship involving frequent contact.

When asked what they wanted from an advisor, the most frequent answers from the high-income individuals were eye openers:

- An individual assessment based upon my personal situation, not some boilerplate pitch.

- I want to work with a fiduciary, otherwise how can I trust their advice? However, I found that most avoid answering truthfully.

- Help me determine my expectations for risk and reward. Help me push through the noise and get to the truth about what I really want.

- Build me a portfolio based on reliable research. Be honest and candid in our relationship.

Take the time to verify an advisor's credentials. An easy way to check out an investment professional is to use the free search tool available on investor.gov, which will direct you to the SEC's Investment Advisor Public Disclosure website: adviserinfo.sec.gov. You can also visit CFP Verify, FINRA's Broker Check website: brokercheck.finra.org or your state securities regulator. Both the IAPD and BrokerCheck databases will automatically redirect you to the other, if necessary. The searches are free and investment professionals or firms are not made aware of searches.[234]

Don't just hire the first advisor you Interview. Many people kind of fall into this mistake after getting a referral from a friend or coworker. Even if the advisor is competent and doing a good job for the person who referred him, you may have completely different needs or a different philosophy about investing and that advisor may be completely wrong for you. This is not to discourage referrals but rather to make you aware of the fact that what works for one person may not work for another and it's especially important to make that distinction when choosing someone to manage your financial future.

Make certain what's in your portfolio reflects your needs and goals. I've frequently had people come to see me and when I reviewed their portfolios, I found some weird investments that didn't make sense given what they had told me about their situation. When I asked one individual how he came to acquire the questionable investments, he said, "Well, I was visiting an old college chum in Oklahoma and he was bragging about how well his advisor was doing for him, so I hired the guy."

"But you live in Seattle," I said, "and from what you've told me, your friend has an entirely different lifestyle. Your circumstances are completely different."

I have encountered individuals who hired an advisor on a recommendation from a friend who implied they were lucky to have this advisor accept them as a client as he normally only accepted new clients with a minimum of a million-dollar portfolio. In one instance, the client had been made so appreciative of being accepted by the advisor that he felt asking any questions about the investment decisions being made on his behalf might upset the advisor. This poor chap was so intimidated, he didn't question the high-commission variable annuity the advisor had slipped into his portfolio, nor the other inappropriate investments purchased to benefit the advisor's pocket instead of the individual's financial goals. This teaches an important lesson: beware of advisors who reluctantly agree to take you on as a client even though your assets don't qualify for the minimums they require of their wealthy clients.

This may sound a bit elementary, but one of the most important things to look for in an advisor is honesty. An advisor can have an MBA, three PhDs in Finance and an impressive performance history, but none of that will do you much good if that advisor doesn't truly care about his or her clients. Without empathy and integrity, none of the window dressing matters. What advisors are really selling is not performance or credentials, it's honesty. It's caring about clients and whether what the advisor is doing is enhancing the lives of those clients. Advisors that spend most of the interview telling you about their accomplishments instead of asking about what your expectations are probably lack the capacity to truly care about their clients.

> "Whoever is careless with the truth in small matters cannot be trusted with important matters."
> Albert Einstein

Chapter Eleven

Asset Allocation

> **"On average, 90 percent of the variability of returns and 100 percent of the absolute level of return is explained by asset allocation."**
> Roger G. Ibbotson

The vast majority of investors fail to achieve market returns for a variety of reasons. If their recent investing experience has been positive, they tend to get overly aggressive with their investment choices. On the other hand, if their portfolio has been suffering losses, they tend to become overly conservative. Either way, they fail to earn satisfactory returns.

Investors—particularly those making decisions on their own—often fail to take into account their financial circumstances, time horizon or tolerance for risk when making investment choices. Decisions regarding investments are often made without regard for the risk they create within the portfolio. Concentrated stock positions, in particular, can eviscerate a portfolio when market downturns occur and there is insufficient diversification or a lack of uncorrelated assets to offset the equity losses.

Asset allocation is a strategy designed to manage systematic risk by diversifying a portfolio among a variety of dissimilar assets, such as equities, fixed-income, cash equivalents, real estate and alternative investments. Because different investments react differently to changing economic and market conditions, a portfolio of uncorrelated assets can provide a balance so that when one category of investment is losing value, another category will offset the loss by making gains. The goal is to reduce the risk of portfolio erosion as a result of being overweighted in a single asset class that suffers a downturn, and to increase portfolio diversification.[235]

Equities, by their nature, can be considerably riskier in the short term than over longer periods because of market volatility. Investment grade bonds have a lower risk profile but often fail to outpace inflation. Achieving the proper mix of equity, debt, real estate, cash equivalents and perhaps alternative investments is the art of asset allocation.

A portfolio can, however, have brilliant asset allocation but miss the mark because it lacks adequate diversification, such as if the equities portion of the portfolio is limited to a small number of stocks or a single sector. A diversified equity allocation would typically include stocks from different sectors of the economy, or include mutual funds or active index funds that seek to outperform their benchmarks.

An asset allocation strategy should not be static but rather dynamic, changing over time in response to the owner's changing lifestyle or investment objectives. It should have sufficient flexibility to adjust to the inevitable market volatility that occurs over long time periods.[236]

I have been a strong proponent of the importance of asset allocation for virtually my entire career, and it's something I practice with great care. Too often, a template based on some outdated or simplified bromide is used to establish asset allocation rather than given the individualized attention it requires. Asset allocation is complicated because it has so many moving parts. Now if an individual starts investing early in life and has sufficient time for the power of time and compounding to do its work, it may preclude the need for thoughtful asset allocation because of the historical performance of equities markets over long periods. The fly in the ointment is that when stocks are down—historically about one year in four—they sometimes stay down for extended periods, testing the mettle of investors to resist moving to cash and missing out on much of the recovery.

Market Movements

The average annualized return for the S&P 500 since its inception in 1926 through 2021 is 10.49%. The average annualized return since adopting 500 stocks into the index in 1957 through 2021 is 10.67%.[237]

A bear market is defined as the S&P 500 or Dow Jones Industrial Average falling by at least 10% from its previous high. The average recorded bear market lasted 289 days. The longest was 61 months, from 1937 through 1942. The bear market from 2007 to 2009 lasted 16 months during which the S&P 500 tumbled by 52%. But episodes like that are rare. The average decline during a bear market has been 32%.[238]

Negative stock market returns occur, on average, about one out of every four years. Historical data shows that the positive years far outweigh the negative years. Between 2000 and 2019, the average annualized return of the S&P 500 Index was about 8.87%.[239]

There have been 26 market corrections since World War II with an average decline of 13.7%. Recoveries have taken four months on average.

As anyone who has tried to time the markets will tell you, markets are unpredictable and can be highly volatile. Timing the market is difficult at best, even for professional traders, and it illustrates the importance of a solid asset allocation, diversification and a long-term investment approach. Missing out on just one or two of the best days each year can make an almost unbelievable difference in investment performance.

(Graphic 11.1 Bull-Bear Markets)

A Bank of America study quantified the value of missed opportunities. Going back to 1930, the study found that investors who missed the S&P 500's 10 best days each decade received a total return of 28%. Those who remained invested throughout the period would have enjoyed a return of

17,715%![240] That's a statistical testimonial to staying invested.

Uncorrelated Assets

Asset correlation is a measure of how investments move in relations to one another. Assets are said to be correlated when they move in the same direction at the same time. Uncorrelated assets do just the opposite; when one is down, the other is up. Modern Portfolio Theory proposes that a portfolio's returns can be enhanced and overall risk reduced by investing in a mix of assets that are uncorrelated, that is, that tend not to move in the same direction at the same time.[241]

A portfolio including uncorrelated assets can generate predictable returns with minimal correlation to the market's major asset classes. The goal is to secure consistent, positive annual returns via diversification that has reduced exposure to any single asset class. It's not an easy balance to attain, but proficient asset allocation can deliver this outcome using the appropriate ratio of uncorrelated assets that are independent of market performance. They tend to make positive returns precisely when needed; when the rest of a portfolio's assets are dropping in value.

I'm often asked what portion of a portfolio should be allocated to uncorrelated investments. Studies indicate that a minimum of 15-20% of a portfolio must be allocated to uncorrelated return assets in order to produce a meaningful statistical reduction in portfolio risk and volatility.[242] Just as endowments and pension plans have to preserve and grow capital over the long-term but also have money available for liability payments (think retirees monthly income distribution from the pension); individual investors must have liquid assets available for emergencies and money for retirement distributions while growing their capital.

Those congruent needs must be taken into account when allocating portfolio investments. Not only should a portion of the portfolio be in liquid assets in case money is needed for an unexpected event, but the asset mix should have an uncorrelated component as well. That is, when one asset is down, another asset offsets the loss by being up. It's nice when people can share similar interests and get along; it makes for a more peaceful and harmonious environment. The same can't be said for the assets in a portfolio. When they all get along, that is, react the same way to market movements, it's not a healthy sign. At any point in time, we prefer some of our investments to be doing the opposite of one another. Every investor knows that over time, stocks tend to go up. What they may not understand is that different stock sectors perform quite differently at any given time.

During a single day, domestic growth stocks were up over 150 points while value, mid-cap and emerging market shares lost almost the same amount. During 2022, the S&P 500 took a beating, down nearly 20% for the calendar year. While the tech sector led the downfall, collectively losing nearly $4 trillion in market value, the energy sector had a spectacular year, gaining more than 60%.

I find it exciting that while getting asset allocation right can be problematic, there is such a broad array of investment classes, each with distinctive attributes, we can fine-tune a portfolio to provide the diversification and low correlation of assets to meet virtually any investor need. Just as certain ingredients in medicine, if taken alone, can be lethal but when combined with other ingredients can be therapeutic, certain investments can be toxic to a portfolio in certain markets but when combined with other uncorrelated investments, can provide more consistent returns while reducing risk.

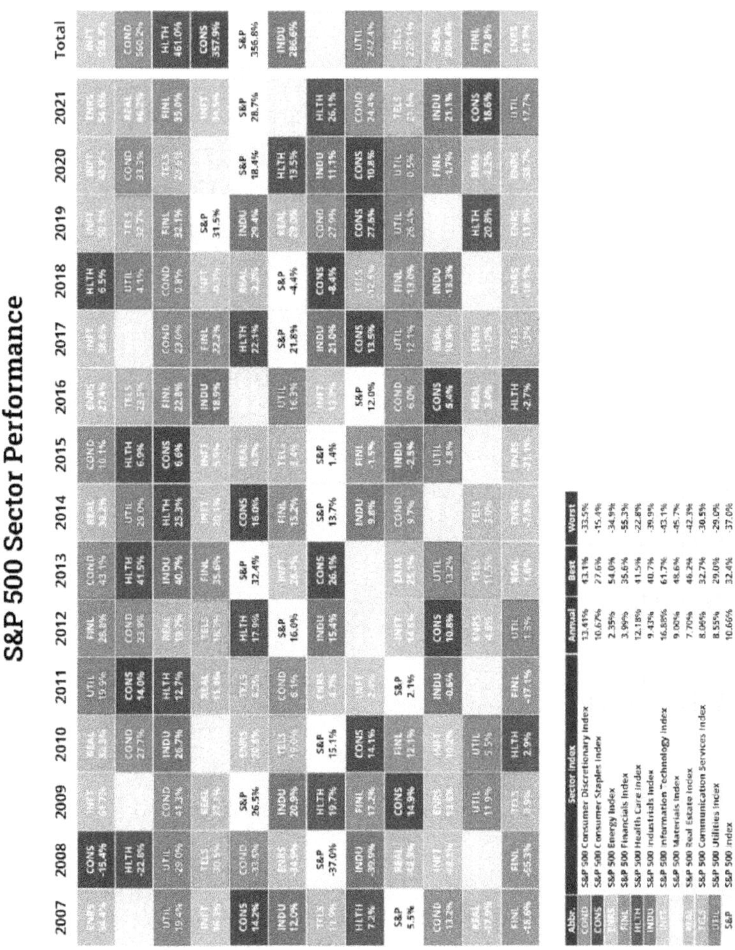

S&P 500 Sector Performance

(Graphic 11.2 S&P Sector Performance)[243]

Efficient Frontier

The efficient frontier is a description of the optimal investment portfolio with the highest expected market return for a given level of risk. It can also be defined as the lowest risk for a specific level of return.

Introduced by Nobel Laureate Harry Markowitz in 1952, the efficient frontier is considered the cornerstone of modern portfolio theory (MPT);[244] It rates investments on a scale of return (y-axis) versus risk (x-axis). An investment's compound annual growth rate (CAGR) is commonly used as the return component while annualized standard deviation depicts the risk metric.[245] Graphic 11.3 is an illustration of the efficient frontier.

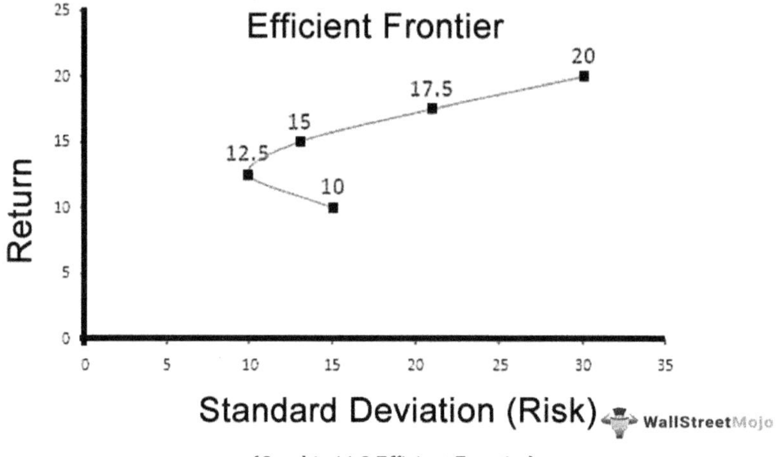

(Graphic 11.3 Efficient Frontier)

The investment being considered is thus plotted on the graph's two axis factors. It is then compared to the curved line of the efficient frontier to determine if it falls above or below the efficient frontier. Of course, different investors will have different efficient frontiers, based on their circumstances and risk tolerance.[246]

An optimal portfolio occupies the *efficient* portion of the risk-return area. Ideally, it meets the requirement that that no other asset mix exists with a higher expected return at the same level of risk—standard deviation of the return. Standard deviation is a measure of volatility and risk—how much an investment's returns can vary from its average return; the amount of fluctuation from its expected return. The higher the standard deviation, the more dispersed its returns are and the riskier the investment may be. The smaller an investment's standard deviation, the less volatile it is;[247] think of volatility as risk.

Prior to Markowitz's work, security-selection models mainly focused on investment returns. Traditional investment advice was to construct a portfolio from securities that appeared to offer the best opportunities for gain with the least risk. Investors following this advice might logically conclude that, as a sector, tech stocks offered optimal risk-reward traits and so would compile a portfolio entirely of these issues. Markowitz was the first to demonstrate how portfolio variance could be reduced through diversification. He proposed that investors focus on selecting portfolios based on their overall risk-reward characteristics instead of merely compiling portfolios from securities with attractive risk-reward characteristics.[248]

> "It's like a crapshoot in Las Vegas, except in Las Vegas the odds are with the house. As for the market, the odds are with you, because on average over the long run, the market has paid off."
>
> Harry Markowitz

The significance of an asset's standard deviation is illustrated in graphic 11.4, which shows that domestic mid-cap stocks had the best (lowest) cumulative rank, that is, the total of all its ranks over the quarter century depicted in the graphic. Cumulative rank, rather than focusing on one year at a time, shows how an asset ranked over the entire period. Following in rank to mid-caps were domestic large-cap, small-cap and large-cap value stocks. The worst rankings were for cash and real estate—as measured by changes in the Shiller U.S. home price index versus REIT returns. The average of each asset (shown by the blue bars) and standard deviation (as shown by the green bars) demonstrates that some assets had significantly greater variability than others.[249]

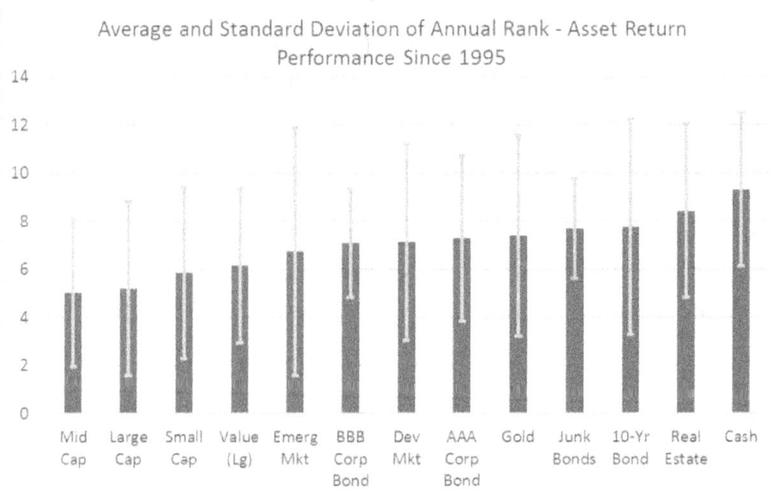

(Graphic 11.4: Asset Standard Deviation)

Asset Allocation vs Security Selection

Asset allocation is the process of deciding how much to invest in different asset classes whereas security selection decides which investments to hold in the portfolio. There are two major types of asset allocation: strategic and tactical. Strategic allocations to various asset classes establish the long-term strategy of a portfolio. Tactical allocations are periodic adjustments—frequently referred to as rebalancing—based on changing market conditions.

In their landmark 1986 paper, "Determinants of Portfolio Performance,"[250] Gary Brinson and colleagues concluded that a portfolio's static (strategic) asset allocation accounted for roughly 90% of the portfolio's total return and volatility over time. Security selection and market timing played minor roles. These findings were subsequently confirmed by Vanguard and other researchers (Ibbotson and Kaplan, 2000).[251]

Brinson's most important contribution may have been the attribution of a portfolio's total return to indexed static asset allocation policy, security selection, and market-timing components. The study showed that, on average, pension funds have not been able to add significant value above their indexed static policy returns through market timing or security selection. Despite the industry's influence of security selection and market-timing strategies on portfolio returns, the amount of skill required to justify active management is very high (Kritzman and Page, 2003). Active returns tend to be unstable and unpredictable over time.[252]

In their 2000 paper,[253] Ibbotson and Kaplan stated that, on average, asset allocation explained 99% and 104% of long-term returns for pensions and mutual funds, respectively. This is based on the premise that a pension fund or mutual fund portfolio's total return consisted of the total return plus the active return minus trading costs. The results demonstrated that, over time, the average fund lost 4% of total return to fees, ineffective active management or poor manager selection.[254]

When I was newer to the industry 30 years ago, the kind of 50-year lookback analysis of the Dow Jones Industrial Average (DJIA) we have for reference today didn't exist. The best you could glean in those days was perhaps 20 years of historical data. Today, we have a half century of data on virtually every asset class in the universe except cryptocurrency. That's a tremendous improvement in terms of interpreting data.

60/40 Formula

For decades, the industry promoted the 60/40 model (60% equities, 40% fixed income) as the standard for retirement portfolio asset allocation. Today there is ongoing controversy about that model. Sadly, much of what is being promoted about it is fear marketing to baby boomers.

In my experience, the average retired or retiring baby boomer who is working with a CFP® has an average of one to two million dollars in their investment portfolio. Too many financial plans for these people revert to a default 60/40 investment model. Our firm has never designed a 60/40 portfolio because it is a generic template targeting modest growth.

The priorities for a typical client of ours with a two-million-dollar portfolio are capital preservation and regular income. On average, they may want $100-120K in annual income. A married couple like this may already be receiving $40-50K annually in Social Security benefits, leaving another $45-75K in income needed from their investable assets.

That means they will need $500-600K in income over the ensuing five years. So, let's allocate that amount into a variety of high-quality bond portfolios, such as those from Nuveen, Vanguard, DFA or one of the many fine fixed income bond managers and make their income distribution secure. If that allocation turns out to be a 60/40 ratio, so be it, but we never base our investment choices on a predetermined asset mix before we know the client's specific needs. We don't target a certain asset mix; as a fiduciary, we look for a way to use reasonable assumptions, knowing we are responsible for our advice and will be held accountable for making prudent decisions for our clients. I guess you could say we work backwards as compared to advisors who start out with a financial template and then try to fit their clients into it.

This is not an indictment of the 60/40 allocation but rather a caution that it should not be an assumed allocation for a certain point of life. On the other hand, the argument condemning it as antiquated for the purpose of promoting some investment product or strategy should not be given serious attention either.

The 60/40 formula works really well for firms trying to rapidly build a client base using dramatic mass marketing techniques stressing fear or greed. Another way to build a large financial practice is to utilize a cookie-cutter allocation approach and have a couple hundred advisors explaining it to thousands of clients. If you want to work with a fiduciary, however, it doesn't make much sense to go to a huge firm like that, unless you are handling most of your own investing and you're willing to pay for the advice.

When we develop a portfolio for the majority of our clients, people who were long-time employees as engineers, managers or executives of major employers in the area, we often find that these people have been working roughly the same amount of time and earning comparable incomes and pension benefits. The appropriate allocation for them is often something close to a 60/40 split. That is never a predetermined allocation on our part but instead the result of our analysis of their circumstances and lifestyle. Of course, the dynamic allocation of their portfolio is going to change over time as we move the portfolio risk and return up or down in response to changing client goals.

Age/Time Horizon

Market declines can compromise investment performance and make recouping losses problematic for those with limited time horizons. After each recession since 1920, it has taken an average of 3.1 years for the stock market to reach pre-recession highs, accounting for inflation and dividends. Even taking into account bad years, the S&P 500 has seen average annual returns of about 10% over the last century.

An investment policy statement should take the investor's age and time horizon into account in developing an appropriate asset allocation. The longer the time horizon, the more an allocation can assume additional risk and take advantage of equities' higher historic returns and growth potential.[255]

Individual circumstances dictate time horizons and are a major consideration in forming an asset allocation. They should ideally be assessed no later than five years prior to a planned retirement. Investment strategy should be predicated on an individual's present and future income needs so that a proper allocation can be made to safe, noncorrelated assets.

Flexibility is something that academics have been talking about for a long time, that is, the odds of investment success go up dramatically if someone is not dead adamant on their retirement date and can adjust the date to the markets.

When someone is roughly five years out from their planned retirement, they might have the flexibility to be more aggressive and increase the odds of getting a higher return. The optimal environment for this is if the individual is not locked in to the retirement date, has the option of continuing to work and has not been burned out by their career. So, if the markets are down and the portfolio does not perform as hoped over the five-year timeframe, the individual could delay retirement, continue to work and wait for the expected rebound. It's a deal with the devil but if the individual has financial resilience, the strategy will work. Often, the wait will not be long.

There exists a rule of thumb to identify the percentage of your portfolio to keep in stocks by subtracting your age from 100. It's a dated paradigm still in use by many advisors that makes no sense to us because it doesn't take into account individual situations. We regularly find that many people in their mid-seventies and eighties don't spend nearly as much money as they did earlier in retirement. They tend to be less active as they grow older and do less things that require significant expenditures. From this observation we've learned to reconsider their allocation in terms of shifting emphasis from income generation to asset disbursement to heirs. Inevitably, we already have an estate plan in place, but once again, rebalancing comes into play, in this instance to meet changing needs as a result of people living longer. For aging retirees, if they still have an IRA building and compounding, allocation can be shifted to meet revised asset dispersion to heirs and the need for revised tax management.

The rebalancing aspect of asset allocation is critical and often overlooked when proponents and dissenters debate whether and/or how often rebalancing is necessary. I believe advisors who ignore rebalancing or do so only casually every two or three years are simply being lazy and should probably tighten up their asset allocation model to take less risk. If, like us, the asset allocation is being rebalanced quarterly—or even semi-annually—the asset allocation model can be somewhat more aggressive because of the rebalancing time frame.

From conversations with do-it-yourself investors, I find very few do a good job rebalancing, if they do it at all. Most seem to recognize they should be rebalancing on a regular basis but instead, tend to be overly conservative with their allocation as a defensive strategy.

Some investments will invariably disappoint but their lack of performance can be offset by other, noncorrelated investments. That's why allocation is so important and so valuable. Something will always be up when something else is down. I find that clients who have been working with us for an extended period develop a level of trust that allows them to satisfy their appetite for increased investment risk in pursuit of higher returns. It's one of the distinct advantages of collaboration with a fiduciary.

Institutional Similarities

The most important thing to remember about asset allocation is to target your liabilities—your monthly income distribution—and invest the funds necessary to fund your distributions in places that have historically shown to be havens for safe money. That would be fixed income, bonds or money market accounts. I omitted CDs because they are not—and have not been—a viable investment for some 15 years now. Instead, we use bonds, and while yields have been low, bond total returns have been satisfactory because of the premiums. When bonds go up significantly in price, there is usually a big selloff, as there was in the Spring of 2020 when COVID-19 hit and the Aggregate Bond Index (AGG) went up over 8% at the time. The AGG includes government Treasury securities, corporate bonds, mortgage-backed securities, asset-backed securities and municipal bonds. It functions for the bond market similarly to how the Wilshire 500 Total Stock Index does for the equity market.[256]

> "We need a mutual fund industry with both vision and values; a vision of fiduciary duty and shareholder service, and values rooted in the proven principles of long-term investing and of trusteeship that demands integrity in serving our clients."
>
> John C. Bogle

Many investors regard bonds as a horrible investment in recent years because they are fixated on the yields being so low. Yes, the yields have been virtually nonexistent for the past 15 years, especially after inflation is factored in but that's not the point. The total return of bonds has been very beneficial during most market crashes. As an asset allocation, we first target a client's risk structure and build our safe money allocation, primarily using different types of bonds with differing maturities. We do this to preserve capital so that the client is never forced to sell stocks for income during a down market. And historically, equities can stay down for extended periods.

Creating an asset allocation for a retiree, like creating an asset allocation for a pension plan, requires planning for liabilities. A pension plan that anticipates average liabilities (distributions to retiring employees) of one hundred million annually may also have to plan for a "pig in a python" year when an unusually large number of employees, perhaps baby boomers of the same age, will be retiring, causing a spike in pension liability. The pension plan must accurately calculate what their liability will be when that spike hits so they can adjust their asset allocation to meet it. It can be a complicated calculation to say the least.

Asset allocation for individuals involves similar calculations when evaluating their IRA and other investable assets against their anticipated future income needs. How much can the individual or couple expect in outlays? Do they want to take annual distributions from their IRA? How many years do they expect that to continue and what is the expected growth rate for their investments? What do we expect inflation to be?

Those are the main considerations we assess when we design a portfolio strategy and asset allocation strategy. Like planning an asset allocation for a pension plan or foundation, as fiduciaries, we must make prudent decisions for our individual clients. Whether they plan to take bi-weekly, monthly, quarterly or annual distributions, we have to ensure the funds will always be available without having to cash out equities at an inopportune time, market-wise. That means making sure that we have enough safe money isolated so that we can meet that expected distribution, just as the institutional plan committees have the responsibility to have funds available for cash calls.

No one wants more of their investible assets than necessary in safe money and low-yielding investments, but an asset allocation, first and foremost, must make certain that safe money will be available when needed, regardless of which direction the markets are heading.

Inflation Always Returns

When I am conducting adult financial education classes, I get asked all sorts of questions, some well thought out. One question I often get is, "What's the best investment to be in when inflation skyrockets?" The answer, of course, is equities. The next best investment is real estate.

This is currently a heated topic. Official government reports put inflation at 8.3% for last year, 2022. Many economists disagree, however, and insist it was well over 12%, which I believe is a more accurate estimate. Assuming the economists are correct, and they have far less incentive to fudge the numbers than the folks in D.C., investors had to overcome quite an inflationary bubble to earn satisfactory portfolio returns last year.

> "Inflation is as violent as a mugger, as frightening as an armed robber and as deadly as a hit man."
>
> Ronald Reagan

Chapter Twelve

Estate Planning

> "The only difference between death and taxes is that death doesn't get worse every time congress meets."
> Will Rogers

I sometimes think our industry should change the description of estate planning to "future planning" or "legacy planning" because a lot of people have an aversion to planning for their ultimate demise. Many people don't realize how much their total assets are worth and the word "estate" has the connotation of someone with significant wealth, not someone who spent 40 years working for a living and through thrift and hard work built a significant net worth over time.

A 2019 survey conducted by Caring.com discovered that only 4 out of every 10 Americans currently have an estate plan in place. According to the survey, only 57% of adults currently have any estate planning documents and, of that, only 1 in 5 millennials (adults ages 22 to 38) currently have any such documents.[257]

There are many reasons why people procrastinate when it comes to planning the end of their life. For one, the prospect of gathering all the documentation necessary can be daunting. The perception of the enormity of the task prevents many from even getting started. It's a bit like postponing a dentist visit because your teeth don't hurt. Some individuals are unable to take action until a deadline looms. Nothing forces people to create wills, trusts or powers of attorney. Nothing will inform you exactly when you need to do it. For the unfortunate, the alarm rings without warning. Then too, if your heirs are not your favorite people, you can subconsciously punish them by delaying financial decisions regarding your money. Finally, the topics of death and money are uncomfortable conversations for most people to have, particularly those who are healthy and don't think they are wealthy.[258]

One of the saddest examples of the consequences of postponement occurs when the individual fails to designate a durable power of attorney and becomes incapacitated. (A durable power of attorney means that the document stays in effect if the individual becomes unable to handle matters on their own.) Having a durable power of attorney in place eliminates the need for a full guardianship by someone appointed to make decisions for the individual.[259]

Not having a will that specifies guardianship can be a tragedy for people with young children. It's not uncommon for married couples to believe naming a relative to be their children's guardian in case of the parents' deaths is sufficient, but the only way to name guardians the courts will recognize is by doing so in a will.

Unintended omissions and distributions can be a devastating effect of estate planning procrastination. It's critical to have documents that accurately reflect a person's final wishes. A poorly drafted will can remain binding even after major changes in a family, such as divorces or deaths. A few words can be the difference between an entire generation inheriting a portion of the estate or being completely left out.[260]

Whether or not you procrastinate, life goes on and incapacity or death may be around the corner. The onset of incapacity without having a plan in place leads to a court proceeding often called a conservatorship. In a conservatorship, your lack of capacity is determined in a court proceeding and the court appoints someone to manage your affairs. Furthermore, planning in advance can allow you to plan for nursing home costs and qualification for Medicaid.[261]

There is a misconception that if you have a will, you have an estate plan, but this is a myth. A proper estate plan also includes health care directives and a financial power of attorney; it often includes a trust to avoid probate, protect minor children, maintain family privacy and protect assets from general creditors or the cost of long-term care.

As unpleasant as it is to acknowledge our mortality, creating an estate plan does not mean that something is suddenly going to happen to you; it means that you value your family enough to do what is best for their future security. More often than not, people who have completed the estate planning process achieve peace of mind knowing that they have planned for their loved ones.[262]

Dying Intestate

If you die without a will in the state of Washington, for example, the state decides who gets your assets through what is called "intestate succession." Having been deemed to have died intestate, the deceased assets will go to relatives, starting with the closest surviving members. Some assets may not be affected by intestate succession if you die without a will in Washington, however. These include assets for which you have named beneficiaries or assets that you co-own with someone else who is still living. These non-probate assets will go to named beneficiaries or surviving co-owners whether you have a will in place or not. Assets not subject to intestate succession:

- Items transferred to a living trust
- Life insurance proceeds with a named beneficiary

- Funds in an IRA, 401(k) or other retirement accounts
- Payable-on-death bank accounts
- Property owned with someone else in a joint tenancy
- Securities held in a transfer-on–death account.[263]

Probate is the legal process for ensuring that the wishes of a person who has died are honored, as stated in his or her will. Through probate, the deceased person's estate is settled, which includes transferring property and assets to heirs and beneficiaries. It also involves paying any outstanding debts, such as loans or taxes, that may remain on the estate. Probate can be formal or informal in Washington. The more lengthy, complicated and costly formal process will be required if any disputes arise among the estate's beneficiaries, heirs, creditors, or other people with interests in the estate. There also may be a dispute about the meaning of written terms or instructions in the will. If these disputes occur, then probate must occur formally, under the supervision and direction of a Washington state court judge. Similarly, a judge must be involved in probate if the estate settlement involves the guardianship of a minor or incapacitated adult.[264]

Probate in Washington typically takes six months to a year, depending on some choices the executor makes (discussed below). It can take much longer if there is a court fight over the will (which is rare) or unusual assets or debts that complicate matters.[265]

People Who Died Intestate

Martin Luther King Jr. played a pivotal role in helping African Americans to obtain full rights and liberty. Since he was a civil rights activist, he frequently received death threats. What is disturbing is that even though he was assassinated quite a long time ago in 1968, his family is still fighting a legal battle regarding the control of his estate. King's children battled over keeping his personal traveling Bible and Nobel Peace Prize Medal in 2014. Moreover, they were at odds regarding how the organization that oversaw the estate should be run.

Steve McNair, the famous NFL quarterback, left this world in 2009 in a murder-suicide. He didn't leave a signed will behind though he had expressed that he wanted his family taken care of in event of his death. His estate was initially tied up in litigation and a battle ensued. While alive he had gifted his mother a home, though he didn't sign the deed in her name. His wife has since sued his mother and evicted her from the house since she couldn't pay the $3,000 rent she now requires.[266]

Princess Diana, after a very public divorce in 1996, died in an unfortunate car accident. She was mourned by the entire world. Diana had a will prepared, which stated that her executors should pass equal shares of all her assets to her two children once they turn 25. In addition, Diana bequeathed her 17 godchildren several possessions from her property. Everything looked smooth until the addition of her "Letter of Wishes". The former princess' Letter of Wishes was a quick amendment to her will, listed to give her godchildren a portion of a quarter of her estate. This could have added up to around 440,000 British pounds sterling, but the issue came from the legality of the document.

The Letter of Wishes itself was neither a legal document nor a codicil, the latter of which would work as an official supplement to her will. The Letter of Wishes was disregarded by her executors and instead, her original directions were directions.[267]

Estate Tax

Federal estate tax is applied to a deceased person's assets in excess of $12.92 million in 2023. It is a tax on property—cash, real estate, stock and other assets—transferred from deceased persons to their heirs. It consists of an accounting of everything you own or have certain interests in at the date of death. The fair market value of the total of these items is your "Gross Estate." The includible property may consist of cash and securities, real estate, insurance proceeds, trusts, annuities, business interests and other assets. Certain deductions are allowed in arriving at your "Taxable Estate." These deductions may include mortgages and other debts, estate administration expenses, property that passes to surviving spouses and qualified charities. The value of some operating business interests or farms may be reduced for estates that qualify. Estates of decedents survived by a spouse may elect to pass any of the decedent's unused exemption to the surviving spouse.[268]

Estate tax differs from an inheritance tax in that it applies to the estate of the deceased, not to the beneficiaries of the estate. The estate's personal representative (sometimes referred to as an executor) is responsible for paying the tax out of the estate's total assets before anything is distributed to beneficiaries.

As people get older, it's been our experience that they tend to spend less. Meanwhile, their assets continue to grow. If they live to an advanced age, they may run up a huge potential tax burden while never having considered themselves wealthy. People tend to overlook the value of their assets until they sit down and make a list of everything they own or have an interest in. The recent runup in real estate values and the prolonged stock market rise alone heightened the estates of millions of investors.

While their estates may still not exceed the federal exemption, depending where they reside, they may incur a substantial state tax obligation. In the state of Washington, where many of our clients live, an individual's estate in excess of the state's $2,193,000 exemption is taxable from 10% to 20%, depending on the amount of excess.[269]

Currently, capital gains tax is due on the appreciation of assets, such as real estate, stock or art when the owner "realizes" the gain (usually by selling the asset). But the increase in the value of an asset is never subject to income tax if the owner holds on to the asset until death because of the **"step-up basis"** for asset valuation.[270]

An example would be if your parents bought an investment property for $50,000 years ago and it is now worth $250,000. If they choose to sell the asset, their tax basis is the original purchase price of $50,000 so they would pay taxes on the gain of $200,000. Because they held the property for more than one year, they would be taxed at the current capital gains rate.

If, on the other hand, the property is passed on to you after your parents have died, you receive a step-up in basis to the current fair market value. If you now decide to sell the property and receive $300,000 for it, your taxable gain on the sale is just $50,000 because your basis was "stepped up" to the value of the asset as of the date of your second parent's death.[271]

Deductions

If you are over the exemption amount, your estate might be able to take certain deductions that lower the value of your estate below $2.193 million, in which case no estate tax will be due. These deductions include:

- Marital deductions. Property left to a surviving spouse, no matter the amount, can be deducted from the gross estate.

- Charitable deductions. Gifts to qualified public, charitable, and religious organizations can be deducted from the gross estate.
- Debts and administration expenses. Debts owed and some administration expenses (funeral costs and attorney's fees, for example) can be deducted from the gross estate.

- Farm deduction. If more than half of the value of your estate comes from real estate (and related items) used for farming, the estate can take a deduction for the value of the farming property.

- Family owned business interest deduction. The value of a family-owned business can also be deducted (capped at $2.5 million) if certain requirements are fulfilled, including that an inheritor of the business must continue it for at least three years following the death.[272]

Estate Tax Strategies

Estate tax strategies often include living trusts, either revocable or irrevocable.

A living trust is one created to exist during the owner's lifetime. It can help manage assets or protect owners should they become ill, disabled or simply challenged by aging. Revocable living trusts permit owners to amend or revoke them should they wish to do so. This provision causes the trust assets to remain in the owner's estate and so, does not help avoid probate, which may not always be necessary depending on the cost and complexity of the estate.

An irrevocable living trust, on the other hand, cannot be revoked or changed, and so, is commonly used to avoid estate tax in addition to protecting assets.

A living trust is legally in existence during your lifetime, has a trustee who currently serves, and owns property which (generally) you have transferred to it during your lifetime. While you are living, the trustee (who may be you, although a co-trustee might also be named along with you) is generally responsible for managing the property as you direct for your benefit. Upon your death, the trustee— or successor trustee if it was you—is generally directed to either distribute the trust property to your beneficiaries, or to continue to hold it and manage it for the benefit of your beneficiaries. Like a will, a living trust can provide for the distribution of property upon your death. Unlike a will, it can also (a) provide you with a vehicle for managing your property during your lifetime, and (b) authorize the trustee to manage the property and use it for your benefit (and your family) if you should become incapacitated, thereby avoiding the appointment of a guardian for that purpose.[273]

A **marital trust** is a type of irrevocable trust that allows one spouse to transfer assets to a surviving spouse tax free, using the unlimited marital deduction, while providing tax benefits not available if transferred outright. Married couples have what is called an unlimited marital deduction. The marital deduction allows the entire estate of the first spouse to die, to pass to the surviving spouse tax free. The idea being that estate tax, if any, is deferred until the surviving spouse's death. A Marital Trust often works in conjunction with a Bypass Trust to capture the deceased spouse's estate tax exemption.[274]

Bypass Trusts—or AB Trusts—are seldom used today, given the $12.06 million federal estate tax exemption, but highly affluent couples still use the strategy, fearing that their estates might someday be subject to the tax. These trusts are much more complicated than simple revocable living trusts, which are designed to avoid probate.

Here's how they work. When the first spouse dies, the trust is split into two separate trusts: the survivor's trust (A) and the bypass trust (B). Property in the B trust doesn't belong to the surviving spouse, but he or she has the right to use it and receive income from it for life. As long as the value of the assets in this trust is below the federal estate tax exemption, no federal estate tax will be due. It may still be subject to state estate tax, however. Everything else goes into the revocable survivor's trust (A). As surviving spouse, you have total control over it and can spend it, give it away, or leave it to the beneficiaries you choose. No estate tax is due on this property, either, because everything left to a surviving spouse is free from federal (and state) estate tax. The tax savings will come at the second spouse's death. Then, the property in the B trust will go tax-free to the couple's "final beneficiaries," commonly their children.[275] The state of Washington is one where bypass trusts are more commonly used.

Some estates use **grantor retained annuity trusts** (GRATs) to pass along considerable assets tax-free. The estate owner puts money into a trust designed to repay the estate the initial amount plus interest at a rate set by the Treasury, typically over two years. If the investment — typically stock — rises in value any more than the Treasury rate, the gain goes to an heir tax-free. If the investment doesn't rise in value, the full amount still goes back to the estate. Such techniques have been described as a "heads I win, tails we tie" bet.[276]

Another strategy involves the **Qualified Terminable Interest Property** trust—or QTIP trust—essentially an A/B trust that is more restrictive than a typical marital trust. In most A/B trust arrangements, the marital, or A portion of the trust, is fully accessible by the surviving spouse. Conversely, a QTIP trust provides limited access to the trust assets for a surviving spouse. Although your spouse may receive income from the trust, he or she cannot decide on the ultimate disposition of the trust assets and cannot withdraw principal from the trust. However, the QTIP trust can be written to provide the greater of $5,000 or 5% of the trust assets to your surviving spouse annually if you wish. Upon the death of your surviving spouse, the trust is distributed according to your ultimate specifications. A QTIP trust does not qualify for the estate tax marital deduction under traditional tax rules due to its restrictive nature. However, the tax code does permit your executor to claim the marital deduction for amounts transferred to a QTIP trust by making an election on your estate tax return.

There are two main reasons why a married individual would choose to establish a QTIP trust. First, it may be unclear what your estate tax situation will be at the time the trust is put into effect. It may be prudent to provide flexibility for your executor to elect between claiming a marital deduction for the amounts transferred to the QTIP or forego that deduction. This will allow your executor to minimize the total estate tax paid by the two spouses combined by choosing to defer the tax on some, but not all, of the assets transferred in trust to a spouse. In other words, your executor can choose the estate tax treatment of the QTIP trust to reflect changes in the applicable tax laws or changes in the value of your assets since you last made your will. It may also be beneficial if your surviving spouse already has significant personal assets. In that case, your executor can take advantage of the graduated tax brackets in the estate tax law for both of you, in turn reducing the overall tax paid between both spouses.

The other, and perhaps more compelling reason, is that you may want to take advantage of the marital deduction for transfers made to your spouse in trust yet want to limit the power or ownership rights he or she has over the trust assets. The restrictive ownership provisions of a QTIP trust are particularly useful for second marriages since you may want to ensure that the amounts held in the trust will ultimately pass to your children or family and not the children or family of your second spouse.[277]

The **family limited partnership** (FLP) is a strategy worth considering for both estate planning and asset protection. A FLP is a business or holding company owned by two or more family members, usually created to preserve a family's generational wealth, providing protection against creditors or lawsuits, and allowing for tax-free transfers of assets. A FLP cannot be used as a stand-alone asset protection plan, however, as by itself, it provides no better protection of assets than a living trust.

A typical FLP arrangement designates both husband and wife as general partners and other family members—including the husband and wife—as limited partners. The general partners might own most or only a small percent interest in the partnership with the remainder in the form of limited partnership interests held, directly or indirectly, by other family members, based on the specific estate planning, asset protection and tax objectives of the family.

Once the FLP is created, assets such as investment accounts and business interests can be transferred into it. These may be real property or interest in entities that own real property. When completed, the husband and wife no longer own a direct interest in the transferred assets but instead own a controlling interest in the FLP, which now owns the assets. Thus, the married couple enjoys equal ownership and control of the FLP and its assets, just as they controlled their assets titled in their own names. But their assets are now fully protected from creditors. As general partner, they can buy or sell assets, subject to the terms of the partnership agreement. They may also have the right to determine what portion of partnership income and assets are retained by the FLP and what amount is distributed to the partners.[278] Limited partners—often referred to as silent partners—have no management responsibilities or day-to-day involvement in the partnership. Limited partners have an economic interest in the FLP, but typically lack control rights.

Combining the FLP with a living trust can be a highly beneficial facet of an estate plan. The FLP owns the family assets and provides protection and discounted valuations for estate tax purposes. The limited partnership interests owned by the general partners' (husband and wife) respective living trusts lets them bequeath their partnership interest while avoiding probate. In using a FLP, it is assumed that the couple will take advantage of the unlimited marital deduction. Upon the grantor's death, the family trust becomes irrevocable, succeeded by two separate trusts: a bypass trust and a marital trust.

This strategy essentially transfers the estate tax liability to the surviving spouse's estate and defers estate taxes. The usual probate complexities, costs and delays are avoided when the FLP interests are owned by living trusts and creditors need not be notified, providing for a quick disposition.[279]

Another potential strategy for dealing with taxes on estates beyond the state exclusions involves using IRA distributions. In particular, the strategy can help retirees of advanced years who are required to take an increasingly higher percentage of their IRA each year as a required mandatory distribution (RMD). It involves buying a life insurance contract, placing it inside an irrevocable life insurance trust (ILET) and letting the ILET take the annual RMDs and pay the policy premiums. The ILET is out of the owner's estate so the insurance policy proceeds remain separate from the estate because the policy is in a separate trust. When the owner dies, the policy proceeds are paid to beneficiaries' tax free. The owner is essentially exchanging taxable RMD distributions for tax-free payments to heirs.

The beneficiaries can use the policy proceeds to pay state estate taxes. For someone with a large estate, the taxes can be onerous. In Washington state, for example, someone with a $5 million estate would owe roughly $360,000 in estate taxes ($240,000 + 15% of the amount over $2 million after subtracting the states $2.193 exclusion).[280] It's an effective but complex strategy that requires the assistance of a financial professional familiar with the nuances.

Wealthier individuals and families may also choose to create a charitable remainder unitrust (CRUT) which allows them to receive a consistent stream of income while avoiding capital gains tax. Many use this structure to donate money to institutions or charities while reducing tax liability. The donor's family members are typically the initial beneficiaries of a CRUT. When the beneficiaries pass on, the assets used to fund the CRUT—typically real estate, stocks, art or other property—pass to the designated institution or charity. To prevent CRUTs from being used simply to avoid taxes, the federal government requires that the charity receive at least 10% of the asset's value.[281]

Gifting

The federal annual gift tax exclusion for 2023 is $17,000 per receiving individual. The federal lifetime gift and estate tax exemption—the amount of money or assets an individual can give away during a lifetime—is $12.92 million.

You can give away $17,000 to as many individuals—kids, grandkids, their spouses—as you'd like with no federal gift tax consequences. Spouses can each make $17,000 gifts.

While a series of $17,000 annual exclusion gifts can add up, they don't count toward the $12.92 million exemption amount. You also can make unlimited direct payments for medical and tuition expenses for as many people as you'd like, with no gift or estate tax consequences.[282]

If a gift exceeds the annual $17,000 limit, that does not automatically trigger the gift tax. If a gift exceeds the annual exclusion limit, the difference is simply subtracted from the person's $12.92 million lifetime exemption limit and no taxes are owed, provided proper filing with the IRS is completed. Exceeding the annual exclusion limit triggers federal taxes ranging from 18% (up to $10,000) to 40% on amounts above $1 million.[283]

Trustees and Executors

Trustees and executors both act as fiduciaries, that is, a person that acts on behalf of another person or persons with a duty to preserve good faith and trust. Being a fiduciary means being bound both legally and ethically to act in the other's best interests.[284]

A trustee is a fiduciary over a trust whereas an executor is a fiduciary over a probate estate. A trustee is responsible for administering a trust to the beneficiaries according to a legal agreement. An executor distributes a deceased person's assets according to a will. Unlike a trustee, an executor cannot act before obtaining a court order.

When a person dies without a will, their probate estate can still be managed, but the person appointed to manage the estate is called an Administrator rather than an Executor. It is the same thing, just different titles based on whether there is a will (Executor) or not (Administrator).[285]

One of the major issues surrounding the use of trusts is choosing a trustee or executor to administer the wishes of the deceased as expressed in the trust or will. Parents often blithely appoint the oldest adult child, an election that can have adverse consequences, particularly in the case of a trust, where the trustee's responsibilities may extend years or even generations into the future. Their choices can have dramatic and far-reaching repercussions for beneficiaries. For one, if the family member trustee lacks financial skills and inadvertently mismanages the trust assets, the family relationships may become irreversibly fractured as a result, not to mention the potential for intra-family legal action.[286]

If a sibling is both trustee and a beneficiary, relationships with other siblings can quickly become strained. Beneficiaries may begin to wonder just what the trustee is doing, what to expect, and of course, when they'll see their money. And because the trustee is "just" a sister or brother, beneficiaries may be inclined to inquire excessively or make outsized demands. On the other side, the trustee/beneficiary may be caught up in the nuts and bolts of handling the trust, and consider his siblings' requests as intrusive or an insinuation that he is not trustworthy. Resentment can build on both sides. In the worst-case scenario, one or more beneficiaries may even resort to a lawsuit in order to have the trustee removed. Most families never recover from this kind of rift.[287]

Some of the common ways trusts implode include poor investment choices by the trustee, beneficiaries that quarrel over the "fairness" of the trust's distributions, a change of heart on the part of the grantor regarding what various beneficiaries should receive but being locked in by an irrevocable trust. Or, the trust grantor remarries, pitting second wives against children from the first marriage. Beneficiaries get divorced or succumb to addictive behaviors. Alzheimer's disease or other forms of dementia throw a monkey wrench into the plan, too.[288]

In the real world, virtually every family has disagreements among members, often for the smallest or seemingly silliest of reasons. Sadly, these differences of opinion can result in the disintegration of otherwise loving relationships and even lead to permanent feuds. The death of a family member can exacerbate these issues. The chances of this happening are greatly increased when the decedent chooses a family member to serve as trustee. Some grantors willingly accept the risk of alienating family members because they are confident the sibling chosen will administer the trust fairly or because they believe the perceived cost savings versus appointing a financial professional as trustee justifies it.[289]

Trust grantors should carefully weigh the potential ramifications of choosing a family member as trustee. I've seen instances where the family member chosen has a history of instability or even addiction, and often, it doesn't work out well.

One client who appointed his three children as co-trustees failed to take into consideration that one sibling, a daughter, had been acting strangely for months. Despite warning from the other two siblings, the father proceeded with the trust arrangement as originally intended. It was less than a year later that the daughter suffered a nervous breakdown and had to be institutionalized, yet she shared equal responsibility with her two siblings for administering her parent's irrevocable trust.

Another error is people acting on the advice of their local banker, who may have good intentions but often lacks the experience to offer sound advice on estate planning nuances such as trusts, powers of attorney and selecting trustees.

As I write this, members of our staff are conducting a client estate planning session in the next room. They are individually checking off a semi-annual review of the client's estate plan, business succession plan, cash flow, beneficiary review (there were two changes since the last meeting) and inquiring whether the action plan established at the last meeting has been implemented as agreed by the client.

A final note about trustees and executors. This may seem like little more than common sense but it's critical for the grantor to notify the person or persons he has selected to administer his will or trust and give them copies of the documentation. Too often, the grantor simply nominates a trustee and fails to share that information with the person chosen.

A client of ours was appointed trustee of her aunt's estate but was never notified. The aunt lived in Florida and when she passed, our client had to fly down from Ohio to oversee the dissolution of the estate. When she arrived at her aunt's condo, she was inhospitably greeted by members of several charities that had been named partial beneficiaries of her aunt's trust. Representatives of the American Red Cross, Salvation Army and two other charities had all gained access to the property and each was determined to get their share of the saleable assets.

Our client was immediately (and rudely) advised not to remove anything from the condo, ostensibly based on the charities' previous problems with relatives of the deceased removing personal belongings in which the charities had a vested interest.

Obviously, they wanted to make certain they were not shortchanged, property-wise, and let the niece know in no uncertain terms they were determined to secure their "fair share" of the estate. The unexpected hostility shocked our client who had only learned she was trustee a few days earlier. This is an example of the importance of notifying the person chosen as executor or trustee and sharing the details of the estate plan with them so there are no unpleasant surprises.

The uncertainties of the future and the complexities of estate planning can catch even a financial professional off guard. An example is a bizarre situation my partner, a seasoned estate planning attorney, found himself in.

A client of his, let's call him Frank, was a successful business owner who remarried after his first wife died. The second marriage lasted some thirty years before he once again suffered the loss of a spouse. Shortly after her death, the couple's daughter showed up at Frank's house and began taking her mother's personal belongings without asking Frank. Understandably upset, Frank reminded her that "I know she was your mother, but she was also my wife for thirty years and this is my house. You cannot simply walk in here and take things without consulting me."

Before leaving in an angry pique, the daughter screamed that Frank was being unreasonable and that she was entitled to take whatever she wanted. The next day, Frank went to the law offices of my partner and demanded the daughter be removed as trustee and beneficiary of his trust and replaced with Karen, the daughter from his first marriage. When asked for a successor trustee in case something happened to Karen, Frank couldn't think of anyone and so asked my partner if he would temporarily act as secondary trustee until he could come up with someone else.

Being a long-time client, my partner reluctantly agreed to the arrangement on a temporary basis but cautioned Frank to come up with a successor trustee as soon as possible, to which Frank agreed.

It was just a few weeks later when my partner learned Frank had passed away. He contacted Karen, who agreed to go over and clean out Frank's house while making sure nothing was removed by the other daughter. After doing so, she felt ill and, unbeknownst to my partner, died suddenly a few days later. When my partner got a phone call asking what he was doing about the estate, he asked, "What are you talking about?" The shocking reply was, "Well, Karen died last week so you are now the trustee of the estate." The ensuing work convinced my partner never again to make that kind of accommodation, even for a lifelong client. A weird, but, true, story.

Without question, family members may find it uncomfortable to participate in a discussion about the disposition of a loved one's estate, but communicating a person's final wishes and explaining the choice of an executor or trustee to family members is vital to avoid misunderstandings and arguments later.

A wonderful example of how to communicate one's final wishes is the case of our now-deceased client, Commander Hill. He and his wife had me come out to their home and explain their final wishes to their four daughters. I asked up front if I was permitted to discuss all the couple's assets, including their IRA values and was told "Yes, tell them everything." Despite his advanced age, Hill was in apparent good health at the time but died unexpectedly a short time after that meeting. I recall how difficult and humbling it was for the daughters to sit and listen to a discussion of what would happen after the deaths of their beloved parents, but having a third person come in to oversee the conversation was a wise choice. It eliminated the tendency for family members to avoid uncomfortable situations, saying things like, "Oh we don't have to talk about that now, dad; you're going to be here for a long time." That meeting made things much easier once both parents passed away.

> "Fear of death increases in exact proportion to increase in wealth."
>
> Ernest Hemingway

Personal Property

Disposing of tangible personal property seems to be the most forgotten part of the average client's estate plan. Perhaps the single greatest source of conflict among surviving family members is over the decedent's tangible personal property. The conflict is often exacerbated by the trauma of a loved one's death, arguments among siblings or in-laws, and the emotional attachment to a loved ones intimate assets. A frequent issue in dealing with personal property is whether the decedent intended to restrict a bequest of "*all my personal property*" to tangible personal property, such as a home, automobile, real estate and personal possessions, or whether the expression was also meant to cover intangible personal property, such as investment accounts and life insurance. It can be particularly dangerous when the dispositive document (dealing with the disposition of property by deed or will) is ambiguous.[290]

Titling Of Assets

The way assets are titled can determine who controls the assets, tax consequences, whether the assets are subject to creditors' claims and who will receive the assets once the owner(s) pass away.[291]

Using my home state of Washington as an example, there are many ways to hold title on a property within the state:

- As a single person. The only requirement is not being married.
- As a sole and separate married person, provided consent is obtained from the spouse via a quitclaim or similar instrument.

- As community property, acquired by a husband and wife during marriage, when not acquired as the separate property of either. Both spouses have the right to dispose of one-half of the property by will. However, if the other spouse dies without a will, all of it will go to the surviving spouse without administration.
- As joint tenancy
- As tenancy in common
- As domestic partners[292]

In general, there are three ways to hold shared ownership of a property within an estate: joint tenancy, tenancy in common and tenancy by the entirety.

Joint tenancy is a legal arrangement in which two or more people jointly own equal shares of a property, each with equal rights and obligations. Joint tenancies are typically created by married couples but can also be created by non-marrieds, relatives, business associates or other parties. The relationship creates a *right of survivorship* so if one owner dies, their interest in the property is directly passed on to the surviving party(s) without having to go through probate or the court system.[293]

Tenancy in common (TIC) arrangements typically have no provision for right of survivorship. If two people are tenants in common of a property and one dies, his share does not automatically go to the other person. Instead, it goes to the party selected in the deceased person's will. The shares in the property may be of unequal size, and can be freely transferred to other owners both during the owner's lifetime and via a will.

Tenancy by the entirety is a type of shared ownership of property recognized in most states, available only to married couples. Much like in a joint tenancy, spouses who own property as tenants by the entirety each own an undivided interest in the property, each has full rights to occupy and use it and has a right of survivorship. Tenants by the entirety also cannot transfer their interest in the property without the consent of the other spouse.[294] Tenancy by the entirety is not an option in all states.

Community Property

In community property states, any assets acquired by spouses throughout their marriage are considered community property, regardless of who buys it. Community property states include Arizona, California, Idaho, Louisiana, Nevada, New Mexico, Texas, Washington and Wisconsin. California, Nevada and Washington also include domestic partnerships under community property law.

Most states in the U.S. implement common law property to determine ownership of assets acquired during a marriage. According to common law property, if one member of a married couple acquires separate property during the marriage, the property belongs to that person alone. The only exception is when the property is listed under both spouses' names. Situations exist where community property law does not apply. These include property given to one spouse as a gift, inherited property, property received through a will or trust fund, property acquired prior to the marriage and property acquired while the spouses were legally separated and living separately.[295]

A Caveat About Inherited Assets

Let's suppose your daughter married a guy you can't stand...but she loves him and so you grin and bear it with him at holiday get togethers, birthday parties and occasional dinners together. But your health is starting to slip—perhaps because of an ulcer from spending time with the son-in-law—

and you don't want this character getting his hands on any of the inheritance you plan to leave your daughter.

This is a situation more common than you might think and there is a land mine awaiting the beneficiary who doesn't know about community property laws. The trap is this: if your daughter mixes the money you leave her with a joint account that is community property with her husband, he automatically inherits half of the money if they use any portion of it for a purchase, home repair, etc. In other words, as soon as they use the money, he is entitled to half.

Of course, you won't know about it then, but if you make her aware of the need to put her inheritance in a separate—and not a comingled—account that only she has access to. Now you can rest easy knowing that guy won't be able to go out and buy a Porsche with the money you intended for her. The same holds true if you gift her while you are alive.

I've had situations where a spouse who inherited money is getting divorced. One of the first things we ask is what happened to the money? Did it go into a joint account? If yes, has any of it been spent on anything you use or enjoy together? If the unfortunate answer to that question is "yes," the other spouse is legally entitled to receive half the remaining money as part of a divorce settlement.

> "I'm not afraid to die, I just don't want to be there when it happens."
>
> Woody Allen

A key to effective estate planning is flexibility. The current administration has proposed the elimination of the step-up basis for inherited assets. (Politicians are eternally searching for new sources of tax revenue.) Let's suppose Congress passes the legislation and the step-up is removed. Now what's your strategy for passing assets on to your heirs? Possibly increasing your gifting while you are still alive? It's important to remain flexible in your planning in response to changes in tax law and other regulations. It's yet another reason not to procrastinate implementing your estate plan. Chances are, grandfathered plans and trusts will be exempted from new legislation.

Chapter Thirteen

Real Estate

> "I'm not in the hamburger business. My business is real estate."
> Ray Kroc,
> McDonald's Founder

Aside from stocks, real estate is the best investment to hedge against inflation. There are many ways to secure exposure to real estate as an investment. These include residential, commercial, industrial, raw land, REITs, investment funds and individual properties.

An investment property is one that's not your primary residence, is purchased to generate income and ideally profits from appreciation. It may also provide tax benefits.[296]

Residential Properties

These include single-family or multi-family homes, mobile homes, condos and vacation homes.

Residential real estate typically involves shorter leases than commercial properties, but that can be an advantage when market conditions change. As a landlord, you have greater leverage in terms of increasing rent with a shorter lease. Residential real estate is generally less vulnerable to economic vagaries.[297]

Commercial Real Estate

These are properties used for retail or office space. They are purchased and rented to businesses requiring space to run their companies or buy and sell goods and services. Common commercial properties include restaurants, retail stores, service facilities or offices.[298]

Commercial real estate usually involves longer-term leases, which can represent cash flow stability and help shelter owners from declining rental rates. A rental environment with sort-term rate increases is more common, however, and it may not be possible to raise rates if commercial property is locked into an existing agreement. The COVID-19 pandemic introduced an unprecedented work-from-home culture, one that continued through 2021. Some industries have been affected more than others. Supermarkets, for example, require employees to be at the store whereas many types of office workers are able to function equally well from home. What impact the pandemic will have over the long term remains to be seen.[299]

Profits from commercial real estate can be earned through income the property produces and from appreciation of the property. Most commercial real estate investors hold their properties for a minimum of several years.[300]

Industrial Properties

These typically include buildings used by companies for the manufacturing, warehousing and distribution of their product. The buildings tend to be large; expensive and tenant needs can change rapidly. Obviously, properties need land and buying land can produce healthy returns, albeit over the long haul. Raw land produces no passive income with the exception of farmland. In addition to paying taxes on a property not generating income, there are zoning and environmental issues to consider, as well as access to utilities and other issues.[301]

Industrial property leases tend to be longer term—10 years or more is not uncommon— depending on the nature of the business. Industrial property tenants tend to be more dependable and have lower turnover than commercial or residential tenants.[302]

Land

Vacant property can be a great investment—but without any buildings to lease, it doesn't generate income post-purchase. Your return will only materialize if you develop the land for business or resell it and make a profit off the property appreciation.

Undeveloped property is typically less expensive than developed property and investors get to execute their vision for the property, subject to land use and zoning requirements. Vacant property can be harder to finance and many investors discover they are forced to self-fund. Also, it may take years to develop the property as a result of securing permits and licenses.[303]

Real Estate Investment Trusts (REITs)

REITs are companies that own different types of real estate, usually commercial properties such as hotels, shops, offices or restaurants. Stock exchanges allow investors to buy shares of these real estate companies where they can invest in the properties the companies own without the risk of personally owning the property. REITs are required to return 90% of their income to shareholders every year, which makes their dividends a reliable source of income while simultaneously diversifying their investors' portfolios. Publicly-traded REITs also offer greater liquidity than any other types of real estate investments. Shares can be sold on the stock exchange at any time investors choose to do so.[304]

To qualify as a REIT a company must:

- Invest at least 75% of its total assets in real estate
- Derive at least 75% of its gross income from rents from real property, interest on mortgages financing real property or from sales of real estate
- Pay at least 90% of its income in the form of shareholder dividends each year
- Be an entity that is taxable as a corporation
- Be managed by a board of directors or trustees
- Have a minimum of 100 shareholders
- Have no more than 50% of its shares held by five or fewer individuals[305]

Equity REITs

Equity REITs are the most common type of REIT. These are real estate companies that own leased properties: office buildings, apartment complexes, etc.[306] Selecting individual equities for investment in real estate can be profitable. Our portfolios have had a real estate investment holding in UMH Properties, a public equity REIT headquartered in Freehold NJ, for the past two decades. The company owns and operates a portfolio of 130 manufactured home communities with approximately 24,400 developed homesites.[307] UMH owns land that they lease back to consumers with manufactured homes on them. This data is for informational purposes and not intended to represent a buy recommendation.

Three of the most successful REIT stocks as measured by revenue growth during the first quarter of 2022 include Crown Castle International Corp, Vornado Realty Trust and Reality Income Corp.

- Crown Castle International Corp.: Crown Castle International is a REIT that operates and leases communication infrastructure. Its assets include over 40,000 cell towers and more than 80,000 miles of fiber throughout the U.S. The company reported financial results for Q1 2022 on April 20. Crown Castle's net income surged more than sevenfold on a 17.3% increase in revenue year-over-year (YOY). A strong 5G leasing market and growth in site rental revenue helped fuel the gains.[308]

- Vornado Realty Trust: Vornado Realty Trust is a REIT that owns, develops, and manages retail and office properties. The company's portfolio includes over 26 million feet of property in New York City, San Francisco, and Chicago.[309]

- Realty Income Corp.: Realty Income is a REIT that owns and manages commercial properties across the U.S. and in Europe. The company seeks investments with the goal of delivering dependable monthly dividends. On May 17, Realty income announced its 623rd consecutive common stock monthly dividend, of $0.247 per share. The dividend is payable on June 15 to shareholders of record as of June 1, 2022.[310]

Mortgage REITs

Mortgage REITs (mREITS) provide financing for income-producing real estate. They buy or originate mortgages and mortgage-backed securities and earn income from the interest on these investments.[311]

Unlike equity REITs, mREITs don't own the underlying property. Instead, they own debt securities backed by the property. For example, an mREIT might buy individual residential mortgages from the original lenders and collect the monthly payments from homeowners who may or may not live in the property. Mortgage REITs tend to be riskier than equity REITs but compensate by paying higher dividends.[312]

Non-Traded REITs

These REITs are sold by brokers. While registered with the SEC, they are not traded on an exchange and so are highly illiquid.[313] We tend not to recommend these to our clients because of their elevated expenses and lack of liquidity. In addition, individual investors have little leverage or control as the boards of directors on non-traded REITs rarely side with shareholders.

Real Estate Investment Funds

Real estate investment funds share some similarities with REITs in that they both invest in real estate using pooled capital. There are some differences, however. For one, REITs are corporations required to distribute 90% of their taxable income to shareholders in order to maintain their tax-advantaged status with the IRS. Real estate funds, on the other hand, are not required to comply with those rules. As a result, many funds attempt to generate returns via capital appreciation versus dividend payments.[314]

Some industries are highly correlated with real estate, such as commercial construction companies, homebuilders and home improvement retailers. Some investors chose to invest in the real estate sector by buying shares in companies tied to the real estate sector.[315]

The principal types of real estate investment funds are mutual funds, exchange-traded funds and private equity funds.

Real Estate Mutual Funds are professionally-managed investment vehicles. These entities may invest in a variety of real estate opportunities, including REITs, real estate-related companies, and direct ownership of real estate.

Real Estate Private Equity Funds are actively managed funds available to institutional and accredited investors.[316]

Real Estate Exchange-Traded Funds (ETFs) provide diversified exposure to REITs and the real estate sector, but do not buy individual REITs. Instead, they purchase and own numerous REITs within a single ETF. Niche areas of the market, such as residential REITs or retail REITs, are also available through ETFs.[317]

There are currently 35 ETFs that focus on REITs and real estate equity. Some of the major REIT ETFs include Vanguard, Schwab, Fidelity and XLRE.

- The Vanguard Real Estate ETF (VNQ) is the largest, with $47 billion in net assets and with a portfolio of nearly 170 holdings spanning all manner of properties from warehouses to malls to hospitals.

- Next largest is the Charles Schwab U.S. REIT ETF (SCHH). Its portfolio differs slightly, with a smaller list of about 140 publicly traded real estate stocks though it intentionally screens out mortgage-related REITs that hold financial instruments instead of physical property.

- The Fidelity MSCI Real Estate ETF (FREL) tracks the MSCI USA IMI Real Estate 25/25 Index, which represents the performance of the real estate sector in the U.S. equity market.

- XLRE is a $5 billion fund whose portfolio is limited to just the largest 30 or so names in the space.[318]

- iShares Mortgage Real Estate ETF (REM) is an ETF that eschews the rest of the REIT universe, instead just zeroing in on a group of 30 or so stocks, such as Annaly Capital Management Inc. (NLY) and Starwood Property Trust Inc. (STWD).[319]

In general, REITs can help diversify an investment portfolio, provide some non-correlated assets, and deliver dividends for income and to help offset the effects of inflation.

Benefits

Income Stream. Real estate investments in various forms can generate an income stream through rental payments. This income, also known as dividend yield, is the focus of real estate investment funds. A metric known as "capitalization rate" (cap rate) is used to assess potential income. Commercial real estate can also provide a non-correlated benefit during an economic downturn. The stock market may go down during this period but owners of office buildings and other commercial properties will continue to collect rental income.

Inflation Hedge. Inflation raises the cost of living for everyone. Residential rentals are included in the Consumer Price Index used to measure inflation. Rent increases are tied to inflation so their value rises in response to inflation.

Diversification. The broad range of property types, investment strategies, noncorrelative properties and locations—both domestic and international—allows real estate to serve as an effective diversification tool in an investor's total portfolio.[320]

Real estate is one method of providing ongoing income, an especially important consideration for retirees and those living on a fixed income. It's also a way to increase the total dividend yield of their investment portfolio, in our case, by making sure clients have four to six percent of their investable assets in real estate and investment trusts.

Depending on the type of real estate investment, it may or may not be correlated to the market. In many instances, it's correlated but not exactly correlated to the stock market so we use it as an alternative to reduce equity exposure in the portfolio. If, for example, a portfolio has 50/50 mix of stocks and bonds, we will typically achieve a 5 percent real estate position by investing 10 percent of the equity portion of the portfolio in a REIT or similar vehicle. We thus secure two meaningful benefits: an additional form of diversification outside of US stocks and a nice dividend yield.

Owning Individual Properties

Contrary to what some people believe, we've never regarded someone's primary residence as an investment. We need a roof over our head but that doesn't make our home an investment. I understand people who argue that they can downsize and take the profit from the runup on their home's value. I've seen people do exactly that, particularly as a result of the significant runup in values over the past couple of years, but it usually doesn't work out where the spreads are sufficient to make a meaningful impact. The new home they are downsizing into has inevitably had the same level of price runup as the home they are selling. Housing is more volatile than most people realize, and homeowners that regard their domiciles as an investment face the same risks as people who invest in stocks via real estate investment trusts.

Owning real estate directly is another option for investing in the asset class. In my experience, those who achieve the best results are investors who avoid hiring a management company, are handy with all sorts of tools and don't mind making repairs. They take satisfaction in ripping out a floor or installing a new bathroom. These might be people who built their own home and enjoyed the experience. Perhaps they have a wood shop in their garage. They're most certainly good at handyman repairs and have the financial means to make a substantial deposit on their properties so as to create adequate leverage.

Investors that use real estate for portfolio diversification and have no problem with a long-term approach can be ideal candidates for single family, duplex or triplex residential ownership, possibly even a small apartment building. We always recommend these investors consult their insurance agent before purchasing because in some areas, like Washington, these properties can qualify as commercial real estate, requiring a commercial insurance policy. For a first-time investor, that may be an unsupportable expense. Investors who own multiple residential properties—typically more than ten—that require commercial policies may have difficulty finding an insurer.

As an investor, you have to understand when you buy and manage rentals on your own that the hoped-for returns are contingent upon buying properties at fair market value or ideally, in a down market, and being able to secure a 15- or 30-year amortization mortgage. That's subject to making a substantial down payment and buying during an interest-friendly environment, of course.

Based on historical norms, buyers can reasonably expect to raise rents every two or three years in response to inflation. Another caution is being extremely cautious about who you choose as renters. If you own multiple properties, it's just a matter of time before somebody rips you off, either through non-payment of rent or destruction. You have to be financially prepared for these eventualities and emotionally able to handle the turmoil of somebody ripping a sink out of the wall or spraying your property with their favorite paint color.

Buying individual properties calls for a calm temperament and an understanding of what you are getting into. Successful investors often had parents that owned rental properties or had a lucrative experience investing in some form of real estate. They tend to be better prepared for the occasional renter causing damage that can be both financially and psychologically devastating.

Investment property management requires a lot of effort and time: advertising your space, interviewing potential tenants, running background checks, chasing slow pay tenants, property maintenance and repairs. All this must be conducted while observing your tenant's "right to privacy," a legal standard that prevents you from dropping by unannounced in most states.[321]

My Experience

My wife and I bought our first investment property, a duplex, when I was just 22 years of age. I learned a lot of valuable lessons from that ownership. If I was a young man just starting out today and wanted to get rich, I would do virtually nothing but leverage investments in real estate. I didn't do exactly that but I did try to take advantage of every opportunity that came my way. I came to recognize that if I put 25% down on a property and borrowed 75% from the bank, all I had to do was collect rents and let the corpus of my portfolio rise with inflation. So, I created spreadsheet calculations projecting a four percent expected growth rate.

My experience as a property investor has been alternately exhilarating and heartbreaking, the latter particularly in my younger years when I lost a lot of money learning how to evaluate reliable rental candidates. The learning process cost me a lot of lost weekends and sleepless nights responding to tenant problems. It took its toll on me in those early years but today, it's a growth and income-producing machine generating almost two hundred thousand dollars a year of rental income and profiting from inflation, which is currently nearing double digits while I pay about four percent interest on the mortgage loans.

Whatever happens in the future, I profited in excess of a million dollars last year thanks to rental income and my properties going up in value. The runup in property values is unprecedented in my adult life and doubtless will not continue at its current manic pace, but historically, it's hard to find an asset class that can match that performance. Even at a steady four percent annual growth, my properties produce annual income in exchange for mortgage payments a fraction of that amount.

Leverage is a critical consideration in real estate. Simply put, leverage is the ability to use a lender's money—typically a bank— to buy assets that generate ongoing income for you and appreciate over time. If, for example, you put 20% down on a property, you are said to have 80% leverage. Compare that with equities, where the same kind of leverage is unavailable. Even when a brokerage allows you buy on margin, they often only lend up to 50% of your portfolio balance—and at elevated interest rates. They can also "call" the leveraged stocks you bought on margin (a margin call) if the stocks go down in value, forcing you to absorb a loss.[322]

It's dangerous to be highly leveraged. Individual investors owning residential or commercial real estate are generally considered to be safe at a 40 percent equity position (60 percent leverage). At least, that's the prevailing opinion of the institutional investors I talk to. Investors who buy a multi-family property or small apartment complex for a long-term investment are potentially in a danger zone if they made a minimum down payment. They would be wise to apply as much towards principal as possible—as soon as possible—to reach a 40 percent debt-to-equity position. Until they achieve that level, they really can't feel comfortable, in my opinion.

It's vital to budget your real estate purchases carefully. If you finance with a lower down payment, you'll have to make a larger mortgage payment because of the larger loan. Deteriorating economic conditions, poor tenant choices, prolonged vacancies and other factors can create financial challenges but you will still be responsible for your mortgage payments, so you have to make certain you can keep yourself afloat in any situation.[323]

Pitfalls to avoid include relying on sustained, high levels of appreciation. Many investors assume what has happened in the past will continue. The financial debacle of 2008 should have dispelled that assumption. There are also numerous examples of investors taking advantage of a low interest rate environment or low down payment offer to buy bad properties. Bad decisions like these can be counterbalanced by one thing: outstanding cash flow. If the rental income, less mortgage costs and expenses of your real estate investments, is generating a hefty return every month, the fact that the properties didn't gain much in value this year won't worry you much.[324]

> “Ninety percent of all millionaires become so through owning real estate.”
>
> Andrew Carnegie

CHAPTER FOURTEEN

PUBLIC SERVICE EMPLOYEES

> "If you put nothing away for retirement, I can tell you, to the last penny, how much you will have when you retire: nothing."
> John C. Bogle

Washington State's Public Employees Retirement System (PERS) has three principal retirement plans, designated PERS 1, 2 and 3. These are lifetime retirement pension plans available to public service employees in the State. Employers and employees alike contribute a percentage of income to the plan, with employees contributing a portion of their pretax salary based on a specified rate, such as 6% in the case of PERS 1 participants.

PERS 1 no longer accepts new members. It was replaced by PERS 2. Employees hired after October 1, 1977 were required to join PERS 2 if they wished to participate in the pension plan. While both PERS 1 and 2 are defined benefit plans, Plan 1 is capped at 30 years of service while Plan 2 has a higher minimum retirement age of 65 for an unreduced benefit and a five-year final average salary period instead of two years in Plan 1.[325]

PERS Plan 3, effective March 1, 2002, is a hybrid plan containing two parts: a pension account and an investment account. Plan 2 members were given the option of staying in Plan 2 or transferring to Plan 3, where the public service employer contributes to the pension and the employee contributes to the investment account.

Washington State law enforcement officers and firefighters have a similar retirement system (LEOFF Plan2). Teachers in the State have the TRS (Teachers' Retirement System) plan, school employees other than teachers have the SERS (School Employees' Retirement System), public safety employees have PSERS (Public Safety Employees' Retirement System). In all, there were 58 public pension systems in Washington as of 2020, according to the U.S. Census Bureau.[326]

An employee's total pension benefit is based on his or her years of service (service credit) and income, defined as the employee's average final compensation (AFC)—the average of the employee's 24 consecutive highest earning months during their career. Monthly benefits for retired employees are calculated using a formula, which is different for the various systems:

For PERS, TRS, SERS 2:
2% x service credit years x AFC = monthly benefit.

For PERS, TRS, SERS 3:
1% x service credit years x AFC = monthly benefit.

As an example, an employee in system 2 who retires at age 65 with 35 years of service credit and a monthly AFC of $7,500 would be entitled to a monthly benefit of $5,250.

(2% x 35 x $7,500 = $5,250)

An employee in system 3 who retires at age 65 with 35 years of service credit and a monthly AFC of $7,500 would be entitled to a monthly benefit of $2,625.

(1% x 35 x $7,500 = $2,625)

There are also separate but comparable retirement plans for other public service workers. The Federal Employees Retirement System (FERS), founded in 1986, provides federal workers with benefits from three different sources: a Basic Benefit Plan, Social Security and the Thrift Savings Plan (TSP). Two of the three parts of FERS (Social Security and the TSP) can go with an employee that leaves the Federal Government before retirement. The cost of the Basic Benefits and Social Security parts of FERS are withheld from employee pay as payroll deductions. The employee's federal agency contributes, similar to the Washington State employers. After retirement, federal employees receive monthly annuity payments for life.[327]

While the pension plan environment for public sector employees shares some of the same elements as its private sector counterpart, there are discrepancies that call for a separate discussion. My home state of Washington is illustrative of the differences and I will use it as an example throughout the chapter. While not representative of every state, my experience working with people moving into Washington from other states has led me to conclude the pension components are typically comparable. Importantly, however, the cost-of-living adjustments (COLA) are subject to caps in some states.

PERS Plan 2

Created in 1977, PERS Plan 2 is a 401a defined benefit plan that guarantees a monthly benefit for life based on earned service credit and compensation while a member of the plan.

A 401a plan is employer-sponsored, generally used by government and nonprofit organizations, where both the employer and employee can contribute. Employees can withdraw funds from the plan in a lump-sum payment or an annuity, or use a rollover to move funds to a different qualified retirement plan, such as a 401k or IRA.[328]

Monthly benefits for PERS 2 retired employees are calculated using the same formula as the original PERS 1: *2% x service credit years x AFC = monthly benefit.*

As with PERS 1, both employer and employee contribute to the plan. Employees are required to contribute a percentage of their wages; employer contributions are also based on a percentage of employee wages. These are not matching funds and cannot be withdrawn if the employee leaves public service. Vesting is five years. (Vesting in this case means that employees that leave the job in five years or less lose all pension benefits while employees who leave after five years receive 100% of promised benefits.) Employees that became a member of PERS Plan 2 prior to the origination of Plan 3 in 2002 have an opportunity each January to transfer to Plan 3.

PERS Plan 3

As mentioned previously, PERS Plan 3 is a hybrid plan containing a pension account and an investment account. The public service employer contributes to the pension and the employee contributes to the investment account.

The portion funded by the employer is invested by the Washington State Investment Board (WSIB). The pension is guaranteed and is not dependent on investment performance. The employee's contribution—ranging from 5% to 15%—is directed to investments chosen from a range of offerings managed by the WSIB. These include a professionally managed target date fund, self-directed investments or a Total Allocation Portfolio (TAP) fund.[329]

The money in an employee's Plan 3 investment account can be rolled into an IRA at retirement to supplement income. Many municipalities and states allow employees to purchase additional pension credits with the investment account money, something akin to buying more pension income.

An employee's service credit is represented by the number of years spent working in public service, with one service credit awarded for each calendar month in which the employee is compensated for at least 70 hours of work.[330] A retiring public service employee may purchase up to an additional 60 months of service credits. The cost is based on the annuity factor for the employee's age and plan. The monthly increase in benefit is based on the same formula used to calculate the retirement benefit.[331]

Plan 3 may be better for younger employees because where most 401a plans vest in 5 or 10 years, employees with 15 years or more before retirement have additional time to accumulate retirement savings in their Plan 3 investment account, which has a market return component and, if assuming the professionally managed option by WSIB (versus self-directed) is chosen, the portfolio will be nicely balanced and diversified, containing some alternative investments, such as real estate and private equity, in addition to traditional stock and bond components. A caveat: if the employee wishes to have short-term access to the funds, such as a 90-day demand, there could be a liquidity issue and a target date fund might be a better option.

Members in either 401a plan (Plan 2 or Plan 3) can add a supplemental retirement savings account, such as Washington's Deferred Compensation Program (DCP) to increase their overall retirement savings. The DCP is a tax-deferred savings program (IRC Section 457) similar to a 403b plan (explained in the next section). DCP offers a variety of professionally managed investment options, including target date funds. The minimum monthly contribution limit is $30 or 1% of earnings. The maximum annual contribution is $20,500.[332]

The Washington State Department of Retirement Systems website offers an easily-understood graphic explanation of the differences between Plan 2 and Plan 3 at: https://www.drs.wa.gov/choice/compare/

There's one Washington State public service pension plan that's different from the other sectors: the Washington State Patrol Retirement System (WSPRS). In this system, troopers become vested and earn the right to a future monthly benefit after five years of service. They can begin receiving that benefit once they turn 55 or once they have 25 years of service completed. The employer contribution rate is a lofty 17.84% for 2021.[333]

The WSPRS is exempt from Social Security and the members enjoy outsized pensions typically ranging from $7,000 to $12,000 monthly of inflation-adjusted income. The pension fund is well funded and the Governor's office has been trying, without success, for years to get the WSPRS pension fund amalgamated into the state's other public service pension funds to help stabilize the shortfall. Of course, the troopers have fought to prevent that change and done so successfully for many years.

Understanding the Different Pension Plan Designations

401a and 401k plans have many similarities. Both are employer-sponsored retirement plans but 401k sponsors are usually private companies while 401a sponsors are generally public sector employers, nonprofits and educational institutions. Sponsors of 401a plans typically enjoy greater control in terms of plan structure and eligibility requirements. They are required to contribute to 401a plans for employees, even if they decide to make it optional for employees to make contributions.[334]

While a 401k allows employees to decide how much to contribute, a 401a can have mandatory or voluntary employee contributions which are deducted from each paycheck, just like 401k contributions. Employers usually decide whether 401a contributions are pre-tax or post-tax, and they also establish the vesting schedule for employer-matched funds, just as they do with 401k's.

In addition, employers typically choose the investment options available to employees with both 401a and 401k plans. Employees who use a 401a commonly have fewer investment options to choose from than 401k participants, but since a 401a is often designed specifically for a select group of employees, a few choices may be adequate.[335]

The previously-mentioned 403b is a retirement plan for certain employees of public schools, employees of certain tax-exempt organizations and certain ministers. A 403b plan allows employees to contribute some of their salary to the plan. The employer may also contribute to the plan and match employee contributions up to a certain amount. The contribution limit for 403b plans and 401k plans is the same but a 403b plan may also include a special catch-up contribution for long-term employees with at least 15 years of service, an increase of up to $3,000 per year with a lifetime limit of $15,000. This makes it possible to save more in a 403b than a 401k near the end of an employee's work years.[336]

Both 401k and 403b are tax-advantaged, defined-contribution vehicles. The primary difference between the two is the type of employer sponsoring the plans. 401k plans are offered by private, for-profit companies whereas 403b plans are only available to nonprofit organizations and government employers.[337]

457 plans are tax-advantaged, deferred-compensation plans sponsored by state and local governments and some nonprofit employers. Eligible employees can make pre-tax contributions. 457's are non-qualified plans, meaning they are not subject to ERISA laws, so withdrawals before age 59½ aren't subject to the 10% penalty tax imposed on most early 401k withdrawals. Some large government employers offer both 457 and 401k plans.[338]

Unlike 401k plans, however, employer matching contributions are extremely rare with a 457, which is viewed as a supplemental savings plan for employees, an option for accumulating additional retirement savings. If an employer does offer a matching 457 contribution, that amount will count towards the employee's annual contribution limit and be subject to FICA tax.[339]

Employees switching from for-profit companies to public sector positions may be able to roll over their IRA, 401k or other retirement account into their new employer's 403b account to maintain the simplicity of managing only one retirement account. This is called an incoming rollover and is dependent upon whether it's allowed by the new employer's plan.[340]

Conversely, employees can roll their 403b into a 401k if their new employer offers a 401k. Self-employed people can also roll a 403b plan into a solo or independent 401k. Those who work for employers not offering a 401k are unable to roll their 403b plan into any type of 401k plan.[341] Rollovers from a 403b to a traditional IRA are tax-free.

Rollovers into a Roth IRA are taxable since the money is being transferred to an after-tax account.[342]

Nonprofit organizations primarily used 403b plans in the past and many still do, but over time the rules have changed and private nonprofits often choose 401k plans as many 403b plans are now subject to the same regulations. The advantage of a 401k is that there are more providers and options to choose from and greater competition tends to stabilize pricing. In addition, a 401k is generally easier for employees to understand and use.

PERS and Social Security

PERS benefits are not affected by Social Security. However, an employee's Social Security benefits may be diminished by a PERS pension benefit. The Government Pension Offset (GPO) and the Windfall Elimination Provision (WEP) are two Federal government regulations that may reduce a Social Security benefit.

With certain exceptions, the GPO offset reduces Social Security spouse, widow, or widower benefits by two-thirds of the amount of the employee's pension. The GPO affects public sector employees that rely on a state-run pension instead of Social Security, that is, people who have a pension from employment that did not contribute to Social Security. The GPO prevents spouses, ex-spouses and survivors from receiving a higher benefit than they would have received if they were totally reliant on their spouse's Social Security benefit.[343]

The WEP is a formula used to adjust Social Security worker benefits for people who receive "non-covered pensions" and qualify for Social Security benefits based on other Social Security–covered earnings. A non-covered pension is one paid by an employer that does not withhold Social Security taxes from the employee's salary, such as state and local governments. The WEP does not affect survivor benefits.[344]

Inflation and Pensions

Defined-pension plans, like public sector 401a plans, pledge to participating employees that they will receive a specified income benefit in retirement. That income is not subject to change, regardless of how long an employee lives, nor is it affected by market movements. However, unlike Social Security benefits that are adjusted for inflation, the benefit from a defined-benefit plan does not protect retirees against the loss of purchasing power due to inflation. Government pensions have a COLA adjustment whereas private businesses do not.

The economy has seen several periods during which inflation has spiraled. Retirees on a fixed-income pension benefit find themselves defenseless against the rising costs of everyday needs. While the annual inflation rate in the United States has averaged 3.27 percent over the last 110 years, there have been times, such as the extended period from 1965 through 1982, when rampant inflation led economists to rethink the policies of the Fed.[345] Graphic 14.1 illustrates this period.

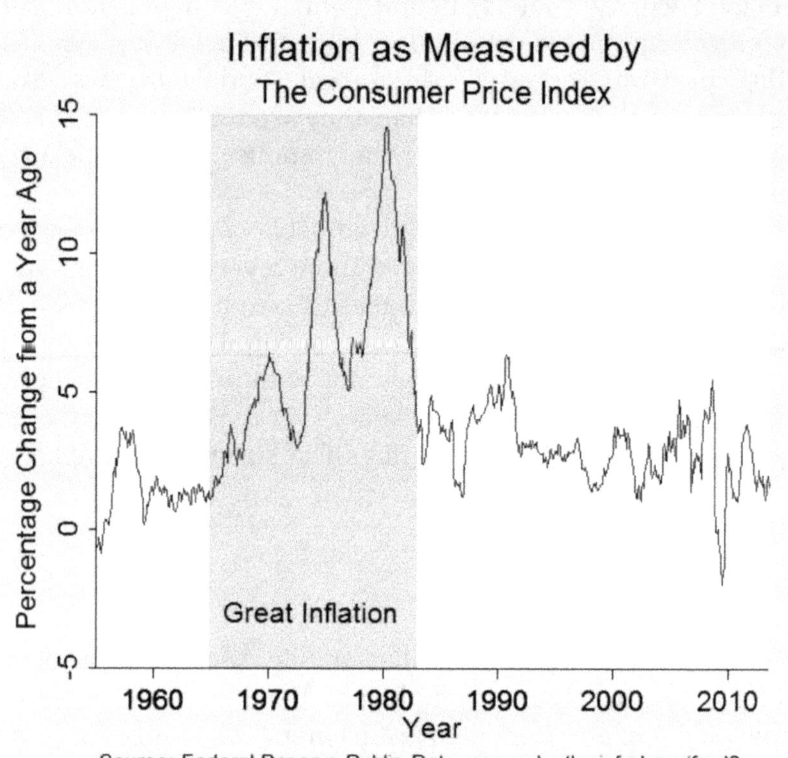

(Graphic 14.1 Inflationary History)

In 1964, inflation measured a little more than 1 percent per year. It had been in this vicinity over the preceding six years. Inflation began ratcheting upward in the mid-1960s and reached more than 14 percent in 1980. It eventually declined to average only 3.5 percent in the latter half of the 1980s.[346] The U.S. inflation rate for 2022 was 6.5% and YTD 2023 is 6%.

During the 12-month period from May 2021 through May 2022, inflation in the U.S. (expressed as the Consumer Price Index) increased 8.6%, the largest 12-month increase since 1981.[347]

You may recall the "Rule of 72" that is usually applied to investment returns. Divide 72 by the annual interest rate to determine the amount of years it takes for an investment to double. The rule also can be applied to inflation, only in reverse. The current inflation rate of 8.6% eviscerates purchasing power by 50% in roughly nine years. For someone on a fixed-income pension, such as a PERS plan 2 living an additional 30 years after retiring, the dire financial implications of this level of inflation are obvious.

This is why PERS Plan 3, which includes an investment account, can be so much more beneficial to public service employees in retirement, particularly if they have an extended period in which to take advantage of market returns, providing a robust defense against inflation.

Washington State has a checkered history when it comes to protecting public service worker pensions from the ravages of inflation. Prior to the introduction of the current SERS Plans in 1977, public sector employees in the state received a pension titled PERS 1, also known as TRS 1 for public school teachers and other school employees, such as custodians, classroom assistants, bus drivers and cooks.

A 2019 opinion piece in crosscut.com[348] details the "raw deal" participants were getting after the State Legislature eliminated Plan 1 COLA in 2011:

> *"For the first 25 years, just as with the other state plans, Plan 1 retirees received increases—most of which were for 3%. However, as part of budget saving during the Great Recession, the Legislature eliminated the Plan 1 COLA in 2011. Until last year (2018), Plan 1 members had not received any adjustment to their pensions since 2010.*
>
> *Without a COLA, Plan 1 retirees have no way to keep up with skyrocketing health care costs, groceries and*

> *basic living expenses. The state actuary found that someone who retired in 1980 has lost over 30% of their pension's purchasing power. The 2018 Legislature granted a 1.5% one-time increase."*

Ultimately, the Plan 1 participants won a 3% COLA increase. Washington Gov. Jay Inslee signed the new law, S.B. 5676, on March 11, 2022.[349]

People go to work in the public sector primarily for financial security. If their pension is exposed to inflationary risk as a result of being capped, their main reason for going into public service work is eradicated.

Washington's 10-year costs of the 2018 and 2020 changes to PERS 1 and TRS 1 were $305 million and $381 million respectively, costs that required increased contributions for state and local government employers. Given Washington's pensions still use a 7.5 percent investment return assumption that's above the 7% national median investment return rate assumption, their cost assumptions may well be understated. Currently, these plans sit at approximately 65 percent funded, a conspicuous departure from the rest of the state's well-funded pension plans.[350]

Benefit Options

It's critical for retiring public service workers to make wise choices regarding their pension. For many, purchasing additional pension credits to increase their monthly income benefit can indeed be a wise choice.

Employees should have the Department of Retirement Services run a couple of different benefit option calculations one year, six months and three months prior to retirement to help ensure they don't make an irreversible mistake. Upon retirement, employees must select from several benefit options: single life, joint and 100% survivor, two-thirds survivor or 50% survivor. On July 1 of every year following an employee's first full year of retirement, the monthly benefit is adjusted to a maximum of 3% per year, as determined by the CPI.[351]

Chapter Three of this book ("Pensions") provides a detailed explanation of the pros and cons of each pension benefit option.

The various public sectors (government, teachers, law enforcement, firefighters, judges, etc.) each have their own retirement system and plan title acronym. While separate pools of money, the various sectors are all managed the same way. Graphic 14.2[352] depicts the various Washington State retirement systems and their acronyms for the various members of the public services sector.

The current employer contribution rate for PERS Plans 2 and 3 is 10.25%. Member contribution is 6.36%. The contribution rates for other sector plans are similar but do vary somewhat. The Pension Funding Council adopts contribution rates and periodically adjusts them to reflect the overall cost of the plan. The Legislature has the final decision on contribution rates.[353]

Plan 3, which includes an investment account, is becoming an increasingly popular plan for state and local governments nationally, largely because legislatures have come to realize that their defined benefit pensions are unlikely to keep up with inflation, particularly for seniors who live into their eighth or ninth decade. The market-based return of a plan 3 type pension gives these retirees a better chance of maintaining their purchasing power as well.

Washington Retirement Systems

Plan Title	Eligible Employees
Public Employees' Retirement System (PERS)	– State or local government employees with at least 70 hours of work p month for at least five months of each yea
Teachers' Retirement System (TRS)	– Teachers compensated for at least 70 hours of work per month for at least five months from September to August
School Employees' Retirement System (SERS)	– Employees of Washington state public school districts or Educational Service Districts (ESD) compensated for at least 70 hours of work per month for at least five months of each year
Law Enforcement Officers' and Firefighters' Retirement System (LEOFF)	– Full-time law-enforcement officers (police chiefs, sheriffs, city police officers, etc.) and full-time firefighters (volunteers or part-time employee are excluded)
Washington State Patrol Retirement System (WSPRS)	– Full-time Washington State Patrol officers compensated for at least 7 hours per month for at least five months of each year
Public Safety Employees' Retirement System (PSERS)	– Employees of state agencies like the Department of Corrections, Gambling Commission, Department of Natural Resources or Liquor Control Board. Visit website for full criteria.
Judicial Retirement System (JRS)	– Judges elected or appointed to Superior Court, the Court of Appeals the Supreme Court of Washington

(Graphic 14.2: WA Retirement Systems)

Taking Personal Responsibility

As I said before, many people enter the public service sector as a means of providing long-term financial security. I certainly would not question their motives. It's a personal decision and one I believe most people make after thoughtful consideration of the private sector alternative. Many people in the public sector have chosen to remain in a Plan 2 here in Washington, perhaps not fully understanding the potential for purchasing power erosion in a fixed-income retirement benefit. In my experience, virtually everyone who opts for this Plan eventually comes to the realization that they are—and will be—beholden to the ability of the state to maintain their benefits and pay claims. Like most other states in the Union, there are many ways that assumption could go badly.

Here in Washington, the economy and the ability of the state to pay pension obligations is contingent upon a relatively small group of large employers, including Microsoft, Amazon, Starbucks and Costco Wholesale. Others have left and the outlook for public pensions could look quite different in a few years. The COLA for some pensions has been capped in the past and it could happen again. If the inflation adjuster is eliminated, a lot of retirees could sink into financial difficulty.

My advice to public service employee clients has always been to assume nothing and take personal responsibility to start putting some of their own saving together as a hedge against the unknown. There are a lot of states that are facing an imbalance in their pension obligations. The past underfunding of pension plans has shifted costs forward to current and future generations. Eventually, someone has to pay but only three groups can be tapped: existing employees or retirees, newer employees or taxpayers. Many states are attempting to limit the hit on taxpayers and older current employees, leaving newer and younger employees with the burden of covering costs for which they were not responsible. A lower assumed interest rate would mean lower burdens on younger employees but would put current tax- payers more on the hook to cover the shortfalls.[354]

As an advisor, I tell clients I think it's wise not to just sit back and hope for the best.

> "I would not be opposed to devising a new system of pensions, in which one part was based on collective provision, but which also gave incentives for people to take out an additional, personal plan."
>
> Jacques Delors
> French Economist

CHAPTER FIFTEEN

STOCK OPTIONS, WARRANTS AND RSUS

Stock warrants and options are securities that have both similarities and differences. Both give recipients the right, but not the obligation, to buy a security at an agreed upon price within a given timeframe.

Stock options are issued to key employees, such as executives, as part of their compensation package and/or as an incentive to remain with the firm, assuming the stock price increases over time. Options may also be issued to consultants or other service providers. Warrants, on the other hand, are typically issued as incentives to outside parties, such as investors and banks, as well as in other financial transactions, but some companies still use warrants as part of employee compensation packages.[355]

Both stock options and warrants may be used by companies to motivate and reward their employees. A corporation can get a tax deduction for letting employees become owners by purchasing stock options or warrants. In either case, at various times, employees get taxed on the value of the stock.[356]

Stock Options

Companies grant stock options as compensation to employees, contractors, consultants and investors. Options are contracts that give the recipient the right to buy or exercise a specific number of shares of the company stock at a preset price—the grant price. The number of options an employee receives is usually based on his or her position, seniority and the firm's perception of that individual's skills and contributions.

Options typically have a vesting period, that is, the amount of time that must pass with the recipients remaining employed by the issuing company before they may exercise their options. For example, someone joining a company may receive 10,000 stock options as part of their employment contract. Their options begin to "vest" on day one of their employment. Vesting refers to the date when recipients can actually exercise (buy) the underlying stock. In most cases, the vesting is staggered, that is, recipients are allowed to exercise a portion of their options at various times. So new employees receiving 10,000 options may have one quarter of their options vest each year for four years, or one quarter after the first year, followed by an equal monthly amount over the next three years.[357]

The obvious benefit of owning stock options is that if the company does well, the exercise price—also known as the strike price—of the stock will be lower than its fair market value by the time the options vest. The employee can then exercise their vested options, buy their company stock for less than market price, and sell at the higher fair market value. Conversely, if the company stock does not rise in value above the strike price, the options can expire as worthless.[358]

For public companies, the FMV is public and determined by the market. In private companies, the FMV is the current value of one share of a private company's common stock. FMV is determined by independent third-party appraisers. It represents what the stock would be worth on the open market. The FMV is determined by a 409a Valuation which is required by law to be updated every 12 months or any time a company closes a funding round. It is calculated either by the company internally or by an independent firm.[359]

The advantage to companies for issuing stock options, aside from motivating employees to remain with the firm, is that it allows the firm to defer a portion of employees' compensation. Issuing options when the price of the stock is lower (in anticipation of it rising in conjunction with the firm's growth and future success) is a cost advantage to the firm, as opposed to issuing options after the stock price has risen. This is due to the value of the stock options being tied to the stock price.[360]

Stock Warrants

Stock warrants are contracts between a company and an individual, whether employee, investor or outside resource. Warrants give individuals the right to trade that company's shares at a certain (strike) price on or before the expiration date.

Stock warrants are alternative investments and there are several types. A call warrant gives the holder the right to buy the stock for the strike price while a sell warrant gives the holder the right to sell the shares for that price. There is no obligation for holders to exercise these rights; they simply have the right to do so.

The stock warrant is good up until its expiration date after which the holder can no longer use it. Up until the expiration date, the holder can exercise the right to buy or sell the shares at any time. Holders of "European-style" stock warrants can only exercise their rights on a specified day.[361]

While stock options are compensatory, stock warrants are often issued by companies to raise capital on the open market. A firm may offer stock warrants to new employees as a benefit of employment or as part of a retention program for existing employees. Companies commonly use the European-style stock warrant when hiring new employees as the recipients cannot exercise for several years, creating incentive to stay long enough to capitalize on the benefit. Some companies issue warrants to make purchases of bonds or preferred shares more attractive. At other times companies issue warrants to fund acquisitions.[362]

Another difference between stock warrants and stock options is that the company issues stock warrants, while traders on the secondary market issue stock options. Stock warrants commonly last between five and fifteen years and better serve as long-term investments. Stock options tend to last for a much shorter period—a few months or years—have more restrictions, and are better as short-term investments.

Stock options have less flexibility than warrants. Options have a limited number of shares issued whereas warrants cover an unlimited number of shares. The two also differ in their tax treatment. Unlike options, warrants do not offer preferential tax treatments. Exercising stock warrants results in taxable income, essentially the difference between the strike price and the share price, minus the cost basis.[363]

Their exercise prices are another difference. While options are priced at fair market value (FMV) at the time of issue, the company can issue warrants at a price lower—or much lower—than fair market value. The reason for this might be to spur investment, attract funding—or more advantageous loan terms—or as inducement for third party participants, such as service providers or advisors.[364]

There are factors that influence the value of an option or warrant, such as the underlying stock price. Other factors are the exercise price, time until expiration, volatility of the underlying security and value as compared to interest available from a risk-free investment, such as a Treasury.[365]

For public companies, the FMV is public and determined by the market. In private companies, the FMV is the current value of one share of a private company's common stock. FMV is determined by independent third-party appraisers. It represents what the stock would be worth on the open market. The FMV is determined by a 409a Valuation which is required by law to be updated every 12 months or any time a company closes a funding round. It is calculated either by the company internally or by an independent firm.[366]

While stock warrants are less common in the US than other countries, such as China, they have gained popularity in recent times with the emergence of special purpose acquisition companies (SPACs). Warrants give investors the right to buy or sell stock at some point in the future, nothing more. Investors buy warrants when they anticipate the value of a stock will rise above the set price within the time the warrant can be exercised. When that occurs, investors exercise their warrants (below market price) and pocket the gain. If the underlying stock does not appreciate, investors lose the money invested in buying the warrant.[367]

Restricted Stock Units

Restricted Stock Units (RSUs), like stock options, provide employees with exposure to the company's stock, but RSUs work differently.

An RSU is a share of stock that employees can earn through a vesting plan and distribution schedule over time. Employers typically grant RSUs to employees based on certain conditions, such as length of employment or performance objectives. Once vesting requirements are met, employees receive their RSUs and own them unconditionally, just like any other shareholder. That is, there is no need for employees to exercise their right to purchase the stock as with an option. After RSUs are done vesting, they are given a fair market value and are considered income. Some of the shares are generally withheld for income tax purposes while the rest are given to the employee who can then sell them. Some plans defer receipt of shares to a later date or allow employees to defer receipt voluntarily. In either case, once employees own the shares, they are unrestricted.[368]

Unlike stock options, which can lose virtually all their value due to a sinking stock price, RSUs almost always retain some value, even if the stock price drops precipitously. RSUs are taxed when the employee receives the shares and at the market value of the shares at vesting.[369]

Exercising Options

There are some things to consider before exercising stock options. Assuming the options have value (the strike price is lower than the market price of your shares trading on the exchange, known as "in the money") you want to do so at the optimum time, given your individual circumstances.

If you think your company will do well in the future, holding on to your options may be a good move, assuming you stay with the company. If your company's share price rises, your options' worth will continue to grow while putting off any tax consequences. If you plan to retire or leave the firm, be aware of the company's post-termination exercise period, which refers to the period after the end of your service with the company during which an option must be exercised before it expires.

Whether your employer is publicly traded or privately owned also matters. Shares of private companies aren't traded on the stock exchange so exercising those options requires employees to pay to fund the purchase, as opposed to being able to sell shares of a public-traded company and cover your cost. Stock options from private companies are less liquid, since they are not traded on an exchange. Employees holding options who hope to cash out when the firm undergoes an initial public offering (IPO) run the risk of seeing the value of their options dramatically reduced if the IPO is undersubscribed or simply flops.[370]

If you don't need the added income from exercising your options and selling the shares (and not compelled to do so as a result of their expiration), you may want to delay doing so.

The opportunity for the options to increase in value as a result of the company's future performance may allow you to do some critical tax planning as well.

CHAPTER SIXTEEN

DIVIDEND STOCKS

> "Do you know the only thing that gives me pleasure? It's to see my dividends coming in."
> John D. Rockefeller

Dividends, in essence, are a bonus paid to shareholders for their equity investment in a company. Most dividends are funded by a company's net profits and paid as an alternative to retaining the profits and reinvesting them in product development or other business interests aimed at growing the firm and its profitability.[371]

When companies have money on their balance sheet, they have several options: they can use it to expand operations, on capital improvements, give it to shareholders in the form of a dividend, or buy back their shares.

Companies that pay dividends tend to be profitable, stable enterprises. Many believe paying a dividend will make their stock more attractive to investors. For shareholders, dividends are a way to participate in the growth of a business, aside from stock price appreciation.[372]

Dividends can be paid as either stock or cash. Most distributions are in the form of cash.

A stock dividend—also known as a stock split—is just what it sounds like: a distribution of additional shares of a company's stock to shareholders as opposed to a cash distribution. Companies have various reasons for choosing stock over cash. There may not be sufficient cash on hand, or the firm may wish to lower the per-share price to prompt more trading and increase liquidity.[373]

Dividend Aristocrats

Companies are deemed dividend aristocrats once they have increased annual dividend payments 25 consecutive years. With the pedigree of unblemished long-term stability, dividend aristocrats are the thoroughbreds of income investing. They are all S&P 500 large-cap stocks with a minimum market capitalization of $13 billion. As of 2023, there are 64 dividend aristocrats.

To remain a dividend aristocrat, a company must raise its dividend payment at least once during the year. Should a company skip a dividend increase, it falls off the list and must wait another 25 years to get back on, becoming the ultimate expression of a long-term investment.[374]

An alternative to buying individual dividend aristocrat stocks is exchange-traded funds (ETF) that contain dividend-raising stocks. ProShares S&P 500 Dividend Aristocrats ETF is the only ETF that strictly tracks the 64 dividend aristocrats.[375]

Dividend Investing Pro/Con

As with any investment, there are advantages and disadvantages to dividend-paying stocks as opposed to stocks that don't pay dividends. Companies that regularly pay dividends—like the dividend aristocrats—are large, stable organizations unlikely to be forced out of business. Their shares tend to do better in down markets than non-dividend-paying stocks and typically endure less volatility. On the downside, omitting non-dividend stocks from one's portfolio could result in missing out on potentially high returns on investments in industries that typically don't pay dividends, preferring to reinvest earnings in research and development of new products.[376]

Let's look more deeply into the pros and cons of dividend investing.

Dividend Benefits

> "A stock dividend is something tangible — it's not an earnings projection; it's something solid, in hand. A stock dividend is a true return on the investment. Everything else is hope and speculation."
>
> Richard Russell

A benefit of investing in companies that pay dividends is that it can provide a buffer from some of the vagaries of investing in equities. The reliability of dividend payments allows investors to pursue growth in a different way than the traditional stock market, where prices fluctuate and growth can be unpredictable.[377]

Dividends tend to be less risky than non-dividend stocks, are less likey to experience wild price swings and retain their value better during economic turmoil or market volatility. Although dividend stocks do not have as much potential for price gains as growth stocks, they do have the potential for value appreciation.[378] Dividend stocks can be an ideal investment for buy and hold investors.

Without reinvesting dividends, a $10,000 investment in the S&P 500 in 1960 would have been worth over $795,800 at the end of 2021. If dividends were reinvested, that $10,000 investment would be worth just under $4.95 million.[379]

Disadvantages

> **"It is an axiom of investment that securities should be purchased because the buyer believes in their soundness, and not because he needs a certain income."**
> Benjamin Graham

Investing in dividend stocks has potential drawbacks. For one, the strategy limits investment returns. Even the most consistent, highest yielding stocks don't generate more than 10% annual returns. While investing in growth stocks has the potential for large, short-term losses, the cap on gains is much higher. A portfolio of dividend stocks cannot match the return potential on growth stocks over an extended period. Even dividend aristocrats cannot provide the total return potential of growth investing.[380]

While most investors consider dividend stocks more conservative than non-dividend investments, with less exposure to volatility and bear market losses than regular stocks, that's not always the case. There have been a few dividend disasters throughout the years. Since dividends are not guaranteed, if a company is experiencing problems, they often reduce or even completely suspend dividends. Here are two major dividend players that imploded in recent years.

Barnes & Noble (BKS), the largest book retailer in the U.S., had been paying a 15-cent quarterly dividend for three years when, in 2008, the firm boosted its dividend to 25 cents, a handsome 5% yield. The company then suspended its dividend in 2011 in order to have money to invest in digital strategies so it could better compete with new industry leader Amazon. BKS stock plunged almost 70% in the two months following its dividend suspension.

Seattle-based Washington Mutual, or WaMu, was the largest savings and loan association in the U.S. The bank made its fortune providing subprime loans to lower- and middle-class consumers considered too risky to secure financing from other banks.

WaMu's dividend in 2007 was 56 cents, a 5% yield. But in December of that year, facing the housing market implosion, and the destruction of its subprime mortgages, the bank slashed its dividend to 15 cents. A year later, the company cut its dividend again to one penny. In September, 2008, WaMu declared bankruptcy, and JP Morgan acquired what was left of the company's operations.[381]

Those investing exclusively in dividend stocks sacrifice diversification and do not necessarily secure reliable income. Dividend policies can change, especially in uncertain times, as the BKS and WaMu examples illustrate. Many dividend payers cut their payments during the pandemic, when dividends from each dollar invested in U.S. markets decreased by 22% in 2020 compared to the same period in 2019.[382]

Then too, the number of firms paying dividends has steadily declined. In 1927, 68% of U.S. companies were paying dividends. By 2021, that number had shrunk to 38%.

Ex-Dividend Date

Ex-dividend refers to a stock that trades without the value of the next dividend payment. A stock is ex-dividend if it trades on or after the ex-dividend date. When a company declares a dividend, it sets a record date when shareholders must be registered on the company's books in order to receive the dividend. The ex-dividend date for stocks is usually set one business day before the record date. Investors that purchase a stock on its ex-dividend date or after do not receive the next dividend payment; the seller gets the dividend.[383]

Taxes

Taxes on dividends vary depending on the type of account and the investor's tax bracket. A dividend's tax rate is based on whether the stock is qualified or not. A qualified dividend is one that meets the criteria for capital gains versus ordinary income taxation. The requirement is for the investor to have held the stock for at least 60 days during the 121 days before the ex-dividend date. For preferred stock, the investor must have held the stock for at least 90 days during the 181 days starting 90 days before the ex-dividend date.[384]

The long-term capital gains tax rate for qualified dividends is either 0%, 15% or 20%, depending on the investor's income. Those earning less than $79,999 per year pay 0%. Those earning between $80,000 and $441,449 pay 15%. Anyone earning more than $441,500 annually pays 20% tax on qualifying dividends. Unqualified dividends are taxed at the short-term capital gains tax rate, which is the same as the tax rate on regular income. The current rates range from 10% to 37%, depending on the investor's income level.[385]

Share Buybacks

Companies that find themselves in the enviable position of having excess cash have the option of distributing it to shareholders in the form of cash payments or a stock buyback.

In a stock buyback, a company purchases shares of stock on the secondary market from investors that wish to sell, although shareholders are not obligated to sell their stock back to the company.[386]

Companies buy back shares of stock to reduce the number of shares outstanding so that each share represents a higher percentage of future company earnings.[387] Once the shares are repurchased, they are discontinued or held internally as treasury shares. Cancelling reduces the number of outstanding shares outstanding, which can have positive ramifications for the company. For example, earnings per share (EPS) are calculated by dividing a company's net profit by the number of shares outstanding. By reducing the number of shares outstanding, the company gains a higher EPS, which many investors regard as an important performance measure. The company's price-to-earnings ratio (P/E ratio), often used as a valuation factor by analysts, may also benefit.[388]

> "I don't like stock buybacks. I think if a company has the money to buy their stock back, then they should take that and increase the dividends. Send it back to the stockholder. Let them invest their money again from the dividends."
>
> T. Boone Pickens

Buybacks affect valuation in two ways. The mere fact that a company is buying back its own stock may be indicative of its confidence in the future. Then too, when buybacks are financed by a debt issue, the company decreases its reliance on equity. Buybacks can significantly change a company's capital structure, increasing its reliance on debt and decreasing its reliance on equity. On the other side of the coin, many analysts do not believe buybacks create value by increasing EPS since the company has spent money (or incurred debt) to purchase the shares, so valuations are automatically modified to reflect both the cash and share reductions.[389]

Corporate executives naturally want to see upward movement in the price of company shares. Aside from their fiduciary duty to increase shareholder value, a portion of their compensation is likely in stock. A share repurchase tends to portray management's belief that the price of the stock will appreciate. Common sense tells us that companies would not want to acquire more of their stock unless they expect the price of that stock to rise.[390]

> "When you are told that all repurchases are harmful to shareholders or to the country, or particularly beneficial to CEOs, you are listening to either an economic illiterate or a silver-tongued demagogue—characters that are not mutually exclusive."
>
> Warren Buffett

Advantages for companies and their shareholders aside, long-term use of stock buybacks have potential drawbacks. Buyback stock prices are almost always considerably higher than their original issue. This price gap means that each share repurchased requires more money than was originally collected when the stock was issued. As a result, buybacks can exert downward pressure on book value per share as well as increase the potential for default. If buybacks force a company into negative retained earnings, the choice to declare cash dividends disappears.[391]

> "In most cases the favorable price performance will be accompanied by a well-defined improvement in the average earnings, in the dividend, and in the balance-sheet position. Thus, in the long run the market test and the ordinary business test of a successful equity commitment tend to be largely identical."
>
> Benjamin Graham

EPILOGUE

As I finish writing this book, the markets are reacting to the second- and third-largest bank failures in U.S. history. Bank and other financial stocks are taking a beating as investors worry the Fed's persistent interest rate hikes may be stretching the banking system to its limits. The government just announced a plan to reassure investors that the banking industry is still sound.[392]

As banks reassure their customers that they will not suffer a similar collapse, many in the mass media are reacting to the events as though we are about to experience a financial collapse reminiscent of the 2008 Great Recession. A politician is calling for reinstating the regulations that made it difficult for smaller banks to survive economic downturns.

During turbulent markets, as we seem to be experiencing more frequently if one listens to the media, it's difficult for investors to maintain their financial equilibrium, if not their financial sanity.

> **"I would like to point to the extraordinary lengths the mainstream media will go to maintain a sensationalist story."**
>
> John McAfee

This is why investors perpetually chasing higher investment returns are susceptible to making poor decisions in response to market volatility. It's why those possessing a sound financial strategy are able to make informed investment decisions, regardless of the economic environment. As was the case with the recent pandemic, events like this can have the potential for a positive result if they impel people to institute a comprehensive financial strategy, one that will allow them to remain calm in the face of economic chaos.

Investors need a sound financial foundation that allows them to ignore the noise that tempts them to make poor decisions. A better understanding of the importance of having an established financial strategy is a good first step. It supports informed decision making as it relates to taxes, retirement distributions, income streams and other critical financial considerations.

Importantly, having a sound financial strategy helps investors resist the fear and greed perpetuated by everyone from the entertainment industry to the nation's largest brokerage firms. It pains me to hear of retirees unable to enjoy the money they've spent decades to accumulate because they are paralyzed with fear regarding their finances as a result of having been fed a continuous diet of economic angst.

Working with our clients, it's my experience that virtually all who have saved for retirement throughout their working years have sufficient resources to do the things they wish to do in retirement. It reinforces the critical need for establishing a regimen of regular saving at as early an age as possible. It's a simple but undeniably important financial tenet.

Most people need professional help dealing with financial matters. The key is to find an advisor aligned with your investment philosophy, personal objectives and risk tolerance. Ideally, you also want one that has been around long enough to guide clients through market declines in multiple economic cycles.

This may sound obvious, but it's vital you find an honest advisor. Advanced degrees in financial disciplines may be impressive but will do you little good if the advisor doesn't have integrity and genuinely care about their clients.

My hope for you the reader is that this book gives you a basic framework to help guide you through your financial life in years ahead.

> "Planning is bringing the future into the present so that you can do something about it now."
>
> Alan Lakein

Endnotes

[1] Jane Bryant Quinn, "4 Unexpected Expenses to Prepare for in Retirement," AARP 12 Dec 2018.

[2] Suze Orman, "Help! I'm 70 and Worried I'll Run Out of Money," AARP Aug/Sep 2018.

[3] Lea Hart, "Americans' biggest retirement fear: Running out of money," Journal of Accountancy 6 Oct 2016.

[4] Jennifer A Kingson, "Companies are racing to dump their pension plans," Axios, 7 Aug 2019.

[5] investopedia.com

[6] www.pbgc.gov

[7] Annual Report 2021, pbgc.com

[8] gao.gov

[9] Alex J Pollock, "Congress Moves to Put Pension Benefit Guaranty Corporation on Taxpayer Dole," R Street 15 July 2019.

[10] Craig Eyermann, "The 5 States with the Most Underfunded Public Employee Pensions," Foundation for Economic Education 13 Mar 2019.

[11] "Washington's public pensions are only 38% to 84% funded, depending on assumptions," Washington Policy Center, 21 Feb 2018.

[12] Anna Petrini, "Recent Reductions in Public Pension COLAs," National Conference of State Legislatures, Oct 2015.

[13] Greg Iacurci, "School lunch, eggs and airfare," cnbc.com, 13 Jan 2023.

[14] 'What Are the Best Retirement Plans?" advisorsavvy.com 12 Nov 2019.

[15] Maurie Blackman, "How Much Will Healthcare Cost You in Retirement?" The Motley Fool, 8 July 2019.

[16] Fidelity: "Why Save In a Roth IRA in Your 20s and 30s." Accessed April 17, 2020.

[17] finance.zacks.com

[18] rbcwm-usa.com

[19] investopedia.com

[20] Kent Thune, "How to Benefit From Using a Mutual Fund Turnover Ratio," thebalance.com 06 Feb 2020.

[21] fidelity.com

[22] etf.com

[23] Andrea Coombes, "Taxes in Retirement: 7 Ways to Trim Your Bill," nerdwallet.com 2 Apr 2019.

[24] wealthsimple.com

[25] nceo.org

[26] betterexplained.com

[27] Alicia H. Munnell, Mauricio Soto, Jerilyn Libby and John Prinzivalli, "Investment Returns: Defined Benefit vs. 401(K) Plans," Center for Retirement Research at Boston College, Sept 2006.

[28] Jerry Kalish, "Investment returns of defined benefit plans and defined contribution plans: which type did better and does it matter"? National Benefit Services Inc., 1 May 2010.

[29] V. Sivarama Krishnan and Julie Cumble, "Defined Benefits Plans vs. Defined Contribution Plans: An Evaluation Framework using Random Returns," Paper resented to the Academy of Financial Services, Oct 2016.

[30] labrg.com

[31] usinflationcalculator.com

[32] Ibid #5

[33] "Your best pension payout options," Consumer Reports, Mar 2014.

---

[34] consumerfinance.gov

[35] A 403(b) plan, also known as a tax-sheltered annuity plan, is a retirement plan for certain employees of public schools, tax-exempt organizations and ministers. irs.gov

[36] investopedia.com

[37] MAGI: modified adjusted gross income

[38] taxschool.illinois.edu

[39] thecollegeinvestor.com

[40] nerdwallet.com

[41] investor.vanguard.com

[42] irs.gov

[43] investopedia.com

[44] Nikhil Adithyan, "Behavioral Finance: Concepts and Why it's Important," The Capital, 11 July 2020.

[45] Jim Holt, "Two Brains Running," New York Times, 25 Nov 2011.

[46] Daniel Kahneman, "Of 2 Minds: How Fast and Slow Thinking Shape Perception and Choice," Scientific American, 15 June 2012.

[47] "What is a Cognitive Bias?" verywellmind.com

[48] Mike Pinder, "16 cognitive biases that can kill your decision making," boardofinnovation.com

[49] Warren E. Agin, "An Introduction to Behavioral Economics and Negotiations," American Bar Association Journal, 3 Nov 2017.

[50] Pon Staff, "The Anchoring Effect and How it Can Impact Your Negotiation, Harvard Law School Daily Blog, 26 Nov 2019.

[51] Bettina Casad, "Confirmation Bias," 9 Oct 2019.

[52] "Behavioral Finance: Confirmation Bias, Cognitive Dissonance, and Recency," seic.com

[53] Saul McLeod, "Cognitive Dissonance," Simply Psychology, 5 Feb 2018.

[54] Hilaire Gomer, "Disposition Effect - an anomaly in behavioural finance," capital.com, 5 Sept 2017.

[55] "Why do we anticipate regret before we make a decision?" The Decision Lab, 2020.

[56] Sam McRoberts, "7 Cognitive Biases That Are Holding You Back," Inc., 20 Aug 2015.

[57] "Gambler's Fallacy," psychology.iresearchnet.com

[58] Ibid #13

[59] "What is Herd Mentality Bias?" Corporate Finance Institute.

[60] G.E.Miller, "Jim Cramer: The Good, the Bad, and the Ugly," 20 Something Finance, 23 Apr 2019.

[61] "What is Loss Aversion?" Corporate Finance Institute.

[62] Why do we think less about some purchases than others?" The Decision Lab.

[63] Brad M Barber and Terrance Odean, "Trading Is Hazardous to Your Wealth: The Common Stock Investment Performance of Individual Investors," Journal of Finance, 2000.

[64] Don A. Moore, "Overconfidence: The Mother of All Biases," Psychology Today, 22 Jan 2018.

[65] finrafoundation.org

[66] David Eckerly, "Recency Bias: The Sneaky Way Your Brain Dupes You into Bad Investment Decisions," Daily Capital, 13 Apr 2020.

[67] Samantha Lamas, "Is Recency Bias Swaying Your Investing Decisions?" Morningstar, 27 Apr 2020.

[68] Christopher Dwyer, "12 Common Biases That Affect How We Make Everyday Decisions," Psychology Today, 7 Sept 2018.

[69] Tejvan Pettinger, "Sunk Cost Fallacy," economicshelp.com, 22 May 2017.

[70] Melissa Lin, "Why Investors Are Irrational, According to Behavioral Finance," toptotal.com

[71] Jim Davis, "$10M settlement closes the books on Frontier Bank of Everett," The Herald Business Journal, `4 Apr 2016.

[72] Benjamin Graham, The Intelligent Investor (New York NY: Harper Business 1949)

[73] "Mr. Market," news.morningstar.com

[74] courses.lumenlearning.com

[75] stern.nyu.edu

Prateek Agarwal, "Business Cycle," Intelligent Economist, 07 Dec 2020.

[76] Christina D. Romer, "Business Cycles" econlib.org

[77] This school of economic thought, which focuses on macroeconomics, is mainly based on interpretations of John Maynard Keynes' most important book, the "General Theory of Employment, Interest and Money," 1936.

[78] policonomics.com

[79] Hyman Minsky, Stabilizing an Unstable Economy (New Haven CT: Yale University Press 1986)

[80] "Five Steps of a Bubble," Forbes, 17 Jun 2010.

[81] "Boom & Bust Cycles: What Are They" analyzingalpha.com, 24 Apr 2020.

[82] William Poole, "President's Message: Volcker's Handling of the Great Inflation Taught Us Much," stlouisfed.org, 1 Jan 2005.

[83] "How do interest rates affect investments?" US Wealth Management, 27 July 2020.

[84] "The Great Inflation," federalreservehistory.org

[85] Allan Sloan, "What do Apple and some well-off senior citizens have in common?" The Washington Post, 23 Feb 2021.

[86] investopedia.com

[87] economicshelp.org

[88] investopedia.com

[89] John A. Tatum, "Does the Stage of the Business Cycle Affect the Inflation Rate?" files.stlouisfed.org

[90] Caroline Baum, "Inflation may be muffled, but the business cycle isn't dead yet," marketwatch.com, 15 Jan 2020.

[91] Claudio Borio, Mathias Drehmann and Dora Xia, "Predicting recessions: financial cycle versus term spread," BIS Working Papers 818, Oct 2019.

[92] Bill Conerly, "Higher Inflation From The Fed's New Strategy—And More Business Cycles," Forbes, 28 Aug 2020.

[93] Lakshman Achuthan, "Stock Prices and the Business Cycle," Economic Cycle Research Institute, 03 Nov 2007.

[94] americancentury.com

[95] Nipun Mahajan, "Is Yield Curve a reliable economic indicator?" medium.com 14 May 2020.

---

[96] newyorkfed.com

[97] Jim Graham, "The Big Three Economic Indicators," discoveroptions.com

[98] "What are the possible causes and consequences of higher oil prices on the overall economy?" Federal Reserve Bank of San Francisco, Nov 2007.

[99] Robert Burgess, "Recession Ahead? Not If You're Looking at Oil," Bloomberg, 27 Aug 2019.

[100] opentextc.ca

[101] seekingalpha.com

[102] Kevin Kliesen, "Leaning Against the Wind: Does the Fed Engage in Countercyclical Monetary Policy?" Federal Reserve Bank of St Louis, 1 Jan 1993.

[103] Lars Tvede, Business Cycles (Chichester, West Sussex England: John Wiley & Sons Ltd, 2006)

[104] ycharts.com

[105] corporatefinanceinstitute.com

[106] ibid #31

[107] William Lazonick, Mustafa Erdem Sakinç and Matt Hopkins, "Why Stock Buybacks Are Dangerous for the Economy," Harvard Business Review, 07 Jan 2020.

[108] Ibid CFI

[109] Jeff Thomas, "Babson's Warning," International Man.

[110] efinancemanagement.com

[111] corporatefinanceinstitute.com

[112] Michelle Baddely, "Herding, social influence and economic decision-making: socio-psychological and neuroscientific analyses," US National Library of Medicine, 27 Jan 2010.

[113] tradersfly.com

[114] BusinessDictionary.com

[115] "Systematic and Unsystematic Risk," Institute of Business & Finance, 29 Jan 2016.

[116] corporatefinanceinstitute.com

[117] readyratios.com

[118] juliusbaer.com

[119] moneyzine.com

[120] firstlinks.com.au

[121] boundless.com

[122] cleartax.in

[123] strategiccfo.com

[124] finra.org

[125] "Concentrate on Concentration Risk," finra.com, 2021.

[126] discovertheodds.com

[127] Bob Collie, "How Big is Longevity Risk?" AAII Journal, Oct 2015.

[128] pbgc.gov

[129] Charles Rotblut, "Managing the Five Big Types of Investing Risk," American Association of Individual Investors, 21 Mar 2019.

[130] statista.com

[131] "Top 5 economic risk factors that must be considered," World Finance, 1 May 2019.

[132] Miranda Marquit, "5 Economic Factors That Influence Stocks," US News & World Report, 5 Aug 2019.

---

[133] Peter G. Peterson Foundation, 2021

[134] corporatefinanceinstitute.com

[135] investopedia.com

[136] finra.org

[137] Emily Cadman, Eric Lam and Katharine Gemmell, "Inflation Risk Is Rising. Here's How to Protect Your Investment Portfolio," Bloomberg Wealth, 9 Feb 2021.

[138] maplecroft.com

[139] John Christy, "Understanding and Managing Political Risk," thebalance.com, 30 Sep 2020.

[140] Lora Jones, Daniele Palumbo & David Brown "Coronavirus: How the pandemic has changed the world economy," BBC News, 24 Jan 2021.

[141] Grant T. Harris, "How Investors Can Navigate Pandemic-Related Risk in Emerging Markets," Harvard Business Review, 15 May 2020.

[142] Rob Berger, "5 Breathtaking Numbers Reveal The Unsettling Cost Of Stimulus," Forbes, 18 Oct 2020.

[143] Jim Tankersley and Alan Rappeport, "Biden's Tax Plan Aims to Raise $2.5 Trillion and End Profit-Shifting," New York Times, 7 Apr 2021.

[144] Lorie Konish, "Biden has promised not to raise taxes on people earning less than $400,000. Here's what he might push for instead," CNBC Personal Finance, 18 Mar 2021.

[145] annuity.org

[146] Nick Kasprak, "Does Lowering Taxes Increase Government Revenue?" The Tax Foundation, 15 Dec 2020.

[147] corporatefinanceinstitute.com

[148] Bob Pisani, "How concerned investors should be about Biden's tax proposals," cnbc.com, 8 Jan 2021.

[149] Janet Smith, "Systematic and Unsystematic Risks: How to Mitigate Them," ezinearticles.com, 26 Mar 2018.

[150] money-zine.com

[151] Evie Liu, "It's Getting Harder to Diversify Your Investments. What to Do About It," Barron's, 8 Jan 2021.

[152] thebalance.com

[153] corporatefinanceinstitute.com

[154] Lawrence Carrel, "Passive Management Marks Decade Of Beating Active U.S. Stock Funds," Forbes, 20 Apr 2020.

[155] Danny Yeung, Paolo Pellizzari, Ron Bird and Sazali Abidin, "Diversification versus Concentration . . . and the Winner is?" working paper series 18, University of Technology Sydney, Australia.

[156] smartasset.com

[157] Tim McMahon, "Inflation Risk," inflationdata.com, 22 May 2018.

[158] finra.org

[159] entrepreneur.com

[160] Patricia Schaefer, "Why Small Businesses Fail," businessknowhow.com, 23 Dec 2020.

[161] investopedia.com

[162] irs.com

[163] Heather Huston, "Tax aspects of selling your business," Wolters Kluwer, 9 Nov 2020.

---

[164] smallbiztrends.com

[165] Cody Webb, "Understanding The Tax Implications Of Selling A Business," cmp.cpa, 10 Sept 2021.

[166] "Sale of a Business," irs.gov

[167] Barbara Weltman, "7 Tax Strategies to Consider When Selling a Business," U.S. Small Business Administration, 21 Feb 2020.

[168] "Sale of a Partnership Interest," irs.gov

[169] Maria Tanski-Phillips, "What Is Washington Labor and Industries?" patriotsoftware.com, 22 July 2019.

[170] Lars Landrie, "What to Know About Washington State's Publicly Funded Long-Term Care Insurance," mossadams.com, 14 June 2021.

[171] Taylor Pepper, "America's Seniors In Debt: A Growing Problem," Forbes, 29 Mar 2021.

[172] "Average Retirement Debt: Older Americans Have More Debt than Ever Before!" newretirement.com

[173] Emily Guy Birken and John Schmidt, "Retirement Planning: How To Get Out Of Debt Before Retirement," Forbes, 29 Mar 2021.

[174] Greg Iacurci, "Retirees can get hosed on taxes," cnbc.com, 12 Nov 2020.

[175] "How to Plan Ahead for Taxes in Retirement," schwab.com, 02 Mar 2021.

[176] ssa.gov

[177] Sarah O'Brien, "Claiming Social Security early? Here's how spousal benefits come into play," cnbc.com

[178] kilplinger.com

[179] ssa.gov

[180] aarp.com

[181] Jeremy Rodriguez, JD, "Understanding the Pro-Rata Rule," irahelp.com, 12 Mar 2018.

[182] fulltimefinance.com

[183] Sarah O'Brien, "Avoid these costly mistakes when rolling over a 401(k) to an IRA," cnbc.com, 4 Jan 2021.

[184] atlas-blue.com

[185] Walecia Konrad, "The Ever-Rising Cost of Long-Term Care Insurance," cbsnews.com, 23 May 2018.

[186] "Long-term care insurance rate increases," insurance.wa.gov

[187] Fidelity Consulting Services

[188] Patricia Barry, "Are There Limits on Medicare Coverage?" aarp.org, May 2014.

[189] healthline.com

[190] statista.com

[191] "What is the lifetime cost of caring for a person with Alzheimer's?" care.com, Nov 30, 2020.

[192] alz.org

[193] Greg Iacurci, "States approving bigger rate increases for long-term care policies," Investment News, 7 May 2019.

[194] topclassactions.com

[195] An ILIT is an irrevocable trust created to hold a life insurance policy.

[196] "How Can I Protect my Assets from a Civil Lawsuit?" brattonlawgroup.com

[197] Julie Boatman, "How to Find the Right Flight Instructor," flyingmag.com 14 Jun 2014.

---

[198] John Schmidt, "How to Choose a Financial Advisor," Forbes 11 Aug 2020.

[199] Coryanne Hicks, "What Is a Fiduciary Financial Advisor?" U.S. News 15 Apr 2021.

[200] ibid Forbes 11 Aug 2020.

[201] bankrate.com

[202] Rickie Houston, "Your Financial Advisor's Conflicts of Interest," smartasset.com 16 Jan 2020.

[203] yahoo.com

[204] *See SEC v. Capital Gains Research Bureau,* 375 U.S. 180, 194 (1963) ("Capital Gains") and Fiduciary Interpretation.

[205] paladinregistry.com

[206] cfainstitute.org

[207] Chris Mamula, "Here's how to understand your financial adviser's conflicts of interest," MarketWatch 31 May 2018.

[208] Ara Jabrayan, "Fiduciary Duty Is Broader Than Many Think," Smart RIA 14 May 2021.

[209] files.consumerfinance.gov

[210] money.usnews.com

[211] James J. Choi, David Laibson and Brigitte C. Madrian, "Why Does the Law of One Price Fail? An Experiment on Index Mutual Funds," scholar.harvard.com

[212] Lance Roberts, "Technically Speaking: Past Performance Is A Guarantee?" advisorperspectives.com

[213] Aswath Damodaran, "Investment Philosophies: Introduction" people.stern.nyu.edu

[214] businessinsider.com

[215] nerdwallet.com

[216] taxdiversification.com

[217] corporatefinanceinstitute.com

[218] Rob Berger and Benjamin Curry, "Understanding How Value Investing Works," Forbes 11 May 2021.

[219] John Heins, Whitney Tilson, "Why Value Investing Is Hard," Kiplinger's 7 Aug 2011.

[220] marketbusinessnews.com

[221] Josef Lakonishok, Andrei Shleifer and Robert W. Vishny, "Contrarian Investment, Extrapolation, and Risk," The Journal of Finance Dec 1994.

[222] corporatefinanceinstitute.com

[223] nerdwallet.com

[224] Robert Armstrong, "The fallacy of ESG investing," Financial Times 22 Oct 2020.

[225] businessinsider.com

[226] blackrock.com

[227] bankrate.com

[228] feeonlynetwork.com

[229] bankrate.com

[230] investor.gov

[231] Amy Livingston, "5 Signs It's Time to Fire Your Financial Advisor," moneycrashers.com

[232] files.consumerfinance.gov

---

[233] Sara Grillo, "The Staggering Disconnect Between What Clients Want and What Advisors Think," Advisor Perspectives 18 July 2018.

[234] investor.gov

[235] finra.com

[236] retireguide.com

[237] "Compound Annual growth Rate (annualized return)" Moneychimp 13 Jan 2022.

[238] Forbes 2 Apr 2021.

[239] thebalance.com

[240] Pippa Stevens, "This chart shows why investors should never try to time the stock market," cnbc.com 24 Mar 2021.

[241] Melissa Phipps, "Correlated and Non-Correlated Assets," thebalance.com 6 May 2021.

[242] Guan Zhen Tan, "Why 2021 Is The Time To Add Uncorrelated Returns To Your Portfolio," Forbes 8 Feb 2021.

[243] "Annual S&P Sector Performance," novelinvestor.com

[244] The Nobel Prize: "This Year's Laureates Are Pioneers in the Theory of Financial Economics and Corporate Finance," 7 Dec 2021.

[245] investopedia.com

[246] Rachel Cautero, "Efficient Frontier: Definition, Benefits, and Uses," SmartAsset yahoo.com 6 Nov 2019.

[247] medium.com

[248] Wei-Ping Chen, Huimin Chung, Keng-Yu Ho and Tsui-Ling Hsu, "Portfolio optimization models and mean-variance spanning," Handbook of Quantitative Finance and Risk Management.

[249] Karl Steiner, "Ranking The Historical Returns of Asset Classes," efttrends.com 18 Feb 2021.

[250] Gary P Brinson, L Randolph Hood and Gilbert L Beebower, "Determinants of Portfolio Performance," Financial Analysts Journal 1991.

[251] Vanguard Investment Counseling & Research

[252] Yesim Tokat, Nelson Wicas and Francis M. Kinniry, "The Asset Allocation Debate: A Review and Reconciliation," FPA Journal 2006.

[253] Roger G. Ibbotson and Paul D. Kaplan, "Does asset allocation explain 40, 90, or 100 percent of performance?" Financial Analysts Journal Jan/Feb 2000.

[254] Adam Butler, "Asset allocation vs. security selection — which wins?" Advisor's Edge 21 Oct 2016.

[255] E Napoletano and Benjamin Curry, "Asset Allocation And Your Portfolio," Forbes 14 Apr 2021.

[256] investopedia.com

[257] Rebekah Freeman, "5 Reasons Why People Procrastinate on Estate Planning," The Hilton Head Sun, 4 Aug 2020.

[258] Eric Martin. "A baker's dozen of why people procrastinate about their estate plan," Matlin Law Group, 30 Mar 2021.

[259] "Problems Procrastination May Cause with Estate Planning," hg.org

[260] Manish Bhaita, "The Costs of Procrastinating on Your Estate Planning," mcb-law.com 22 Oct 2019.

[261] "Estate Planning is Too Important to Procrastinate," Academy of Estate Planning Attorneys, cathompsonlaw.com 27 Jun 2018.

[262] Linda Cammuso, "Estate Planning: Procrastination Could Have Harmful Results," thefiftypluslife.com, 05 Feb 2018.

[263] dicksonlegal.com

[264] probateadvance.com

[265] nolo.com

[266] Sherrie Johnson, "12 Celebrities Who Died Without a Will—And Their Disputes," joincake.com 25 Aug 2020.

[267] Matthew Odgers, "Ultimate List of Celebrities Who Died Without an Estate Plan (2022)," opelon.com

[268] irs.gov

[269] dor.wa.gov

[270] Chye-Ching Huang and Chloe Cho, "Ten Facts You Should Know About the Federal Estate Tax," Center on Budget and Policy Priorities, 30 Oct 2017.

[271] Donald J. Murn, "What is Step-Up in Basis & Why is it Important?" axley.com, 20 Jan 2022.

[272] Mary Rudolph, J.D., "Washington Estate Tax," nolo.com

[273] americanbar.org

[274] burnerlaw.com

[275] Mary Rudolph, J.D., "What is a Bypass Trust?" alllaw.com

[276] Zachary Mider, "How Wal-Mart's Waltons Maintain their Billionaire Fortune," Bloomberg, 12 Sep 2013.

[277] Carlo Lombardi, "The Benefits of QTIP Trusts," library.wilmingtontrust.com

[278] stimmel-law.com

[279] assetprotectionattorneys.com

[280]dor.wa.gov

[281] Valerie Keene, J.D., "What Is a Charitable Remainder Unitrust?" nolo.com

[282] Ashlea Ebeling, "New Higher Estate And Gift Tax Limits For 2022," Forbes, 11 Nov 2021.

[283] Patricia Villanova, "Gift Tax, Explained: 2022 and 2021 Exemption and Rates," smartasset.com, 21 Jan 2022.

[284] investopedia.com

[285] Albertson & Davidson, LLP, "What is the Difference Between a Trustee and an Executor?" aldavlaw.com, 21 Sep 2021.

[286] "Should You Choose Family or a Professional Trustee? Know the Pros and Cons," Czepiga Daly Pope & Perri, czepigalaw.com, 26 Aug 2021.

[287] "When the trustee and beneficiaries are siblings, everyone needs to know the ground rules to stay on good terms!" karplaw.com

[288] "When the trustee and beneficiaries are siblings, everyone needs to know the ground rules to stay on good terms!" karplaw.com

[289] Gerry W. Beyer, "Keeping It In The Family: Pitfalls of Naming A Family Member As A Trustee," lawprofessors.typepad.com, 7 Dec 2021.

[290] John J. Scroggin, "What Dead Celebrities can Teach us about Estate Planning," *FPA GA Regional Symposium*, fpaga.org

[291] jpmorgan.com

[292] mindyhibbardrealestate.com

[293] investopedia.com

[294] Legal Information Institute, law.cornell.edu

---

[295] quickenloans.com
[296] nolo.com
[297] Learn.roofstock.com
[298] "The 4 Main Types of Real Estate Investment Properties," listwithclever.com, 19 May 2022.
[299] Joshua Kennon, "Different Types of Real Estate Investments," thebalance.com, 04 Mar 2021.
[300] "Understanding the 4 Main Types of Investment Real Estate," Fifth Third Bank, 06 Dec 2020.
[301] ibid #1
[302] ibid #3
[303] ibid #3
[304] Paul Esajian, "The Best Types Of Real Estate Investments," fortunebuilders.com
[305] reit.com
[306] Ibid #8
[307] umh.reit
[308] "Crown Castle Reports First Quarter 2022 Results and Increases Outlook for Full Year 2022," crowncastle.com, 20 Apr 2022.
[309] investopedia.com
[310] "623rd Consecutive Common Stock Monthly Dividend Declared By Realty Income," realtyincome.com, 17 May 2022.
[311] Ibid #8
[312] nerdwallet.com
[313] Ibid #13
[314] Matthew DiLallo, "What Is a Real Estate Investment Fund?" fool.com, 13 May 2022.
[315] moneycrashers.com
[316] Ibid #15
[317] seekingalpha.com
[318] Jeff Reeves, "7 Best REIT ETFs to Buy," money.usnews.com, 10 May 2022.
[319] money.usnews.com
[320] preqin.com
[321] rocketmortgage.com
[322] G Brian Davis, "What Is Leverage in Real Estate and How Does It Help Investors?" sparkrental.com, 04 Apr 2022.
[323] investopedia.com
[324] James Kimmons, "Risks to Avoid When Using Leverage in Real Estate," thebalancesmb.com, 20 Nov 2019.
[325] nasra.org
[326] ballotpedia.org
[327] opm.gov
[328] investopedia.com
[329] drs.wa.gov
[330] Ibid #1
[331] co.benton.wa.us
[332] Ibid #1
[333] drs.wa.gov
[334] humaninterest.com

[335] fool.com
[336] Rachel Hartman, "What Is a 403(b)?" money.usnews.com, 14 July 2021.
[337] Ibid # 3
[338] irs.gov
[339] fool.com
[340] nbsbenefits.com
[341] Iinvestopedia.com
[342] irs.gov
[343] Tom R. Hager, "Understanding Social Security For The Public Sector: The Government Pension Offset," Forbes 1 Oct 2018.
[344] ssa.gov
[345] tradingeconomics.com
[346] federalreservehistory.org
[347] bis.gov
[348] Alan Burke, "Retired teachers in WA are getting a raw deal from state lawmakers," crosscut.com, 30 May 2019.
[349] Pete Levine, "Washington state retirees win pension COLA increases through persistence," afscme.org, 11 Apr 2022.
[350] Ryan Frost, "Washington State Grapples With Public Pension Cost-of-Living Adjustments," Reason Foundation, 9 Aug 2021.
[351] piercecountywa.gov
[352] smartasset.com
[353] seatacwa.gov
[354] Richard W. Johnson, C. Eugene Steuerle, and Caleb Quakenbush, "State Pension Reforms:
Are New Workers Paying for Past Mistakes? Urban Institute, July 2012.
[355] Casey W Riggs, "Stock Options versus Stock Warrants—What's the Difference?" strictlybusinesslawblog.com 2 Nov 2012.
[356] investopedia
[357] Derek Silva, "How Do Employee Stock Options Work?" smartasset.com 19 Sept 2022.
[358] Daniel Lee, "Everything You Need to Know About Stock Options," Harvard Business Review 05 Aug 2021.
[359] esofund.com
[360] upcounsel.com
[361] smartasset.co
[362] smartasset.co
[363] contractscounsel.com
[364] The Carta Team, "Stock options vs. warrants: Everything you need to know," carta.com 12 Feb 2021.
[365] pulley.com
[366] esofund.com
[367] Robin Kavanagh, "What are stock warrants and why do companies offer them? Businessinsider.com
[368] Eric Rosenberg, "Stock Options vs. RSUs: Key Differences Between the Two," investorjunkie.com 22 Apr 2022.
[369] schwab.com
[370] nerdwallet.com
[371] investopedia.com

---

[372] Coryanne Hicks, "The Ultimate Guide to Dividend Stocks," U.S.News 13 Oct 2022.

[373] Shauna O'Brien, "What are Dividend Stocks?" dividend.com

[374] Cory Mitchell, "10 Best Dividend Aristocrats Of 2023," Forbes 1 Mar 2023.

[375] Stefon Walters, "What the S&P 500 Can Teach Us About Reinvested Dividends," Motley Fool 27 Aug 2022.

[376] "Investing in Stocks With Dividends vs Stocks Without Dividends," corporatefinanceinstitute.com 9 Dec 2022.

[377] "The Pros & Cons Of Dividend Stock Investing," suredividend.com 23 Nov 2022.

[378] "Why You Should Consider Investing in Dividend Stocks," nirmalbang.com

[379] ibid #5

[380] "The Pros & Cons Of Dividend Stock Investing," suredividend.com 23 Nov 2022.

[381] dividend.com

[382] investor.gov

[383] ibid #12

[384] investopedia.com

[385] "What Are Dividend Stocks?" Forbes 28 Sep 2022.

[386] Benjamin Curry, "What Is A Stock Buyback?" forbes.com 7 Feb 2023.

[387] seekingalpha.com

[388] ibid #15

[389] Justin Pettit, "Is a Share Buyback Right for Your Company? Harvard Business Review Apr 2001.

[390] "What is a Share Repurchase?" corporatefinanceinstitute.com 27 Dec 2022.

[391] Andrew S. Bargerstock, "The Downsides of Stock Buybacks," Strategic Finance 1 Sept 2022.

[392] Stan Choe, "Bank stocks tumble; others rise on hopes of easier interest rates," Associated Press 13 Mar 2023.

www.ingramcontent.com/pod-product-compliance
Lightning Source LLC
LaVergne TN
LVHW020533100826
845148LV00010B/1442

9781506911540